generous
spaciousness

generous spaciousness

Responding to Gay Christians in the Church

WENDY VANDERWAL-GRITTER

BrazosPress

a division of Baker Publishing Group
Grand Rapids, Michigan

Published by Brazos Press
a division of Baker Publishing Group
P.O. Box 6287, Grand Rapids, MI 49516-6287
www.brazospress.com

Printed in the United States of America

Library of Congress Cataloging-in-Publication Data is on file at the Library of Congress, Washington, DC.

ISBN 978-1-58743-355-9 (pbk.)

Unless otherwise indicated, Scripture quotations are from the Holy Bible, New International Version®. NIV®. Copyright © 1973, 1978, 1984, 2011 by Biblica, Inc.™ Used by permission of Zondervan. All rights reserved worldwide. www.zondervan.com

Scripture quotations labeled KJV are from the King James Version of the Bible.

Scripture quotations labeled Message are from *The Message* by Eugene H. Peterson, copyright © 1993, 1994, 1995, 2000, 2001, 2002. Used by permission of NavPress Publishing Group. All rights reserved.

Scripture quotations labeled NASB are from the New American Standard Bible®, copyright © 1960, 1962, 1963, 1968, 1971, 1972, 1973, 1975, 1977, 1995 by The Lockman Foundation. Used by permission.

Scripture quotations labeled NIV 1984 are from the Holy Bible, New International Version®. NIV®. Copyright © 1973, 1978, 1984 by Biblica, Inc.™ Used by permission of Zondervan. All rights reserved worldwide. www.zondervan.com

Scripture quotations labeled NKJV are from the New King James Version. Copyright © 1982 by Thomas Nelson, Inc. Used by permission. All rights reserved.

Scripture quotations labeled NLT are from the *Holy Bible*, New Living Translation, copyright © 1996, 2004, 2007 by Tyndale House Foundation. Used by permission of Tyndale House Publishers, Inc., Carol Stream, Illinois 60188. All rights reserved.

14 15 16 17 18 19 20   7 6 5 4 3 2 1

For my treasures:
Nathan, Renate, and Arianna

Contents

Acknowledgments

The journey to get this book to this point has been rich and full because of the many relationships I've been privileged to engage. I'm sure that these few words of acknowledgment and thanks will be insufficient and incomplete. Nonetheless, there are some key people without whom this book would not have been written. Thank you to my former New Direction colleagues David and Brian. I learned much from your stories, have shared some of those insights in this book, and am grateful for the many hours we spent in conversation and reflection together. Thank you to Christine and the community of ex-gay survivors—your stories continue to impact me. Thank you to the literally hundreds of gay and trans sisters and brothers who trusted me enough to allow me into your lives. Your courageous faith and tenacious resiliency has not only shaped my ministry but has had enormous significance in my own spiritual life. Thank you to the team at New Direction for your unconditional support of this project. Thank you to John for your long-term service on the board. You were an example of generous spaciousness before I even coined the term. Your encouragement and nonanxious presence was an immeasurable gift. Thank you to my home fellowship, the good people of Meadowvale Christian Reformed Church. Thank you for walking with me through the years: "a long obedience in the same direction." Thank you for being so faithful to pray and care for me and my family. Thank you to Carl. Your unwavering support of my work with New Direction was a great gift to me. And thank you to my children. You teach me every day through your love. If I had not been able to experience a more fearless, generous sense of God, I'm not sure where I would be today. But I am grateful beyond words to live in the "unforced rhythms of grace" where I can rest in the quiet confidence that God is truly love and delights in nurturing generous spaciousness in us.

Introduction

An Unpredictable Adventure

In a memorable preview for the movie *Doubt*, Meryl Streep playing Sister Aloysius declares to the priest she is accusing of inappropriate conduct with a male student, "No I don't have proof, but I have my certainty!" For those who have seen the movie, this declaration is contrasted with the final poignant scene in the film when the indomitable nun breaks down and with tears confesses, "I have doubts. Oh, I have doubts!" Like the cracking and crumbling of the paradigms and systems inherited from modernity, Sister Aloysius dares in a moment of abject desperation to expose her authentic voice—a voice that acknowledges the limitations of certainty. In this final scene, we see a fragile new hope for Streep's character to enter more deeply and intimately into relationship with the other nun she confides in and, even more significantly, with the God with whom she can be honest.

This book, too, has come from such a place of brokenness and hope. The breaking and deconstruction of not only rigid certainty but also the systems that created and sustained such certainty, is a journey that is both terrifying and exhilarating. Being the leader of a national organization with the legacy of promoting and defending a clear and certain position (which is not only the traditional position that says sexual intimacy is reserved for marriage between one man and one woman but also the evangelical ex-gay position that says freedom and change are possible for the same-sex-attracted person), makes it particularly threatening to go to that honest and authentic place, where doubt and questions and uncertainty live, with an utterly childlike expectation that God will be with you in that place. But that is indeed the journey that God compelled me to take, albeit with much fear and trembling on my part. And it is a journey that has allowed me and the organization I lead to emerge as a place of generous spaciousness.

I became the director of a Canadian ministry called New Direction in the spring of 2002. I often say that I was naïve but willing. New Direction had been part of the Exodus network since the mid-eighties. Exodus[1] was an international group of like-minded ministries committed to the proclamation that freedom in Christ is available to those who experience same-sex attraction. For most of New Direction's history, the ministry had been a counseling center for Christians who were experiencing unwanted same-sex attraction, a facilitator of pastoral care for families with gay loved ones, and a point of consultation and referral for churches and pastors encountering people affected by homosexuality.

When I came to the ministry, I was a relatively recent seminary grad who'd spent the intervening years with my young children. I was itching to get into my first ministry position while mindful of juggling the demands of a young family. New Direction seemed like the perfect fit: It was part-time, I could work from home, and it was focused on an area of pastoral care that I was passionate about. Though some ministry colleagues surmised that I could potentially blacklist my ministry career by taking a leadership role in a ministry addressing such a controversial issue, I sensed God's call. I'd been reading Henry Blackaby's book, *Experiencing God*, around that time, and I very much felt that God was on the move, wanting to do something with New Direction, and that he was simply nudging me and asking me to join him in what he was intending to do. I suppose, looking back, there was a generous helping of reckless idealism in my discernment process. I have no doubt that God called me, but I now wonder if it had as much or more to do with what he wanted to do in me than with what I could do for the ministry.

The journey of serving God and his people in my role with New Direction over these years has been full of surprises. Many of those surprises have been startlingly painful. I certainly didn't expect that I would be confronted with the need to unpack so many layers of my own assumptions—many of which I didn't even realize I had. It has been profoundly threatening at times and (most significant) deeply humbling. In the traditional constructs of liberal and conservative, I've been critiqued by those who thought I was too liberal and others who thought I was too conservative. I increasingly found myself drawn to move beyond the restrictions of labels, such as liberal/conservative, and to find a space within what theologian Hans Frei termed, "generous" orthodoxy.[2]

Part of my movement, admittedly, came with a weariness of living within the constrictions of what felt like nearly constant interrogation of the true extent of my orthodoxy. I began to long for a more spacious place. I can't count the number of times I was cornered by someone demanding to be assured that I did believe homosexuality to be a sin (once or twice the question instead was whether I supported the full inclusion of gay people into ordained ministry and sanctified marriages—with the same sort of cut-and-dried expectation). These orthodoxy tests came devoid of any interest in engaging in conversation, let alone relationship. My questioners reflected a system of black and white, right and wrong, that I came to realize was often motivated and driven by anxiety, anger, and pride rather than by anything that might resemble the fruit of the Spirit. Such questions, more often than not, had no relational connection to a person for whom the question might deeply matter. This kind of questioning often left me feeling objectified. The inquisitors weren't really interested in hearing how God was leading me in the complex realities I faced on a day-to-day basis; they didn't really care about what God was teaching me and the ways he was excavating my heart. What mattered to the questioners was that I verbalize a clear stance, which allowed them to give either a confident "thumbs up" or a "thumbs down" to my ministry.

Peter Rollins, an Irish philosopher/theologian, makes the helpful distinction between focusing on *what* you believe and the manner in which you live out *how* you believe it.[3] In Rollins's estimation, much of the Western church, still living in the shadow of modernity, puts its emphasis on *what* we believe. Having lived and ministered in such a system for a number of years, I am increasingly convinced that this focus can lead to compartmentalized lives. I've grown weary of triumphalistic warriors for truth—who know and believe all the "right" things but exude pride, self-centeredness, and a devaluing of anyone who disagrees with them. I would rather engage someone who might have some spotty theology but who oozes humility, kindness, generosity, and true and deep love for their enemies. And while this may sound a little too hippy-drippy, this isn't just about warm fuzzy feelings—this is about walking in the way of Jesus.

In addition to feeling stuck in the black-and-white certainty of the broader Christian community, I was also experiencing a sense of restriction with the ex-gay system.[4] I remember when one of the leaders in the Exodus network had a brief appearance on *Dr. Phil*, a daytime television show that focuses on interpersonal and psychological issues. Also appearing was Justin Lee, executive director of the Gay Christian Network.[5] The two had very little airtime, but in the few moments I witnessed, I was horrified by what I heard. In a nutshell the ex-gay leader proclaimed (not in these exact words but with this insinuation) that everyone could change their orientation and that if this didn't happen it was because the individual didn't try hard enough or have enough faith. After the show aired, on the Exodus leaders' discussion boards, I tentatively asked what others thought of the show. (I considered myself the new kid on the block and didn't want to start out too critically, so I thought it best to test the waters with an open-ended question.) To my utter surprise, no one, even the people I considered to be more moderate, offered any critique of the Exodus leader's comments. We all knew that though sexuality could be fluid, and we knew individuals who had experienced shifts in the direction and intensity of their attractions, there were clearly people who would experience same-sex attraction persistently and this was *not* due to a lack of faith or motivation. Yet even in this private and confidential discussion, no one spoke up and declared what we all knew to be true—radical reorientation at an attraction level is *not* the typical experience.

I found myself asking more questions and feeling the pinch of trying to function in what felt like a very closed and static system. Ex-gay ministries began with the intention of offering a redemptive and caring response to Christians in conflict over their experience of same-sex-attraction or for those experiencing dissatisfaction with the behavioral or relational choices they were making. But some thirty years after ex-gay ministries began, I was now an insider within the system, and I could feel myself becoming agitated and unsettled and unable to continue with "business as usual." Alan Roxburgh[6] describes this kind of experience as *liminality*, where "liminal" means an in-between or transitional state, and "liminality," in this case, is that confusing and uncertain place of questioning established structures, hierarchies, and tradition. I felt that we had lost our center, gotten distracted, forgotten to put first things first. Our team at New Direction began to long to move forward by charting a distinct course—one that could embrace and build on good and true teaching from the past, while having the courage to step out with redemptive innovation.

I wasn't the first or the only one to experience the tension such liminality fosters. Some Exodus leaders were quietly working within the system to renew and transform their particular corners of it. Some leaders chose to exit either to pursue different ministry opportunities that had nothing to do with homosexuality or to leave ministry altogether (in some cases with a good measure of health; in others broken, burned out, and bitter). Still other leaders made a dramatic shift in not only their praxis of ministry but also in their belief systems. These leaders garnered a certain notoriety within the ex-gay ministry field (that went unnoticed by the majority of the evangelical Christian community) and were quite simply disassociated, cut off, and disregarded as having no further usefulness or contribution to offer.

As I reflected on this, it felt as if the system of ex-gay ministry had an unhealthy level of control. This control was often presented as "guarding the truth," but its defense of truth seemed more driven by fear and anxiety than by love. I became more acutely aware of the perpetuation of an "us and them" mentality or perhaps even more an "us *versus* them" mind-set. Some of these so-called enemies were people within the church; they were people who differed in theological, philosophical, and ethical positions but who also continued to name the name of Christ and were, therefore, our brothers and sisters. This seemed completely inconsistent with Jesus's revolutionary motif of loving our enemies. It seemed that the ex-gay movement was spending the majority of its energy on what it was *against* and had forgotten what it was called to be *for*. This was a posture with which I was increasingly uncomfortable and dissatisfied.

Neal Plantinga writes, "The sobering fact is that reforms always need reforming. Rescuers need rescue. . . . Repentant sinners need to repent even of some dimensions of their repentance, such as their pride in the humility that has driven them to their knees."[7] I didn't have a complete picture of what this reformation in evangelical ministry to gay people needed to look like or how it would be expressed, but that change was needed I had no doubt.

In January 2008, I was asked to give a keynote address at the Exodus leadership conference.[8] With perhaps more tentativeness than the situation warranted, I took the opportunity to raise questions I was wrestling with and to offer initial ideas about how ex-gay ministry could engage a postmodern context. In particular, I spoke of three key distractions that I observed were creating the greatest barriers in our engagement with Christians of differing perspectives as well as with the broader gay community. These were the discussions and debates around *causation*, *orientation change*, and *political involvement*. I spoke to men and women I considered colleagues and friends, fellow laborers in Christ, many whose passion and commitment I deeply respected. When I had taken the role of Exodus regional representative for Canada a few years earlier, I had sensed that despite my questions and concerns, it was better to engage and serve from within than to stand and critique from without. And so my address was intended to encourage and challenge—with the goal that all of us would continue to move forward into the new ways God was asking us to function in ministry. Afterward, a good number of leaders were eager for more discussion. The president of Exodus, Alan Chambers, told me there was a lot more to unpack and that I would need to speak again.

But even as I prepared with my colleagues in mind, I was considering another audience. I had invested in coming to know this audience in both the personal relationships God brought across my path and the internet world of blogs and social media. The make-up of this audience was not monolithic but had one thing in common—they took issue with ex-gay ministry. I have always considered that listening to one's critics is a crucial form of feedback for any leader. I wanted to understand what critics of ministries like New Direction thought and felt. I wanted to mine the truths that were being exposed by those who were often disregarded in ex-gay circles.

I found these critics to be a rich resource. Engaging with the thoughts of gay activists, with those who had experienced painful and soul-crushing experiences in ex-gay ministry, and with gay Christians who held different theological perspectives than I, was at times very challenging and threatening, stretching my need and capacity for discernment. But it was also significant and valuable for the ways it forced me to think and rethink.

As it turns out, I was very grateful to have had this kind of preparation because after we posted a podcast of my Exodus address, I was contacted by the editor of a website called Ex-Gay Watch (XGW), which is a watch-dog site dedicated to monitoring the ex-gay movement. In the past, I had been warned about them by other network leaders. This editor had listened to my address, followed my discussion with commenters on another blog by Christian psychologist Warren Throckmorton,[9] and asked if I would be willing to write a guest post for their blog. Via email he said, "I think it is worth your time and effort to give people who visit XGW some hope that there are ministries that do get it (or at least understand where they don't), not that everyone will agree entirely (won't happen). . . . I'm asking this mostly on discernment; I sense God in what you say, and I know how powerful that can be. Please pray about this and don't make a snap decision. I know we do not see eye to eye on these things entirely, but let God deal with that."

Clearly, there was a climate of suspicion and mistrust between the Exodus network and a site like XGW, and I didn't consider myself at that time to be very savvy in this whole arena of engagement. I wondered if I would get in way over my head and what the fallout might be. But as I prayed and had others pray with me, we sensed God's opportunity in all of this. So on February 25, 2008, my post on XGW went public.[10] It begins with an introduction by David Roberts:

Recently we became aware of Wendy Gritter's keynote talk (mp3) at the Exodus leadership conference in January. Wendy is the executive director of an Exodus member ministry in Canada called New Direction. While it is what most here would describe as an ex-gay ministry, many things about it are unexpected. For one, you won't find them using that term, "ex-gay" or many others associated with an Exodus ministry. Whether this is for show, or a sincere attempt to be different, you are free to explore here.

Many of her suggestions echo our own pleas to ex-gay ministries over the years; stop political lobbying, stop emphasizing "change," genuinely respect . . . those who are comfortable with their sexual orientation (even though this may come from a personal understanding of Scripture which diverges from your own), recognize and remove the underlying tone which says that ex-ex-gays just didn't try hard enough, and on and on.

We thought Wendy might just be a breath of fresh Canadian air and asked her to write a guest post to spur on discussion. What might Exodus, or any ex-gay ministry, be like if they were to take these suggestions to heart? What does it mean that an ex-gay ministry which may just "get it" more than any so far, grew out of a country largely unfriendly to the kind of fundamentalism that often surrounds their US counterparts? How close does New Direction come to your idea of what a fair ex-gay ministry should be, if it is to be at all?

Wendy will be available to respond off and on in comments, so don't spare the hard questions. Her post follows:

Thank you for the invitation to write this piece. To be honest, my knees are knocking a bit.

I want to begin by saying I'm sorry. I'm sorry for the pain that some of those who follow this site have experienced from leaders like me and ministries like the one I lead. I'm sorry that some of you connected with this site who identify as Christian have had your faith questioned and judged. I'm sorry there is a felt need for a site like XGW. I'm sorry that it feels like legitimate concerns have not been listened to. I am sorry for the arrogance that can come across from leaders like me.

I suppose I'm not what some would assume to be your typical ex-gay leader. I'm not gay, not ex-gay, not ex-ex-gay.[11] Not male. Not Southern Baptist. Not Republican. Not even American. I'm a Gen X postmodern whose perspectives are, depending on who you talk to, too liberal or too conservative, unorthodox or too orthodox, heretical or vibrantly Christ-centered.

The ministry I lead is over 20 years old. I've been at the helm for the last 6 years—although truth be told, the first 2 years I was just trying to get my head around what the heck God had called me to. It's been the wildest learning curve of my life.

I deeply believe that God's intention for sexual expression is the covenant of marriage between one man and one woman. God has also deeply convicted me of my own pride in assuming that I had a perfect pipeline to God, and everyone who disagreed with me was simply deceived by the enemy or putting their own wants and desires ahead of commitment to God. I have had the opportunity that many conservatives have not had—and that is to come to know people who have deeply and honestly sought God through prayer and Scripture and come to a different conclusion than I. Their faith was neither trivial nor superficial, and though there were points of disagreement, I respect their deep commitment to God. And so, I've come to a place where I'm grateful that God has humbled me and given me the opportunity to listen, learn and engage with those who come to different perspectives.

I don't think my job is to change the minds of all those who think differently than I do. As an eclectic Calvinist, I believe God is the one who convicts and reroutes us in our minds and hearts. My job is to walk in step with the Spirit and do my very best to do what he tells me to do. I find a lot of affinity in the words attributed to St. Francis, "Preach the gospel at all times. If necessary, use words." As I work and serve, I find more often than not that what the Spirit whispers for me to do is to simply focus on serving and loving those he brings across my path.

I do think there needs to be a safe place within the Christian community for those who experience same-gender attraction who have wrestled with Scripture and come to believe a traditional biblical sexual ethic. I believe we have a long way to go to eradicate hateful and homophobic environments and responses in the Christian community. We have a long way to go to demolish the pervasive hierarchy of sin. And we have a long way to go to counter-act the perpetual sense of shame that many experience due to the reality of their same-gender attraction.

I work toward the day when a follower of Jesus who experiences same-gender attraction can be honest and open about that reality and receive support and encouragement in living a life that is pleasing to God. And I feel particularly called to do that within the conservative church.

I also feel called to speak to the conservative church about some of the ways I believe we have been distracted from the primary calling to support and encourage deeply devoted disciples of Jesus Christ.

1. We have been distracted by the politics around homosexuality. I do think there is a place for Christians to engage in the public arena. God calls his followers to be a blessing to all nations and to represent him by being the presence of *shalom* on the earth. Unfortunately, in many of the Christian political efforts regarding homosexuality there is little evidence of *shalom*. The result is that many who need to hear a gospel of good news perceive God's people to be hypocritical and unloving ("you say you love us—but you're fighting to prevent/take our rights"). This has perpetuated a sense of alienation that I believe grieves the heart of God.

2. We have been distracted by a focus on orientation change. The heart of Christian ministry was summed up by Jesus when he said, "Go, make disciples, teaching them to obey everything I've commanded you." The point of a ministry like the one I lead is to support and encourage disciples of Jesus in their journey to live out their sexuality in a manner that they believe is God-honoring. If in that process they experience a deeper ability to love their opposite gender spouse (if they were already married) or a greater capacity to engage an authentic romantic, sexual, marital relationship with someone of the opposite gender, that is a gift that can be gratefully received. But such gifts can't be predicted, they can't be guaranteed, they don't follow a set of instructions, or come after just the right combination of root identification and eradication. There is a sense of mystery that necessitates an attitude of humility, discussion of realistic expectations, and serenity. So at the end of the day, "change is possible" is not really the main point. Life in Christ is.

3. We have been distracted by the question of causation. While there is clearly a place for research on this topic, and those involved in ministry should have the integrity to stay abreast of current research, by and large the conclusions (or lack of

conclusion) on this matter are peripheral to the call of Christian ministry. Because there is currently such inconclusiveness on this question, conservative Christians would do well to humbly acknowledge this fact rather than being perceived as ill-informed, blinder-wearing, or agenda-promoting.

In light of some of these distractions, New Direction Ministries, under our current leadership, has laid out some distinctives for ministry:

1. We are pastorally-focused, not politically driven.
2. We are relationally-focused, not program driven.
3. We are discipleship-focused, not change driven.
4. We are partnership-focused, not empire driven.

Our Core Values are to be relational, respectful, relevant and redemptive.

I acknowledge that there have been people who have connected with our ministry who have left feeling hurt, confused and uncertain about how to go on with their lives having not experienced change. I wish I could pass the buck and say all of that happened before my time. Sexuality is incredibly complex. People are complex. Their stories, their experiences, and their journeys are unique. In the midst of this complex uniqueness, as ministers of the gospel we don't always get it right, we don't always discern appropriately. I hope that as a ministry, we are learning and growing and improving. I hope that we have created an environment that is open and safe regardless of what happens with someone's attractions. I know our staff are open to engage people where they're at. If people disengage from the ministry, which could happen for a multitude of different reasons, we hope that they would always feel they could return for a hot cup of coffee and be received with warmth, caring, and respect—regardless of where they might land on the ex-gay ~ ex-ex-gay continuum. When we can, we try to follow up with those who have left while respecting their privacy and right to be left alone as well. We believe God loves unconditionally and, though regularly faced with our own limitations, we seek to imitate him.

I see a lot of triumphalistic "name it, claim it" kind of stuff in the church, and it always makes me nervous. I don't particularly see evidence that the Christian journey should be about getting all the things we want—or even about our individual happiness. We see in Jesus Christ someone who poured himself out for the world, and he calls his followers to imitate him. Frankly, Christians aren't very good at pouring ourselves out for others, especially for those who disagree with us. The world sees this—and it compromises our ability to share the love and life of God with our neighbors. At the risk of being misunderstood or called heretics, we want to engage, listen, and be the presence of Christ with those who hold differing perspectives. We want to hang out with all the folks that make church leaders nervous (and frankly want to be the kind of people who make church leaders nervous)—because we know that is who Jesus was and what Jesus did. We do this, in part, because there is more common ground than might be initially apparent. And I think there could be more understanding and respect.

I've been very encouraged by some of the conversations I've had over the years that were respectful, charitable, and gracious. For all the caricatures Christians may have of gay people, I have encountered a whole array of responses—some not so nice—but many kind and thoughtful. I'm very grateful to those who, though personally holding a gay affirmative perspective, have acknowledged a place and even a need for a ministry like New Direction. And in those conversations, you've earned the right to keep us sharp and on our toes. You've been an interesting accountability partner at times—and my hope is that I will continue to be open to hear any appropriate critique that is offered. Likewise, I hope that in my engagement and offering of input, I will also earn the right to speak—particularly with those who name the name of Jesus Christ. The perception of polarization and enmity between Christians of differing minds on sexual ethics is damaging to a unified Christian witness to an increasingly post-Christian, skeptical generation. I want to be part of doing something about that.

So, we seek to be a nuanced, moderate voice in this area of ministry. The attempt at introducing this level of nuance has, in part, been impacted by listening to the critique of people like those represented at XGW. The listening process has, at times, been difficult and frustrating. It can be discouraging to feel "lumped in" with others, despite real attempts to chart our own distinct course. It can be painful to reach an impasse and feel there is no way through. It is disappointing to be accused of being disingenuous in attempts at bridge-building.

But I'm grateful for this journey nonetheless. Because in the process, we have felt compelled to put "first things first" and recognize when second place things were encroaching on an essential focus on Jesus Christ. One of the contributors to XGW at one point, somewhere, said something like, "The mission of ex-gay ministries should be to support those, who for religious reasons, seek to not be mastered by their experience of same-gender attraction." I think that is pretty darn close to what I would suggest too.

I am deeply passionate about contributing to a climate where anyone questioning, struggling, or embracing an alternative[12] sexual identity can encounter the presence of Jesus Christ. My focus in this area of engagement is unapologetically Christ-centered. Some might say that by the very nature of holding a traditional sexual ethic, I contribute to the inaccessibility of the gospel for gay and lesbian people. I believe the power of the gospel is not thwarted by a call to radical discipleship. And my prayer is that as we, at New Direction, commit ourselves to loving, serving, and building bridges with same-gender attracted people, Jesus will be seen in and through us.

Thank you for the opportunity to share my heart for Christian ministry from a conservative perspective. I look forward to further conversation.[13]

What followed this post was a storm of comments, some positive and some incisively critical. And suddenly, I was in a whole new ballgame. Things I'd thought and prayed about were now in front of my face in very personal, yet very public, conversations. Near the beginning of his book *Generous Orthodoxy*, Brian McLaren identifies some key practices when engaging different perspectives; he encourages the

> consistent practice of *humility, charity, courage* and *diligence*: *humility* that allows us to admit our past and current formulations may have been limited or distorted. *Charity* toward those of other traditions who may understand some things better than our group—even though we are more conscious of what we think we understand better. *Courage* to be faithful to the true path of our faith as we understand it even when it is unpopular, dangerous and difficult to do so. *Diligence* to seek again and again the true path of our faith whenever we feel we have lost our way, which seems to be pretty often.[14]

These were the practices that I tried to keep in front of me in this new territory. I prayed for much grace, that I would not get defensive, and that I would say nothing that would misrepresent Jesus. I was so mindful of how public this conversation was and deliberately tried to redirect my responses again and again back to a central focus on the person and work of Christ.

These experiences marked pivotal moments of transition in this adventure God has me on. One of the earliest vision statements for New Direction, many years before I came into my role, was to be a "bridge between the gay community and the church." But over the years, informed by the larger network and system of which it was a part, the ministry became inwardly focused—offering pastoral care for those within our ranks, those who agreed with our theology and absorbed our psychoanalytic theories about homosexuality. We were perceived as adopting a rather defensive posture, and despite very clear boundaries keeping us out of the political arena, we were expected to be on the front lines of standing against the onslaught of the "gay agenda." Such a narrow and perceived-to-be adversarial stance failed to embody that original missional vision of being a bridge. But now God was opening new doors and providing a practical laboratory to bring together my restlessness, dreams, and learning, and I walked through those doors with sometimes tentative, sometimes bold steps.

I have become convinced that the polarization of the church over the issue of homosexuality has been to our impoverishment on multiple levels. I believe there are crucial things we need to learn from one another to most effectively reach, disciple, and live in community with our neighbors. I am both compelled and haunted by Jesus's final prayer with his disciples as recorded in John 17:23, "May they be brought to complete unity to let the world know that you sent me and have loved them even as you have loved me." I believe there are helpful models of difficult but rich conversations within the larger body of Christ that can help to give shape and form to a hopeful vision of fruitful common ground.

In the midst of this journey, I have been so grateful to encounter and connect with mutual pilgrims who could resonate with some of my restlessness and the seemingly crazy roller-coaster rides God calls us to. This book is for such souls. Those who love God with a deep passion. Those who are gay or those who deeply love those who are gay, or experience same-sex attraction.[15] Those who have wrestled with gut-level incongruities and persevered to search for a faith that is authentic and real. This is a book for those who find themselves caught up in the agony of uncertainty when so many of the Christians around them seem disaffected or simply closed to tension and questioning. This is a book for those who love the body of Christ (and by this I don't necessarily mean the institutional church but the call of our relational Triune God to know him in the context of relationship with other disciples of Christ) with an honest, sometimes critical but enduringly loyal, commitment. And this is a book for those who are deeply immersed in the mission of God to bless the world through his people. For those who have become disillusioned with the Christian faith and the church's response to gay people, this book is also for you, and I pray that you will find a reason to hope and reengage in these pages.

This is a book written with the church in mind, in particular, those congregations in which much diversity exists and for whom simplistic, black-and-white answers on these questions will not suffice. I see this book as a word in a transitional season. I believe these questions surrounding homosexuality are best engaged as part of a much bigger conversation about the expression of the Christian faith in our Western culture and global reality. I see it connected to the larger systemic questions around equity and diversity that touch so many aspects of our common life together. My hope is that many of the particular questions this book engages will cease to be such sources of anxiety and tension in the near future. However, as I look back over church history and see the pattern of turmoil in times of significant change, I am reminded of the many years leading up to, in the midst of, and in the aftermath of seasons of change. In light of that, my prayer is that this book will be of help to the church in this journey.

Certainly, my own journey is far from over. I'm not in the harbor, tied to the dock. I'm still out in the wind, navigating the waves and tides, in the thick of day-to-day conversation, engagement, and service. I fully expect God to continue calling me to deeper humility, charity, courage, and diligence.

While I am neither a theologian nor a psychologist (the kind of people who tend to write on this topic), I am a practitioner with over ten years of experience in focusing on this area of pastoral care and cultural engagement. I write as someone at the grassroots, listening for the whisper of the Spirit, seeking to be alert to the surge of life within various parts of the body, having engaged relationally with a diverse spectrum of individuals and communities. I'm not interested in joining the chorus of voices clamoring for this position or that perspective. This book is decidedly not about *the* right answer or solution for the church on the theological topic of homosexuality. It intentionally positions itself at a different starting point. It values the spiritual formation inherent in the experience of exploring intimate relationship with God and with each other as we wrestle through these difficult questions and challenges and face the inevitable differences that result. Its posture seeks to be one of openness that is inquisitive, personal, relational, and dependent on the Spirit. This book is about generous spaciousness.

Walter Brueggemann has said that what is needed in the body of Christ is an embodiment of the gospel that is "dramatic, artistic, capable of inviting persons to join another conversation, free of the reason of technique, unencumbered by ontologies that grow abstract, unembarrassed about concreteness."[16] Brueggemann is speaking here of the poetic voice, a voice that can speak beyond our entrenched systems, our arrogant certainties, and the veneer that covers our core anxieties and deepest fears. I envision such a voice to have a wildness and beauty that can touch the parchedness pervading our discussions around our gay brothers and sisters in the church. I pray for such a voice to permeate the pages of this book. I am hopeful for the ways God will resurrect fresh imagination and creativity through this project.

In my experience, the complexity surrounding matters of sexuality, the unique realities affecting each individual and situation, and the unknown factors and unanswerable questions necessitate a humble recognition of the inadequacy of our best attempts. Seeking a poetic voice, such as Brueggemann describes, is not a search for the definitive, final say on the matter. Rather, the poetic voice calls for a rediscovery

26

of wonder—the wonder that incarnates the welcoming, accepting, re-deeming heart of God for all his creation.

I've read a lot of books covering the intersection of faith and ho-mosexuality. Many of them proffered answers. Many of these answers were profoundly unsatisfactory as I encountered one unique individual after another. In light of this, I have tried to write in a manner that shares the insights and experiences gathered over my years of personal conversations and pastoral engagement. But I have avoided attempting to formulate a one-size-fits-all response. My hope is that this book will give you permission to confront the tensions and air the questions you should ask, and allow you to encounter a spacious place in which to continue to press into the heart of God. I believe that engaging in these areas will allow us to live out Jesus's summary of the law: to love the Lord our God with all our heart, mind, soul and strength, and to love our neighbor as ourselves.

1

Reevaluating Evangelical Ex-gay Ministry

I remember well the catch-22 conversation. It was in the context of my temporary job as an office worker just prior to going to seminary in 1995. I was earnest and idealistic and, looking back, had a heaping helping of naiveté. This job had long stretches of boredom when my coworker and I had plenty of opportunities for far-ranging conversations. She was a plucky single mom in a tough situation, trying to find a better life for herself and her young daughter. We didn't always see eye-to-eye, given her agnosticism and my evangelicalism, but I respected her intelligence and common sense and appreciated her kindness. One afternoon our conversation turned to the subject of our gay friends. I lamented the church's poor track record in welcoming gay people and expressed my desire to serve as an advocate for them in the church. At the time, I felt that I was quite open, quite generous in my attitudes and opinions. My coworker thought I was full of crap. "But you believe the Bible says homosexuality is sin, right?" she challenged. I stammered and stuttered through my response, trying to reiterate my true heart, which I believed to be genuinely loving toward gay people. She wasn't having any of it. With candid bluntness she said, "They won't believe you care about them as long as you believe homosexuality is a sin. You can't have it both ways."

It was a question that would haunt me and tear at my heart. Could I not find a way to love gay people and continue to hold a traditional understanding of biblical teaching regarding homosexual behavior? This tension is what I often encounter as I speak with Christians. One pastor described getting to know a gay couple who daily went to the same local coffee shop he did. Over time, cordial greetings evolved into a sense of real relationship. At one point this couple, knowing he was a pastor, asked if he would perform a marriage ceremony for them. My pastor friend told them that it crucified him to have to say no. This demonstrates the depth of the tension one can feel. "I deeply love my gay friends—but I cannot violate what I believe the Bible teaches."

In the eighteen years since I had that conversation with my coworker, there has been rapid change within our culture at large and within the Western church in both its attitudes and engagement with gay people. In general, rapid and extensive cultural change "exhausts our physical, mental and spiritual resources by its sheer magnitude."[1] We live in uncertain times that have eroded people's sense of and ability to trust. Some consider this a skeptical and cynical generation. Competing philosophies, theologies, ecclesiologies, and epistemologies have shaken many of our faith communities. Gone are the days of monolithic congregations with general doctrinal consensus. Today, there is great diversity in perspective in the pews.

For some, the uncertainty that accompanies such change elicits a sense of loss and a longing to go back to simpler and more predictable times. This can manifest itself in dire warnings and denunciations of people who propose more progressive responses. For others, this is a time of adventure, dreaming new dreams and taking risks to step into new expressions of redemptive community. Some people feel the need to distance themselves from established institutions and traditions. People's responses to change can be stressful and unpredictable. But learning to listen to one another, engage in dialogue, and discern together what the Holy Spirit is saying to a particular people, in a particular place, at a particular time is an effective incubator for spiritual formation and growth. The truth is we need one another. Iron sharpens iron. As we encounter the need to honor one another, submit to one another, and extend grace to one another, our capacity to love enlarges.

After a number of years leading an organization with an ex-gay focus, I became compelled to reassess the structure of our ministry. Its foundation and development were based on evangelicalism, Christian counseling, and a quarter century of entrenched enmity between the church and the perceived agenda of the gay community. We'll discuss each of these below.

The Journey of Evangelicalism

Evangelicalism can be understood as a movement within Christianity that has four key aspects: an emphasis on personal conversion and intimate relationship with Christ, living out the values of the gospel in one's daily life with a particular focus on sharing one's faith with others, a high regard for biblical authority, and a central focus on the death and resurrection of Jesus. This movement, from the beginning, crossed denominational lines and therefore celebrated unity with some degree of diversity. For the last few decades, evangelicals have been feeling the tremors of change, struggling through an identity crisis, with the desire to be both faithful and relevant.

Ex-gay ministry sprouted from this soil, and it internalized some of these tensions. On one hand, ex-gay ministries were seeking to be innovative and relevant in their engagement with a marginalized group, the gay community, that the church at large wanted nothing to do with. On the other hand, these ministries wanted to be a beacon for radical discipleship and a corrective to the perceived slide into moral relativism that seemed to be threatening evangelical churches.

Fighting for recognition, acceptance, and support within the larger ministry of the evangelical church, ex-gay leaders struggled to know how to present their pioneering but controversial work in a way that

31

would activate the imagination of their fellow evangelicals. If such activation happened, evangelicals could always be counted on to be passionate in their involvement.

This is mirrored in many ex-gay ministries. There is a lot of passion. Many of the leaders themselves have journeyed to make sense of their same-sex attraction and the commitments and values of their faith. They know how arduous the journey can be, and their evangelical faith compels them to help by serving and ministering to others just starting down the path. But there are times that such passion, and the lack of appropriate education and training, has the potential to harm.

I did a fair amount of teaching and speaking in my early years at New Direction. While I had finished my master of divinity degree, my educational training did very little to prepare me for the ex-gay environment I found myself in. I've always considered myself a pretty quick study, and so upon taking my position, I dug in with gusto. I read everything in the ministry's library, listened to recordings of seminars, and spent hours in conversation with staff and with ministry recipients. And I prayed. A lot. And then I hit the ground running. Determined to raise the profile of the ministry, to equip the church, to fulfill my call, and to serve well, I pursued opportunities anywhere that would have me. What I didn't realize then is that I was simply regurgitating what I had learned from the internal system of the ministry, with little to no exposure to informed critique. I simply assumed that everything I had learned was true. The information had been researched and compiled by knowledgeable and experienced ministry leaders, who loved God; so of course it must all be useful and accurate and helpful.

My intentions were good. I wanted, passionately wanted, the church to reach out to and minister effectively with gay people. I wanted to break through the complacency and apathy that grips so much of the church. I wanted to bring hope where there was discouragement. I wanted to be an advocate for gay people where there was judgment, anger, and fear. I wanted to convey the heart of my evangelical faith—that in Christ there is redemption, transformation, healing, and wholeness. And while these are things I continue to passionately desire, I have had to face the truth that I inadvertently taught theories about homosexuality that have since proven to be deficient, and I promoted ministry interventions that had the capacity to cause much personal harm to the individual. Though not aware at the time, I have come to see that many ex-gay ministries inflated the claims of these theories and promoted personal testimonies to support their convictions that God would redeem gay people in the manner that fit their paradigms. Having learned from these mistakes, I now want to help the church do better.

One of the hallmarks of evangelicalism, and by extension ex-gay ministry, is the vigilance with which it guards its own internal content as both normative and binding. One could say that a lot of energy is spent on boundary maintenance—discerning who is inside and who is outside of the boundaries of shared commitments. This is in contrast to nonevangelical ministries that exhibit a more generous inclusiveness and that may have more fluid and flexible boundaries, understanding and accepting wider points of view while still sharing common values. However, in evangelicalism and in ex-gay ministry, anything that seemed to deviate from the commonly held beliefs and understandings about homosexuality and healing were considered invalid and potential deceptions from the enemy. To investigate or inquire beyond these commonly held assumptions was dangerous territory, where one would be vulnerable to error. And while there is diversity within the networks in the ex-gay movement, for the most part, the fundamental boundaries are clearly marked and maintained. Anyone who ventured beyond them was suspect.

Although there are very intelligent people within the ex-gay network, with some holding PhDs, I often sensed a general anti-intellectual flavor among the membership. In some conversations, I encountered a type of capitulation to the expert: "My pastor says . . . ," or "Andy Comiskey[2] says . . . ," or "Frank Worthen[3] says . . . ," or "Leanne Payne[4] says. . . ." Such a mentality breeds an ironic blend of both a lack of confidence and arrogance. On one hand, the individual doesn't feel adequate in his or her own ability to think and discern and have confidence in his or her own assessments. But on the other hand, the individual can possess a rigid arrogance, believing that the position and perspective of a specific expert is the only one that can be right.

33

Having grown up in a Reformed denomination, I was both attracted to and, at times, challenged by an evangelistic fervor that I'd not experienced growing up. There were aspects of evangelical faith and belief expressed in other denominational traditions that appealed to me; for example, I was grateful to be exposed to a deeper engagement with the Holy Spirit through the charismatic and Pentecostal traditions. As I have hit my midlife stride, I'm grateful to have had the opportunity to learn from many different expressions of the body of Christ, as well as embrace the rich gifts my own tradition has to offer. One of the gifts of my particular denomination is its commitment to intellectual rigor. And it was this aspect of my heritage that was a key contributor in motivating me to question, think, research, and explore how different systems and paradigms might impact the expression of Christian ministry and mission with gay people.

It's funny, though, how we can turn away from our own heritage when we've become immersed in a new system that maintains order and orthodoxy through fear and deferral to experts. For a number of years that is where I was in evangelicalism. I absorbed both the fear of compromise and the fear of being labeled as one who had compromised. After all, the stakes seemed so high: I didn't dare question the rock solid position on homosexuality held by ex-gay practitioners lest I be responsible for gay people going to hell, society breaking down completely, and angering and disappointing God.

Psychology and Christianity

In my early days with the ministry, a gentleman in my denomination sent me an article written by Lewis Smedes, who was a well-respected theologian in the Christian circles in which I'd grown up. The article was titled, "Like the Wideness of the Sea?" and refers to the lyrics of a hymn comparing God's great mercy to the wideness of the sea. The question mark Smedes added to the phrase was to provoke readers to ask themselves, "Does God's great mercy really extend to gay people?" In the article, Smedes compares the contemporary pastoral concerns regarding homosexuality with the church's response to those who had divorced and remarried. He suggests that divorced people who have remarried and gay people in committed same-sex relationships are similar in five ways:

1. Both divorced [people who have] remarried and [gay] partners are seeking to fulfill a fundamental, God-implanted human need for a shared life of intimate, committed and exclusive love with one other human being.
2. Both are fulfilling their God-given human need in the only way available to them, not what the Creator originally intended for his children, but the only way they have.
3. Both are striving to do the one thing the Lord considered supremely important about all sexual relationships: they are living their sexual lives within their covenants with each other.
4. Both are trying to create the best lives they can within the limits of personal conditions they cannot change.
5. Both want to live as followers of Christ within the supportive embrace of the Church.

Smedes concludes, "Yes, it does seem to me that our embrace of divorced and remarried Christian people did indeed set a precedent for embracing Christian homosexuals who live together."[5]

If I try, I can almost physically recall the anxiety I felt as I read the article. My thoughts raced, "Of course, Dr. Smedes—distinguished and respected ethicist and theologian—didn't understand as I, an Exodus network leader, did that change was indeed possible. Of course, Dr. Smedes, despite his many years of teaching and pastoring, had simply become sentimental in his engagement with people. Obviously, he was putting his own misguided compassion ahead of reverence for the holiness of God." Not long after reading the article, a friend and I lamented how Smedes had slipped down the slope of moral relativism. How arrogant I was. How unwilling, or perhaps unable, I was to name my own anxiety as being the biggest barrier to engage the thoughts presented in the article. There was too much at stake. Too much to lose. God *needed* me, I convinced myself, to be his gatekeeper, to be a watchman on the walls.

Despite some differences in theological perspectives within the ex-gay movement, this system I was a part of drew a very clear line in the sand regarding points directly related to homosexuality. For example, at that time Exodus International's doctrinal and policy statement read,

Exodus upholds heterosexuality as God's creative intent for humanity, and subsequently views homosexual expression as outside of God's will. Exodus cites homosexual tendencies as one of many disorders that beset fallen humanity. Choosing to resolve these tendencies through homosexual behavior, taking on a homosexual identity, and involvement in the homosexual lifestyle is considered destructive, as it distorts God's intent for the individual and is thus sinful. Instead, Christ offers a healing alternative to those with homosexual tendencies. Exodus upholds redemption for the homosexual person as the process whereby sin's power is broken, and the individual is freed to know and experience true identity as discovered in Christ and His Church. That process entails the freedom to grow into heterosexuality.[6]

Within evangelical circles throughout the late 1980s, 1990s, and early 2000s, ex-gay ministry was the predominant ministry paradigm addressing homosexuality, and it prided itself on being both the guardian of orthodox belief about sexuality and the practical extension of redemptive ministry to those affected by homosexuality.

Many ex-gay ministries espouse a variety of psychoanalytic theories in the development of ministry interventions. The most notable example of this is their embrace of the work of Elizabeth Moberly, a British psychologist who wrote *Homosexuality: A New Christian Ethic* in 1983. She hypothesizes that same-sex attraction is caused by a disruption and sense of rejection, either real or perceived, in a child's relationship with his or her same-sex parent. This disruption and sense of rejection causes a deficit that Moberly posits leads to a reparative drive. At the onset of puberty, this reparative drive to find connection and affection with a significant other of the same sex becomes eroticized. Moberly suggests that the drive itself is not so different from the kind of bonding that heterosexuals experience in friendship and camaraderie. Her theory, therefore, suggests that to repair this need for same-sex love and connection, those who experience same-sex attraction need to focus on building nonsexual intimate friendships with people of the same sex and work on strengthening their sense of gender security in order to diminish same-sex sexual attractions.

This particular theory, caricatured by the idea of the absent father and domineering mother, shaped evangelical ministry to gay people. Having listened to many people's firsthand experiences, I can tell you that many Christian individuals in such support groups felt they could identify with the kinds of experiences Moberly described. I think this sense of identification, combined with a longing to find some key to unlock the door to their presumed hidden heterosexual potential, was a big part of the ongoing energy in ex-gay circles for this theory. However, this theory has been heavily critiqued and disputed. Gay individuals who do not identify with the assumptions of this theory, those who had good relationships with their same-sex parent and same-sex peers, have been part of deconstructing the credibility of this model. For many gay people, their life experiences simply do not match Moberly's causal theory.

Many local practitioners, through pastoral ministry initiatives, such as support groups and one-on-one meetings, apply these theories in people's lives despite failing to hold basic credentials in psychology or therapeutic counseling.

Three evangelical psychologists who have made particularly significant contributions in their work with same-sex-attracted clients are Mark Yarhouse, Warren Throckmorton, and Janelle Hallman. It is interesting to note, however, that all three have taken moderate positions in distancing themselves from what is termed a reparative therapy model. Yarhouse and Throckmorton developed a "Sexual Identity Therapy Framework."[7] One of the important contributions of this framework was demonstrating to colleagues in the American Psychological Association that some clients prioritize their religious identity over their sexual identity. In other words, honoring the values, goals, and autonomy of the client means to support the client in living consistently within their chosen religious identity. While Yarhouse,[8] Throckmorton, and Hallman[9] (who brings particular expertise in working with same-sex-attracted women) continue to articulate a clear position that sexual intimacy is reserved for the marriage covenant between one man and one woman, they all seem to have evolved in their position on the ability to change sexual orientation.

Christian counseling may be helpful for those who are questioning or struggling with their sense of sexual identity or who have additionally experienced past trauma, such as abuse, dysfunctional family dynamics, or bullying and harassment. But it is critical that counseling be initiated and desired by the individual (and not just by the family or pastor). Future ministry initiatives with sexual minorities will be well served by putting Christian counseling and therapeutic practices within the proper perspective, as an additional resource and service for those who particularly request and require it.

A History of Enmity: The Church and the Gay "Agenda"

It is a common perception that the church hates gay people. This generalized, unqualified statement is not helpful. Its origin, however, arises from the manner in which the church, and in particular the evangelical church, has responded to public and civil matters of equity in relation to LGBTQ (lesbian, gay, bisexual, transgender, queer) people. Patrick Chapman, in his book *Thou Shalt Not Love: What Evangelicals Really Say to Gays*, outlines a thorough history of the evangelical church's message in public forums on gay issues. He says, "In evangelical circles it is referred to as the 'gay agenda,' seen by many evangelical leaders as a stealthy attempt by homosexuals to abolish Christian morality and undermine American society. . . . Therefore, many evangelical leaders encourage their followers to oppose homosexuals' attempts to gain equality."[10]

Chapman's book was published in 2008, and one might argue that the pendulum has since swung toward gay marriage. In Canada, where gay marriage has been in place since 2005, civil rights for gay people are not typically a front and center issue. Some would argue that the more critical issue is freedom of speech for those who in good conscience seek to speak about their particular convictions against homosexual practice. But despite the movement toward a more gay-positive climate, the residue of the evangelical community's protests and resistance to issues like gay marriage continues to negatively affect the perceptions and mind-sets of many.

New Direction policy has always been to avoid overt involvement in political matters. But in the past, we were associated with the actions of American organizations as they spoke publicly against overturning sodomy laws, against hate crimes legislation, and against gay marriage. The Christian witness never benefits when Christian organizations are known more for what they are against than what they are for. This is part of the history that makes reconciliation, bridge building, and nurturing generous spaciousness more challenging and complex.

My particular background gives me an insider perspective on the development of ex-gay ministry as the church's response to sexual minorities. However, ex-gay ministry was not the only response of the church. Below, I briefly introduce several long-standing, affirming ministries and organizations. After years of fighting for basic civil rights for gay people and for safe and welcoming places within the Christian community, many of these organizations are now contemplating what the next leg on their journey will be as the context around them continues to change.

The Metropolitan Community Church (MCC) denomination was founded by the Rev. Troy Perry in Los Angeles in 1968. The church was fully affirming of LGBT people and focused on social action generally and civil rights for gay people particularly. MCC is considered by many to have spearheaded the quest for marriage equality. The theological bent of MCC churches can be somewhat diverse, but many would consider them to be relatively conservative and evangelical. Often caricatured as the "gay church," some MCC congregations are in transition as affirming churches now exist in other denominations. Brent Hawkes, longtime MCC pastor in Toronto, beamed as he told me that the fastest growing demographic for their congregation is young heterosexual couples with children. (Today there are over 250 MCC churches in twenty-three countries.)

Evangelicals Concerned (EC) is "a national volunteer organization and fellowship of Christians concerned about addressing the integration of Christian lifestyle and homosexuality." Their goal is to "live lives of Christian love and discipleship while helping other evangelicals better understand homosexuality and gay people better understand the Gospel."[11] EC was founded by Dr. Ralph Blair, a psychotherapist, in 1975. EC runs annual conferences as well as regional Bible studies and gatherings for mutual encouragement and support.

Soulforce, another affirming ministry organization, "is committed to freedom for lesbian, gay, bisexual, transgender, and queer people from religious and political oppression through relentless nonviolent resistance."[12] Founded in 1998 by the Rev. Dr. Mel White, Soulforce was developed as a social justice and civil rights organization inspired by the principles of nonviolence as espoused by the Rev. Dr. Martin Luther King Jr. and Gandhi. Soulforce seeks dialogue with Christian organizations and churches through initiatives such as their Equality Ride (which seeks dialogue with Christian college campuses), American Family Outing (which seeks dialogue with megachurches), and Seven Straight Nights for Equal Rights (which allows straight allies to stand with them). When dialogue is denied, Soulforce conducts acts of nonviolent resistance, such as vigils, sit-ins, protest rallies, and marches.

During my early time with ex-gay ministry, I absorbed the notion that these organizations and ministries were to be avoided. However, refusing to even review and reflect on their work with prayerful discernment meant that I missed the opportunity to be challenged and stretched by their sense of calling and mission.

2

Of Doubt, Tension, and Anxiety

Simply said, it was a system that was strangling me. I would wake up in the middle of the night with visceral, gut-level angst, crying out to God, "If I am wrong, show me!" The weight of what I represented—calling all gay Christians to a chaste, celibate life—was crushing me. "If I am wrong, show me, for I am calling people to a very narrow path, a path that I know I fail to fully walk in my own life." I did not have words to describe this mixture of doubt and dread. In those moments, in the middle of the night, I keenly sensed God's presence, but he never wrote on the wall, "Wendy, you're right," or "Wendy, you're wrong." Either one would have been fine. I just wanted release from the tension of uncertainty. Rather, in those dark moments lying in bed with tears streaming down my face, in my mind's eye I could see only Jesus. His face was obscured with shadows; he was on the cross and I was at his feet, and I could see that he, too, was weeping. This was the only response I ever received in these recurrent episodes of agonized pleading for certainty, and though the deep questions remained unanswered, in those exquisite moments, there was a glimpse of peace. And while initially I would have much preferred clear writing on the wall, over time I grew to treasure these encounters, more content to simply be in Christ's presence than gain the knowledge I was seeking. These experiences were transforming me in ways I did not fully understand.

Perhaps those who only encounter a few gay people might find it hard to relate to my anguish. But I had accumulated years of conversations, years of personal relationships with hundreds of people and their families, and I could not avoid the depth of pain that these unanswerable questions caused. For a long time, I simply determined to believe with greater passion. I reminded myself of the cost of discipleship, the call to carry one's cross.

Barriers that Prevent Necessary Questions

I could feel my heart being compartmentalized into separate rooms, with certain doors I dared not open. As much as I tried to believe the "right" way, to be loyal to the system of truth that had been instilled in me from infancy, I was feeling more and more fragmented and fearful. At these lowest points, I could sense the Spirit's whisper, "Stay present in the uncertainty." As much as I wanted to scream, "No, I can't; I need some resolution," I increasingly knew that this place was where God wanted me. I knew that I could not live and be fully alive with locked doors in my soul. And while I did not understand what was happening or what the outcomes might be, as I continued to listen, pray, reflect, and write, I could sense that God was transforming me. He was taking me from a place of fear and desperation to a place of increasing fearlessness and bold love.

Reading Peter Rollins's book, *How (Not) to Speak of God*, gave me language for my experiences of the previous seven years. He says,

> In contrast to the modern view that religious doubt is something to reject, fear or merely tolerate, doubt not only can be seen as an inevitable aspect of our humanity but also can be celebrated as a vital part of faith. Doubt has often been disparaged, or merely tolerated, because it is seen as leading to an inert state of undecidability in which nothing can be believed

42

or acted upon. Yet in reality it is only in the midst of undecidability that real decisions are made. . . . Doubt provides the context out of which real decision occurs and real love is tested, for love will say "yes" regardless of uncertainty. A love that requires contracts and absolute assurance in order to act is no love at all. . . . Only a genuine faith can embrace doubt, for such a faith does not act because of a self-interested reason (such as fear of hell or desire for heaven) but acts simply because it must.[1]

In my wrestling to know Christ more deeply and follow his leading in my ministry, I was confronted by a multiplicity of self-interested motivations. Most profound was my deep desire to do the right thing, believe the right thing, serve in the right way, lead in the right way. I wanted to do it right to avoid wrath, to avoid punishment, to avoid the overwhelming despair I would feel if God looked on me with disapproval, disgust, and disappointment. At one Exodus leadership conference, I spoke with a pastor who had just given a rousing, motivational address on confidence in God's grace. Nearly at the point of breaking down, barely able to verbalize the turbulence in my soul, I told him I was afraid of disappointing God. This Southern pastor looked at me with great compassion in his eyes and said, "Honey, he is not disappointed with you." I couldn't help but wonder if he would have had this kind and compassionate response if he knew that I was questioning (to the very depths) the framework upon which Exodus was built.

In a very practical sense, there were also external pressures. The board, staff, ministry recipients, and constituency who supported the work of New Direction trusted me to embody the beliefs and value system of the ministry. I keenly felt the burden of their trust, and I did not want to break it. I truly did not want to hurt or confuse these people who I loved and cared about.

Having been in ex-gay ministry circles over the years, I knew the pain that those within the system felt when someone seemingly defected "to the other side." And I remembered how easy it was for me to feel threatened and defensive when I encountered people who appeared to have moved from a traditional understanding of Scripture's boundaries for same-sex sexual behavior toward a more inclusive and affirming stance. I remembered feeling quite justified in my judgments of them because, after all, I felt they had distorted the truth. I lamented people's lack of certainty, attributing it to them being either deceived by the enemy or selfish and fleshly. I felt that I needed to be very guarded, that I needed to be very careful to not be tricked or fooled into deceptive thinking.

And if this was true for me, someone who was not personally wrestling with the experience of same-sex attraction, I can only imagine how intense these feelings might be for someone who experienced unwanted same-sex attraction and was seeking to live in alignment with traditional beliefs. One such woman made this comment on our blog: "It is WAY too hard to take that journey of obedience unless there is strong reinforcement from brothers and sisters in Christ. Also, there is often an inability for many 'strugglers' (for lack of a better term) to engage with those who are gay affirming because it's too much of a stumbling block for them."[2]

When someone became affirming, there was a sense that the person's defection made the loyalty more difficult of those who were continuing to hold to traditional standards at great personal cost. And while one might argue that people need to stay true to their convictions because of their own internal motivations, I could empathize with these feelings and did not want my actions to cause this kind of personal betrayal.

I also didn't want to be responsible for destroying the ministry that God and others had built over more than twenty-five years. If I dared to air my questions, if I dared to deconstruct, rethink, articulate my uncertainties, it could easily (and did) lead to a loss of donors. And without funds, the ministry organization would cease to exist. I felt responsible for the livelihood of my staff and the maintenance of the organization.

Then there was also the matter of my own reputation. When I originally took the role with New Direction, there were friends in ministry who advised against taking on this topic of homosexuality because it could pigeonhole me. Well, if they thought that then, how much more of a hit would my ministry career take if I were publicly labeled a traitor to orthodoxy? It felt as if I would have to give up any future hope of ministry service.

Whether or not these fears were realistic, they represented the pressures that weighed on me day in and day out. By the end of seven years, I was completely burned out and desperate for God to move.

I knew of a man who I suspected would be able to understand. Jeremy Marks founded Courage, an ex-gay ministry in the United Kingdom, in 1988. "Jeremy startled the evangelical world by publicly repudiating the ex-gay movement, proclaiming that it did more harm than good. *Courage* then embraced an unequivocally gay-affirming approach, recognizing the despair that had resulted for so many sincere Christian folk who had tried the 'ex-gay' approach."[3] After this, Courage's membership in Exodus was terminated, they were rejected from other evangelical groups they'd been a part of, and they suffered tremendous financial loss as donors quickly pulled their support. All of this happened in 2000, two years before I came into my role with New Direction, but I had read about it. In spring 2009, I called Jeremy. I hoped that I would find a safe place to share the pain of ambiguity that had become my daily companion. I found Jeremy to be a humble, kind, and compassionate man—a brother in Christ. He listened with empathy and understanding. He offered to send me the book he'd written, and in turn I sent him a copy of our newly released DVD set, *Bridging the Gap*.

In his book, I encountered a mutual pilgrim, our journeys being similar in some ways and quite distinct in others. He introduced me to the writings of James Alison who said,

> When you are *not* aware that there is Another, bigger than us, who is holding all of us in his hand through the upheaval and that ultimately we are safe, there is room, we can be wrong, and we can learn to get it right; when you are *not* aware of that, then you are frightened of disagreement and what you need to do is to produce a unanimity of opinion, of ideology, you need to get everyone to agree, and have those who are in, in, and those who are out, out.[4]

I was understanding in deeper and deeper ways that the questions and doubts I was experiencing were not antithetical to faith but rather an expression of a robust and daring faith, and this gave me courage to continue to deconstruct the systems that had become so stifling. But it may be helpful to offer some context to what caused these doubts in the first place.

Ex-Gay Ministry's Focus on Orientation Change

When I came into ex-gay ministry, I was initiated into a world that most people in the evangelical community understand in only a cursory way. I have found that people have one of two basic reactions to ex-gay ministry. Either they agree that God can heal people and point to ex-gay testimonies as evidence. Or they know people who had negative experiences with ex-gay ministry and feel that essentially no one experiences change.

In the 1990s, the critique from gay activists began intensifying. They argued that there was no scientific evidence that orientation could be altered successfully. And they claimed that the people who most ferociously defended the success of ex-gay ministry to effect orientation change were the very people who held leadership positions within ex-gay ministry. These leaders claimed that they themselves had experienced same-sex attractions but had overcome them through their commitment to Jesus Christ. The critique was that orientation change was supported only by self-report, and those who reported personal success clearly had vested interests, given that their livelihood depended on the evidence of their healing. In 2002, my understanding from listening to past Exodus seminars and printed articles was that one third of the people who attempted orientation change experienced significant change, one third experienced moderate change, and one third experienced little to no change.[5]

The mentality within ex-gay circles was that those who questioned orientation change did not know as intimately as ex-gay leaders did the lives of those who had indeed moved successfully into heterosexual marriage. A common response by the leaders to critics was, "If orientation change isn't possible, then why were my ten years in the gay community the most miserable of my life, but the last six years with my wife the best I've ever had?"

In the early years, I had the opportunity to build relationships with a lot of people in ex-gay circles. I never interrogated my friends about the intimate details of their sex lives or sexual desires. But I did see mature men and women with solid families and deep commitments to their opposite-gender spouses. It wasn't so much about technical proof of orientation change but more the sense that, for those who wanted to follow Christ, an ex-gay life was possible. I also met ex-gays who were single. Some were open to a romantic relationship with someone of the opposite sex. Others, often those who had been engaged in the journey for some years, were quite honest about the reality of their ongoing same-sex attraction and had seemingly come to a place of peace with living a single life.

These friends' lives reinforced my convictions that heterosexual marriage or celibacy were the two God-honoring options available to those who experienced same-sex attraction. My friends demonstrated to me that living consistently with a traditional understanding that precluded same-sex sexual behavior was possible.

What I did not realize was that I had closed myself off from engaging with those who had very different experiences. I had discounted any other experience than what I had encountered in ex-gay circles.

Gay and Christian?

A common question I heard was whether or not someone involved in a gay relationship could truly be a Christian. Many in ex-gay circles viewed salvation from an evangelical perspective: one is saved through belief in Jesus Christ as Savior and Lord. However, passages such as 1 Corinthians 6:9–10, often caused evangelicals to question whether someone in a gay relationship was ever really saved to begin with: "Do you not know that the wicked will not inherit the kingdom of God? Do not be deceived: Neither the sexually immoral . . . nor male prostitutes nor homosexual offenders . . . will inherit the kingdom of God" (NIV 1984). They often quoted verse 11 of that text to suggest that if someone was truly a Christian they would no longer be involved in homosexual behavior, "And that is what some of you were. But you were washed, you were sanctified, you were justified in the name of the Lord Jesus Christ and by the Spirit of our God" (NIV 1984 and NIV).

This question was often the litmus test posed to me by audience members in churches where I was invited to speak. In my response I clarified the distinction between justification (our being reconciled to

God because of Jesus's atoning work) and sanctification (the process of becoming holy) and indicated that our sexual behavior fell into the realm of sanctification. I emphasized that only God can truly know where an individual's heart is. I would say, "He knows whether they are turning toward him, or just playing games, or too wounded to move forward, or too rebellious to move forward. What I do know is that it is God's heart that none should perish but that all would return to him and be restored to him. Since I do not know the condition of a person's heart, I will take them at their word if they profess to be a Christian and I will keep encouraging them to draw near to God."

Looking back, I often failed to lead and instead responded out of the fear of failing people's orthodoxy tests. I often stifled the questions that came up in my own heart and was too intimidated by those who were so sure and certain. In my first year with the ministry, I was at an event where I had been invited to speak on a panel. During the break, an older woman came up to me and challenged me on a statement I'd made differentiating between attraction and behavior. She was convinced that the experience of same-sex attraction was sinful and that I was dangerous. The experience shook me. I was unprepared for how personal these challenges could be. I had taken my role with New Direction because I felt a deep love for gay people and wanted to serve them through both effective pastoral care and advocacy on their behalf within the church. I was completely naïve about the pressures and personal attacks I would face.

Ex-Gay Survivors

As scared as I was to fail the orthodoxy tests, inside my own heart and mind I continued to push the boundaries of my own assumptions. I started reading stories of ex-gay survivors. Peterson Toscano and Christine Bakke launched a website called "Beyond Ex-Gay" in 2007. Here I was confronted with the lives of gay people who shared journeys of pain, self-loathing, shame, and seasons of nearly shipwrecked or completely abandoned faith. I was heartbroken. I could no longer do the mental gymnastics that accused those who left the ex-gay path as those who "didn't have enough faith or hadn't tried hard enough."

Stories like Eugene's (below) motivated me to continue to question and explore:

Not wanting a life of one-night stands (which seemed at the time to be my only alternative), I joined a Living Waters[6] program. . . . [I]t was a godsend . . . to be able to talk about all these feelings that I'd kept hidden (even from myself) for so long.

In retrospect that group was exactly what I needed at the time. It did, regrettably, leave me with the impression that I'd start growing into my "natural heterosexuality" any day, but it also forced me to confront a number of issues in my life including problems I'd had with my father and stepfather, and the healing I experienced as a result of all of that left me emotionally healthier, if no less attracted to other guys. . . .

Still desperate to be rid of my same-sex attractions, I joined another local Exodus-affiliated ministry. This one was different, with no formal curriculum and less emphasis on orientation change, but I decided to give it a try anyway. Working in that atmosphere I was forced to confront all of the anger I'd been harboring toward God (both for my failure to change and for the friends that he'd so abruptly ripped out of my life), which in turn enabled me to be completely honest with him (and with myself) for the first time in my life.

Through that process God was able to get through to me (again for the first time) that he really does love me exactly the way I am, whatever my flaws and regardless of whether I'm ever able to fall in love with a woman. . . .

The freedom that came with that understanding empowered me to take a closer look at everything I'd been told about homosexuality. The more I examined what I'd learned from Exodus and the church, the more I began to see how heavily their entire case rested on faulty assumptions, false stereotypes, outdated psychological theories and fatally flawed studies.[7]

Encountering Gay Christians

At the beginning of 2007, I chose to go to a conference being held by the Gay Christian Network (GCN). I had read their website and understood that they welcomed gay Christians who held to both traditional and affirming perspectives. In GCN language, this is described as Side A (affirming) and Side B (traditional). I understood that the majority of the folks (approximately 95 percent) who connect with GCN are Side A or undecided. That meant that only 5 percent were Side B. What intrigued me initially about GCN was that they were living as a diverse community. They were modeling a safe place to authentically hold convictions while being relationally present in a supportive, encouraging posture to those who held different convictions. And, far from these being abstract, theoretical differences, they were deeply personal, deeply threatening differences. Yet in this community, real human beings—all on their own journeys and at different levels of maturity and commitment—were living out a tangibly Christocentric life. They were putting their love for Christ and their love for their fellow brothers and sisters in Christ ahead of their own need for the security of homogenous agreement.

In light of this, I called the director of GCN, unsure of what I would encounter. I wanted to be honest about my role and why I wanted to come to the conference—quite aware that if my presence was known it could compromise the sense of safety for participants. I could be perceived as a "wolf in sheep's clothing." So I introduced myself on the phone as an Exodus leader who really wanted to come to the conference just to listen and observe and be present, open to what God might want to show me. I assured the director that my intention was to maintain a very low profile. To his credit and my amazement, Justin Lee demonstrated an open and trusting response to my request. He encouraged me to come to the conference, and later when I met him there, he was genuinely warm and welcoming.

At the conference I had the opportunity to worship with a group of two hundred people. I was one of only a handful of straight people and quite likely the only straight Side B person there. As I sat at the back deliberately focused on simply being open to whatever God wanted to say, I found myself overwhelmed with a kaleidoscope of emotions. When one Side B presenter had completed his keynote address, there was sustained applause. It wasn't a rousing standing ovation, as some of the other Side A presenters had received, but it was a warm and genuine response nonetheless. I was quite touched by this. In many other parts of the church, where wars over homosexuality have escalated to the point of

50

viewing those with a different opinion as the enemy, here was a group of gay Christians graciously and generously applauding one who differed so significantly from them, on such a deeply personal matter. They received him as a brother in Christ, appreciative for his offering, trusting that he had given out of a spirit of love and friendship in community together. I sat there and wished that somehow the warring church at large could glimpse this moment of shared fellowship and worship. And as this group lifted their voices in praise, their bodies fully engaged in worship, partner with partner, friend with friend, brother with brother, and sister with sister, I glimpsed a beauty that was a fragrant offering. To this day, I can't quite put into words what I sensed God saying to me in that experience. And I don't offer my experience as evidentiary. But in choosing to make myself available and open to experience worship with my brothers and sisters, I had a sense of God's understanding and grace over the group. My heart was opened in a new way to see with different eyes the good fruit that was present in the lives of gay Christians.

Jesus said, "By their fruit you will recognize them. Do people pick grapes from thorn bushes, or figs from thistles? Likewise every good tree bears good fruit, but a bad tree bears bad fruit. A good tree cannot bear bad fruit, and a bad tree cannot bear good fruit. Every tree that does not bear good fruit is cut down and thrown into the fire. Thus, by their fruit you will recognize them."[8] This image came to my mind again and again as I encountered gay Christians who hold an affirming perspective. I was often encountering good fruit—the fruit of kindness, graciousness, patience, forgiveness, self-control, and faithfulness. I was encountering robust faith, rich prayer lives, missional fervor, and passionate worship. A closed system necessarily finds ways to discount such fruit as *appearing* to be authentic but actually being counterfeit. But I could not justify such an ultimately subjective, selfish, and spiritually violent evaluation. As far as I knew, the fruit that I was seeing and experiencing was the real deal—and if it wasn't, that could only be God's call.

For those of us who are straight and who don't spend a whole lot of time processing, wrestling, hiding, or managing our heterosexuality, I think there will always be a gap in our understanding of what it is like to be persistently attracted to the same-sex. We might like to try to step into a gay person's shoes, but we can't really fully grasp the multilayered complexities of the process of discovery and coming-out.

At this first GCN conference, I intentionally chose to be relatively anonymous, with most people simply assuming I was gay. For two and a half days, I chose to set aside some of my most significant identi-fiers—wife, mother, New Direction leader. I found it exhausting. It took a lot of energy to be vigilant about what came out of my mouth, particularly when meeting new people—which I did a lot of—because those identifiers were so ingrained as part of my "get to know me" script. As I reflected on that conference experience, I think one of the things God wanted me to experience, albeit in a very limited fashion, was the burden of hiding significant parts of your identity. Being a wife or a mom or a ministry leader doesn't define me, but these identifiers do describe very important parts of me. And keeping those identifiers under wraps was really hard—I felt diminished in some way. God birthed a deeper empathy in me that weekend for those who invest great energy in such vigilance day after day and year after year.

Building relationships over the last years with gay Christians has allowed me to experience, in very tangible ways, the wideness of God's mercy. I do *not* have the sense that "God has mercy for *those* gay Christians"—with an undertone of pity. Not at all. Rather I have been confronted with my *own* impoverished view of God, one that often expected a stinginess in God's mercy rather than lavish acceptance. My new experience with the wideness of God's mercy was not so much about learning that my gay Christian friends experienced God's mercy but that I came face-to-face with the limitations I imposed on *how* to experience God's mercy. My gay Christian friends dared to believe that God's mercy surrounded their lives. They often lived a more robust and generous faith than I did. I had wasted so much of my spiritual journey being mired in shame and fear and unworthiness. I had often failed to have such free and childlike faith to step out of those slimy pits and move with confidence into the things God desired for me.

As I engaged with Christians who had been involved in ex-gay minis-try and had acutely negative experiences, I heard their stories of feeling that they were drowning in the same kinds of slimy pits of fear and shame that I had experienced. I got to know men and women who regretted wasting many years investing all their emotional, spiritual, physical, and often financial energies trying to achieve the right kind of transformation (eradicating their experience of same-sex attraction). The irony of this is that, for some, trying to achieve sexual wholeness became a narcissistic focus—the focus of their lives and faith was caught up in their sexuality.

One friend spent more than fifteen years in various support groups, in therapy, and attending conferences, all in the drive to become straight. At one point, his counselor confronted him and asked, "If your attractions never go away, would you still follow Jesus?" His initial response was, "No." In his mind, this was the deal: He would obediently follow God, submitting his sexuality to the lordship of Christ, and God would heal him so that he could get married and have a family. Eventually, my friend determined that his relationship with God was the most important thing in his life regardless of what happened to his attractions.

Now at this point, some people are quick to point out 2 Corinthians 12:7–9: "I was given a thorn in my flesh, a messenger of Satan, to torment me. Three times I pleaded with the Lord to take it away from me. But he said to me, 'My grace is sufficient for you, for my power is made perfect in weakness.'" But when people thrust these verses into the face of someone who is wrestling to understand why God does not seem to be answering their prayers for healing, the Scriptures become a weapon rather than an invitation to find rest in the Lover of their souls.

Through my experiences with so many different followers of Jesus who were navigating the integration of their faith and their sexuality, I became much more aware of the questions, doubts, tensions, and anxieties punching holes in the ex-gay system I'd been handed when I joined the New Direction team. It was increasingly clear to me that people need the grace of generous spaciousness as they navigate making sense of their experience of same-sex attraction.

3

The Power of Stories

One of the wonderful things about this time of upheaval in our culture and in our churches is the reconnection to the power of story. Stories shape our lives. These stories, when we take time to listen well, reflect deeply, and risk challenging the assumptions within, can lead us to places where God can rekindle our imaginations to dream beyond our own ideas and fears and move into new landscapes.

When we tell our own stories, sharing the brokenness of our lives, or when we listen to the stories of others, we take a step toward more fully becoming the body of Christ, a body that rejoices when a member rejoices and mourns when a member mourns. In stories we can also testify to the inner healing and new life we've received from the Holy Spirit.

However, there are times when our life stories can be misused. In our telling, we may leave out certain details of our stories that would paint a more complicated picture of who we truly are. Or ministry leaders may choose to promote certain life stories that highlight the success of their kind of ministry. Or we think that one particular individual's life story applies to all persons who are similar to him or her. Or we think that our own story applies to all others who are like us. In this chapter, we'll explore the good things about stories, and we'll consider some cautions related to stories.

Personal Testimonies

Story has historically been used extensively in ex-gay ministry in the form of testimonies. Such testimonies often followed a relatively predictable pattern: first, childhood wounds and traumas were outlined (as they fit the general psychoanalytic theories of causation), then negative experiences with gay relationships were described, followed by an account of the ways God had intervened to draw the person away from homosexual behavior. Sometimes these testimonies included honest accounts of ongoing struggle; sometimes the language used was more triumphant and victorious. Many of the very public testimonies concluded by introducing the audience to the individual's opposite gender spouse and perhaps children.

When I was first exposed to ex-gay ministry, I was astounded by these testimonies as they bore witness to profound devotion to Christ and to lives willing to embrace struggle and sacrifice, and they were often told with staggering vulnerability—a vulnerability that many Christians would never consider practicing. I had the opportunity to meet a good number of the individuals whose testimonies were widely circulated in ex-gay circles, and I discovered that these individuals were very real and genuine followers of Jesus. So while the testimonies may have sounded a little formulaic, they were shared with a deep desire to honor Christ and encourage others. The longer I hung around such circles, however, the more I became aware of the complex layers to this phenomenon of the ex-gay testimony. Two typed pages describing God's victory, I discovered, was not a complete account of the ongoing reality of life. I met people who, despite confident testimonies, lived lives of such tight-fisted control that their determination to overcome their homosexuality absorbed most of their lives—nearly all their emotional and spiritual energy. There always seemed to be issues to work on, deeper roots to tackle, and regressions to address.

My Own Story

I could relate to this. Although I didn't experience same-sex sexual attraction, I too felt that I was a very broken person in need of healing. For more than a decade I lived in the vein of Christianity that focused on inner healing. I became accustomed to telling my own story in a manner that highlighted all the root issues and focused on the benchmarks of what God was doing in me. This is how I would share my story:

My world crashed before I even had words to describe it. My mother, after a brief and intense battle with cancer, died when I was just sixteen months old. Growing up I was an insecure child, susceptible to bullies, and often felt unacceptable, misunderstood, and alone. My father remarried, and by the time I was nine, there were five daughters in our family. Real or imagined, I sensed that my younger half-sisters were preferred over me and my older sister. My response was to try to fill the shoes of the son my dad didn't have. My dad and I would do renovation jobs together, chop wood, and work in the garden. We shared many personality traits, so he and I had always had a special bond.

My childhood was a typical mix of good and painful memories. But life changed pretty significantly for me when I was twelve. I was entering puberty and feeling quite insecure about being a "late bloomer." That hot July, my mom and dad brought home my new baby brother. Six children, stresses of unemployment, the costs of Christian school, a rebellious older sister, and my own identity crisis. Who was I now that Dad didn't need me to be his son? Will I ever really become a woman?

When I was thirteen, I met a new teacher at school. She was smart and seemed so confident and sure of herself. And to my utter surprise—she took an interest in me! I went over to her house to babysit her kids, and we would talk and talk and talk. It seemed like for the first time in my life someone was really listening to me—really valuing my thoughts and ideas. She chose me to be in her canoe for a weeklong school trip. And by the end of the week, it was a done deal: we were soul mates, kindred spirits, no one else understood me as she did, no one cared for me as she did. And though I didn't know it at the time—I was smitten. I had allowed my heart to open up, and all the need and all the fear and all the insecurity of my whole life rushed in with the reckless hope that I would finally be loved.

What I didn't know in those early days—and could not see for many years—was that this was my initiation into a life-strangling codependent relationship. Though the relationship was never a sexual one, as I look back it is very clear to me that if she had introduced a sexual element, I would have been a sitting duck. I was so vulnerable during those years. The relationship lasted for nearly ten years, and by the time it ended, I had turned my back on my family, my heritage, and my church, just to be close to her.

The relationship ended badly. She had gone through a difficult period in her life and, finally facing the full extent of the unhealthiness of our relationship, told me, "You've ruined my life—I don't ever want to speak with you again." I was devastated to the point of being suicidal. After so many years of my life being enmeshed with hers, I didn't know who I was, didn't know what I believed, didn't know where I was going—I was a sorry mess. At this point in my life I had essentially no support network. I was finishing university and had no money and no connections. I was alone, vulnerable, and felt broken beyond repair.

The Value and Limitations of Inner Healing

So my experience of deep brokenness was not unlike the brokenness in the stories that Christians in ex-gay ministries were telling. At that point in my life, I found that I didn't have the resources within myself to recover from the loss of that relationship (unlike all the claims of the self-improvement material I was reading). My pain was a whole lot deeper and more entrenched than something that could be changed by just learning to think positive thoughts. I couldn't heal myself. I couldn't even fully heal through loving, healthy relationships—as important as those are. I needed someone bigger and more powerful, someone more trustworthy and perfectly loving, someone who I could know that I know that I know loves me, won't leave me, and sees me in a way I can't even see myself: as whole and confident, as someone who can love and contribute and make a difference, as someone whose life matters.

So I turned to books on inner healing to try to make sense of the chaos of my life. I attended charismatic healing services, went to weeklong prayer retreats, was trained in four different prayer ministry methods, and experienced hours of personal prayer counseling.

In the context of this paradigm I dared to become hopeful that God could pick up the shattered pieces of my life. I learned about codependence, soul ties, bitter roots, judgments, and unforgiveness. I walked through the process of inviting God into the dark places in my heart. I learned more deeply about practicing the presence of God (in ways that continue to shape my spiritual life today). I became more intimately acquainted with the Holy Spirit and was exposed to the gifts of the Spirit in new ways. All of these things are God-given treasures that have enriched my life.

For many years, this inner healing paradigm was the filter through which I saw the Christian life. But I was unaware of the blind spots that were developing in me, such as being unable to embrace mystery and acknowledge the limitations of inner healing or the tendency to assume those involved in such prayer ministry had a superior faith. Now I am a "post–inner healing" follower of Jesus. The prefix "post" has become a common (some would say overused) way to describe moving beyond the limitations, excesses, and abuses of a particular system or movement without completely tossing out that which is true, good, and helpful within that system. It is with this understanding that I say I am a post–inner healing follower of Jesus. I am not a *non*-inner healing Christian; I have experienced far too much growth and restoration in my own life to ever discount this aspect of ministry. I am not an *anti*-inner healing Christian either; I continue to see great value in inner healing prayer ministry when it is entered into with discernment and engaged in with wise, experienced, and tempered servants of God—those willing to look beyond the paradigm of inner healing, who have more than one tool in their ministry toolboxes, who have personal acquaintance with suffering, who don't have so much personally vested in the fruitfulness (also known as "success") of their ministry that they can step back when needed, and who minister from a place of humility and trust.

Because I have seen and experienced limitations, excesses, and abuses within this paradigm (in particular as it is applied to the area of gender and sexual identity) and because God has challenged me regarding my own blind spots, I have moved beyond an exclusive emphasis on inner healing.

But there are circumstances in which inner healing through therapy or prayer may be extremely helpful. There are individuals who have experienced wounding and confusion in their sexual development, which has resulted in same-sex involvement, despite what seems to be an enduring heterosexual orientation. Good counseling and wise prayer ministry can be a source of great comfort and growth for such an individual.

I know a man I'll call Jim, who experienced molestation as a preteen boy, perpetrated by an older boy in his neighborhood. As part of these encounters, Jim was introduced to gay porn. Jim had no recollection of any sense of being different or attracted to his own gender growing up. But after that season of involvement with this older boy, he went on to have a number of same-sex encounters as a young adult. These encounters left Jim feeling empty and ashamed. Was this due to a sense of connection with the molestation incidents? Was this due to an internalized homophobia? Was this due to the inherent emptiness of anonymous encounters? Was this due to the inner conflict between his orientation and his behavior? Was this due to his conscience? Was this due to a complex combination of all of these things? Regardless of exactly why, Jim knew that he didn't want to continue to have promiscuous same-sex encounters and sought help. Jim would say that he has experienced much healing in this area of his life. He is now married with children and considers his sexual experimentation to be a resolved part of his past. Over the years I have heard many similar stories, and I believe that appropriate counseling and inner healing for people experiencing sexual confusion or trauma can be of great help.

One Story Does Not Fit All

Jim is now passionate about mentoring young people and is involved with the youth in his church. He is sensitive and compassionate with

60

students who are struggling with confusion and questions about their sexual identity. Because of his personal experiences, he feels he has something to offer such students. The challenge for Jim is to be open to different outcomes for the young people he engages. Will Jim be able to recognize that his experience is not a universal one, and his personal response won't apply to every student who is processing questions around their sexual identity? The healing that Jim experienced seemed to be related to particular trauma. As Jim experienced a sense of resolution in this area of woundedness, he felt a sense of sustainable closure on his interest in same-sex sexual behavior. But does that mean Jim experienced a change in his sexual orientation? Or does it mean that Jim experienced healing in an area of trauma, which has allowed him to experience greater wholeness in his heterosexual orientation?

Part of the challenge in trying to address these kinds of questions is the variety of perspectives around the concept of sexual orientation. Some consider sexual orientation to be a psychological determination of the direction of attraction an individual experiences. Others will include in the assessment of orientation the gender of partners an individual engages in sexual behavior with. Still others will focus solely on an individual's self-concept and self-definition.

The American Psychological Association states that sexual orientation

refers to the sex of those to whom one is sexually and romantically attracted. Categories of sexual orientation typically have included attraction to members of one's own sex (gay men or lesbians), attraction to members of the other sex (heterosexuals), and attraction to members of both sexes (bisexuals). While these categories continue to be widely used, research has suggested that sexual orientation does not always appear in such definable categories and instead occurs on a continuum (e.g., Kinsey, Pomeroy, Martin, & Gebhard 1953; Klein 1993; Klein, Sepekoff, & Wolff 1985; Shiveley & DeCecco 1977). In addition, some research indicates that sexual orientation is fluid for some people; this may be especially true for women (e.g., Diamond 2007; Golden 1987; Peplau & Garnets 2000).[1]

Since sexual orientation is understood differently by different people, the question of change is also understood differently. We see this in

Jim's story. Some people would say that Jim has changed. What they mean by this is that Jim used to be involved in same-sex behavior, which is to them an indication of sexual orientation, and now Jim no longer has the desire for, nor has he been actively involved in, such behavior. They may point to this story as evidence that reorientation is possible. They may even use this story to suggest that all people who desire or are involved in same-sex sexual behavior can change, as Jim did. But others would say that Jim was never gay in the first place. That is, Jim never experienced persistent attraction to his own gender, and therefore did not experience a same-sex orientation. They would say that the change Jim experienced was very positive for Jim and was consistent with his beliefs, values, and goals for his life, but says nothing to the experience of those who are gay. Still others would say that Jim is simply lying and that he does continue to experience same-sex attraction but is simply suppressing it and claiming what is really a nonexistent healing.

I think part of the reason for this kind of cynical response to Jim's story is the way that testimonies of change have been used in ex-gay circles. The stories told often fail to include the nuances among the varying experiences of attraction, behavior, and orientation that people experience. In some stories, change meant that the person no longer engaged in same-sex sexual behavior, while the assumption of the listener was that the person no longer experienced same-sex attraction.

The response to such testimonies is also complicated by the political undercurrents that often energize the telling of such stories. If people can rid themselves of same-sex attraction, then (some people reason) same-sex attraction is a *choice*, and "the government should have no obligation to protect their civil rights or honor their relationships." But, if sexual orientation is more *intrinsic* and beyond an individual's control, then (some say) "it is unethical to discriminate against them and to deny legal recognition to same-sex relationships."[2]

One tendency that I became aware of was the way the Christian community at large seemed to misuse testimonies. I encountered many Christians, often family members of gay loved ones, who heard one individual's story and projected that experience on all gay people in general and on their loved ones in particular.

Years ago, I received a phone call from a man who wanted to know why he was sent one of our newsletters. While I tried to explain the different possibilities for why he might have received the newsletter, he became a bit agitated. I asked him to describe the envelope the newsletter came in. He said it was a blank envelope with no return address. I gently told him that we had not sent the newsletter and that someone must have anonymously forwarded their copy to him. At that point, he became quite emotional and shared his story. He was gay and had been estranged from his family for many years after first coming-out. But that Christmas he had actually spent time with his parents and siblings and had announced his engagement to his partner of eighteen years. He was sure his father was the one who sent the newsletter to him because in that particular edition was the story of a young man who told of his joy and contentment in his ex-gay path. (As an aside, the young man in the newsletter is now in a committed gay relationship.) The man raged into the phone, "After all these years, eighteen years with my partner, my dad thinks one story of some kid is going to change my life?" I could hear the strong emotion in his voice as he articulated his realization that the acceptance he'd experienced at Christmas was just a charade. He assumed that his engagement must have motivated his father to try one more time to change him. We talked for a little while, and I learned that he and his partner were involved with an affirming church and had a circle of supportive friends. But the pain of alienation and judgment from his family was palpable. I sensed his profound resignation as he ended our conversation.

4

A Complex Spectrum

Views of Same-Sex Sexuality

Ordering the Disordered?

The expectation that God will reorder that which is perceived to be disordered reveals a simplistic and erroneous belief that God must and will always remove or transform that which is believed to be inconsistent with his original intentions in creation. Generally speaking, such an idea is not usually imposed on those living with Down syndrome or cystic fibrosis or autism. In most cases, when encountering such conditions that seem to vary from what we presume to be God's original design, Christians accept the condition and whatever accommodations need to be made in light of such a condition. There are exceptions of course, and prayers for healing may be offered for any condition someone deems undesirable. But it seems that when it comes to an experience of sexuality that is believed to be disordered, there is the expectation that God will "reorder" things.

I have a friend who is blind who came to know Christ as an adult. He tells many (sometimes humorous) stories of Christians who want to pray for his healing. With the patience of Job, my friend has endured lectures and prayer sessions, despite not having asked for or initiated them. My friend is content with his life. He has a robust acceptance of his blindness. He sees the gifts he has that others don't because of the different way he navigates life. One has to wonder what drives well-meaning Christians to insist on pursuing a gift of healing for a man who has found the peace and presence of God in his situation. While they might not be able to imagine ever being blind and may feel a sense of pity for him, none of these responses has anything to do with my friend. They are all about the other person. Despite all the prayerful interventions, my friend is still blind. And despite all the discomforts and expectations of those around him, my friend continues to live with a beautiful serenity that embraces his unique reality with grace and gratitude.

Conditions like Down syndrome or blindness are obviously very different from sexual orientation. Many gay people would understandably bristle at the idea of their orientation being compared to a perceived disability. And indeed, this is an important distinction. Same-sex orientation is not a disability like blindness, it is not a disease like cancer, nor is it a disorder like autism.

Views of Same-Sex Attraction

Same-sex attraction is different from opposite-sex attraction, but how are we to understand this difference? Paul Egertson (1935–2011) was a retired bishop in the Evangelical Lutheran Church in America and also the father of a gay son. In an article he wrote for parents, he presents four common ways in which homosexuality is viewed within different parts of the Christian community.[1] He says some Christians view homosexuality as *rebellion*, some see it as an *illness or addiction*, some see it as *brokenness*, and some see it simply as a *difference*, a natural variant.

Same-Sex Attraction as Rebellion

Some view the experience of same-sex attraction as a "conscious and defiant rebellion against the laws of God and nature," and the appropriate response is to call people to repentance. While a gay person might wonder how he or she can repent from a *feeling*, those who hold this view may insist that this is a matter of repentance and that with repentance will come deliverance. When probed as to the nature of this deliverance, some may suggest an emergence of heterosexual desire. Others may suggest a diminishment of same-sex attraction. However, since same-sex attraction is viewed as against God's nature, sanctification would work toward the eradication of it, even though people holding this view recognize that this may not be a realistic outcome for some people. God's redeeming work of regeneration is seen to be a return to the perfect created order, even though this transformation may be incomplete this side of heaven.

The disconnect comes when a gay person recounts years of prayer, repentance, discipline, therapy, and so on, with little to no change in their experience of same-sex attraction. Within this view, the only logical response is to claim a lack of correct technique or knowledge, motivation or discipline. Such a response, however, is deeply hurtful and discouraging to someone who has prayed, fasted, searched the Scriptures, and desperately wanted to experience transformation.

Same-Sex Attraction as Illness or Addiction

Another common view that I regularly encounter is the comparison between homosexuality and conditions such as alcoholism. In this view, same-sex attraction is considered to be a susceptibility to moral weakness. It is assumed that any attention given to either attraction or same-sex behavior will inevitably lead to addiction and therefore ought to be dealt with through abstinence and sobriety. For gay persons, this translates into: refusing to describe themselves as gay, committing to celibacy, and avoiding gay friends or gay-friendly places, books, films, and so on.

One of the disconnects of this view is the idea that suppression and avoidance will help an individual live in alignment with a traditional view. Such suppression and avoidance invite people to live compartmentalized lives that often eventually implode or explode in ways that cause a lot of damage and hurt. Another disconnect comes when considering how Scripture addresses celibate singleness. Clearly, there is high regard given by Jesus and the apostle Paul to the state of singleness. In fact, it could be argued that this is the preferred state. However, there is also a sense of accommodating those for whom singleness is too heavy a burden. Following Jesus's words on divorce and remarriage,

> The disciples said to him, "If this is the situation between a husband and wife, it is better not to marry."
> Jesus replied, "Not everyone can accept this word, but only those to whom it has been given. For there are eunuchs who were born that way, and there are eunuchs who have been made eunuchs by others—and there are those who choose to live like eunuchs for the sake of the kingdom of heaven. The one who can accept this should accept it." (Matt. 19:10–12)

Given that Jesus extends grace to others regarding celibacy, some struggle with imposing celibate singleness on gay people, especially when it is done without regard for their legitimate needs for companionship and family. Others look at lifelong celibacy as a specific gift given by God and recognize that some gay people may not have been given this spiritual gift. One of the challenges here is to remember that celibacy is about more than refraining from sexual intimacy. Many people are called to abstain from sex, even if it would not be their first choice: Some marriages are essentially sexless for a variety of legitimate reasons, and some single people would love to be married but have not found the right partner. While these people are currently abstaining from sex, they are not being called to lifelong celibacy; celibacy means that one is prevented from exploring the possibility of finding a life partner, a companion in the journey, one significant other to share all types of intimacy with (of which sexuality is only one).

Same-Sex Attraction as Brokenness

For gay people and friends of gay people these first two explanations may seem unsatisfying in light of their lived reality. They know that changing their sexual orientation isn't as simple as repenting of a nonvolitional feeling. And they know that many deeply committed and earnest efforts to reorder attractions have caused deep pain, a sense of failure and shame, self-loathing, and essentially no change in the direction of their attractions. They recognize that the experience of same-sex attraction is intrinsically different from the challenges that addictions raise.

Additionally, as people wrestle with Scripture, they may not see specific guidance related to the actual experience of same-sex attraction. While there are general admonitions related to temptation, it is a point of contention whether same-sex attraction itself should be considered a temptation or whether there are aspects of same-sex attraction (as with opposite-sex attraction) that can *lead* to temptation. Because the science regarding the cause of same-sex attraction is inconclusive, because research in the area of orientation change reports marginal positive results, and because longings for intimacy, belonging, companionship, and family are healthy and normal, many people want to view homosexuality in a way that better incorporates these truths.

Today, many Christians consider homosexuality to be a result of the fall into sin, outside God's original design for humanity, but not outside his grace. Sometimes the language of brokenness is used to express that this experience of sexuality (though not volitional) is a reality in our fallen world. Those who adopt such a view do not place blame on the affected individuals, are often quick to call for compassion, and see same-sex attraction as a "cross to bear," just as other innocent victims who suffer the fallout of sin's impact live with less than desirable conditions.

In wrestling through the possible options for faithful discipleship for the same-sex-oriented person, it may be helpful to consider the variety of ways we extend grace and accommodate those experiencing other such conditions. For example, for those who are paralyzed, we build wheelchairs. For those who grieve infertility, we may support fertility interventions or adoption. And while none of these conditions parallels the experience of same-sex attraction, accommodations of grace in these matters can encourage us to consider similar options for gay people. The idea, therefore, is to seek an extension of grace that will make life as full as possible, given this particular "thorn in the flesh" this side of heaven. For those who hold the conviction that sexual intimacy ought to be reserved for heterosexual marriage, they might endorse options like covenantal but nonsexual friendships or living in intentional community. Gay people who particularly long to be parents but do not anticipate being in an intimate relationship may consider fostering children or being a spiritual mentor/parent to others.

Others will support committed same-sex unions as an extension of such grace or as a better alternative to promiscuity or a pattern of abstinence-indiscretion-abstinence that can wreak havoc on a person's spiritual and emotional well-being. Some will see committed same-sex unions as a sort of pastoral concession: not God's best, but needing the grace of God. Others may view same-sex relationships in a more positive light that could be described as a redemptive accommodation where God's gracious blessing is believed to cover the relationship.[2]

One of the challenges of viewing homosexuality as brokenness is that it seems to carry an inherent sense of condescension in how gay persons are viewed. Does such a view perpetuate an "us and them" mentality or create an invisible line that places gay people in a second-class category? Is a gay person less than a straight person due to something they did not choose? Does such a view perpetuate hetero-normative privilege? The trajectory of Scripture breaks down this kind of favoritism and invites us to view one another as equally valuable and as image bearers of God: "My brothers and sisters, believers in our glorious Lord Jesus Christ must not show favoritism. . . . If you really keep the royal law found in Scripture, 'Love your neighbor as yourself,' you are doing right. But if you show favoritism, you sin and are convicted by the law as lawbreakers."[3]

Same-Sex Attraction as Difference

In light of this call for equity, some view homosexuality as "one of the varieties of nature, one of those delightful differences that regularly appear in counterpoint to the ordinary norm."[4] Consider other minority conditions, such as left-handedness (which describes me) or eyes of two different colors (which describes my sister). Egertson reminds us that such minority conditions were often viewed in the past as deviant. My mom, who started out left-handed, had her hand tied behind her back as a child to train her to be right-handed. With her it worked—she has some of the most beautiful right-handed penmanship I've ever seen. She made a few feeble attempts to repeat the training process with me, but to no avail. Today I'm as left-handed as can be.

Over time, many minority conditions assumed to be deviant or even evil have been gradually accepted as simply natural variations—and indeed ones that can be delightful, creative, useful—and should be embraced and celebrated. Some suggest this is the appropriate way to view homosexuality. For a minority of people, same-sex sexuality is their reality, and they bring a unique perspective to the table as they view people and relationships through a different lens than most, and this is a valued and special contribution.

This chart summarizes the variety of ways that Christians view same-sex sexuality:

View of same-sex attraction	Response
Rebellion	Repentance
Addiction	Abstinence
Brokenness	Accommodation
Natural Variant	Celebration

Even in describing these four different understandings of homosexuality, I am mindful that there are individuals who will protest that they do not fit into just one of these particular categories but perhaps a hybrid of two. How we view homosexuality is affected by so many different factors; it would be impossible to describe all the points on a continuum to describe everyone's views.

Clearly, the distance between the first category of understanding and its call to repentance and the fourth category and its call to celebration is immense. Even gay Christians differ widely in how they view same-sex attraction. Given these differences, it is no wonder that there are also differing opinions and confusion among straight Christians. These different starting points can lead to unhelpful assumptions, misunderstandings, and miscommunication. In any conversation around matters of sexual identity, it is important to first clarify basic understandings and perspectives.

Despite attempts at such clarification, there can be a significant gap when a straight person, working from theoretical ideas, tries to dialogue with a gay person, who is speaking from intimate personal experience. For the most part, straight Christians cannot imagine ever experiencing same-sex attraction. Part of this may be the "ick" factor some straight people, especially men, experience when they imagine a same-sex sexual act. Such visualization reduces the complex experience of same-sex attraction to a sex act and fails to consider that sexual attraction is a multifaceted combination of the spiritual, emotional, romantic, and physical.

Most straight people don't think about how much they view and experience the world through their lens of sexuality. It seems so intrinsic to them. But it is there, informing, influencing, and impacting the way they relate, engage, think, and see. To say that this is something that they should try to get rid of, change, or ignore would be like amputating a fundamental part of themselves. Yet, many in the Christian community ask exactly that of gay people.

Sexual Fluidity

Because there is such a variety of perspectives regarding how to understand sexual orientation, it is perhaps easy or convenient within the Christian community to deny the enduring nature of a person's orientation. This seems to be further complicated by discussion of sexual fluidity. Sexual fluidity suggests that for some people (women in particular) love and desire are not rigid categories but rather may evolve and change throughout the various stages of life and relationships. Or to put it another way, fluidity means "situation-dependent flexibility in sexual responsiveness."[5]

Research on sexual fluidity seems to have brought more complexity to the conversations about faith and sexuality. For some, this research simply reinforces the conviction that God will reorder, as part of his sanctifying work, any sexual desire that is perceived to be disordered. For others, who may have spent significant time and energy trying to change their sexual orientation through therapy or support groups, this research seems to dangle a carrot in front of their noses, and they aren't sure if they should keep trying to bite it or not. Let me expand on that a bit.

Consider a friend of mine who is a Christian woman in her late thirties. She has never been married and has never been in a long-term same-sex relationship. She has tried to date men but always felt that it was not a fit and would eventually break off the relationship out of care for the man. Her honest assessment of her sexuality is that she is predominantly attracted to women. But she wonders how much bisexual attraction she could muster and if that would be sustainable in a marriage relationship. She wonders if that would be fair to a potential husband. She desires to be in a lifelong, covenant relationship and would love to have children. Biologically, she doesn't have much time left to bear children. Should she attempt to exploit the possibility of sufficient sexual fluidity in order to try to enter a sustainable and life-giving heterosexual marriage?

Mixed-Orientation Marriages

There are certainly men and women who live in mixed-orientation marriages. This describes the marriage of two people of opposite gender where one or both of the spouses experience enduring attraction for the same sex. In some cases, a spouse may have a same-sex orientation; in other cases, a spouse would say he or she has a bisexual orientation. Such relationships are entered, sustained, or terminated for diverse and complex reasons.

There continue to be deeply unfortunate situations of a closeted same-sex-oriented individual marrying a straight spouse with the hope that marriage will change their same-sex attraction. Of all the people I have talked to who went into marriage with this expectation, none of them experienced the hoped-for change. Alternatively, the straight spouse may have been told that the same-sex attraction of their partner was a thing of the past that they didn't need to worry about. The same-sex-attracted spouse may have genuinely believed this at the time. But this is a promise that no one with past experience of same-sex attraction should make. While the initial years of marriage may feel as if there has been a diminishment of same-sex attraction, there can be a later resurgence of same-sex attraction, sometimes with even greater intensity than previously experienced. This may result in the same-sex-attracted spouse feeling unable to continue to carry the secret and potentially experiencing profound depression, anxiety, or suicidal ideation. A same-sex-attracted spouse may live for years in this incredibly difficult place due to the fear that disclosure will result in rejection and relational break-down. Secrecy around same-sex attraction can be toxic to the individual and to the relationship.

For others, disclosure of same-sex attraction after years of marriage comes when the same-sex-attracted spouse has been living a double life. The same-sex-attracted partner may have been involved with gay porn or chat rooms or has had a same-sex affair and has either been found out or confesses because of fear of being found out. When such disclosure happens in the context of infidelity, it is very painful and difficult to process.

There are also situations, particularly in the faith community, where there has been honest and authentic disclosure of same-sex attraction prior to marriage. The same-sex-attracted individual often holds the conviction that a gay sexual relationship would be inconsistent with scriptural teaching. Such marriages may prioritize spiritual and emotional intimacy and hopes of conceiving and raising children over sexual pleasure and intimacy. I asked one gay Christian man, who had been married to a woman but who now has a male partner, if he thought a mixed-orientation marriage could ever really work. He said he thought they were generally a bad idea. But he added that if both partners had relatively low sex drives and if raising a family was a core desire, such a marriage could be a life-giving option for some people. In many churches and communities, there are couples quietly living out this reality, some with great vibrancy and fulfillment.

A former colleague of mine is in a mixed-orientation marriage. For a number of years Brian was very active in public speaking and sharing his life's journey. He had gone the ex-gay route and had learned a lot and processed a lot of things about his life, but his sexual attractions did not change. He says that his years of therapy and support groups led him to a better relationship with his dad and his same-sex peers, and improved his sense of confidence and security in his masculinity, yet he was "as gay as ever." For a while Brian referred to himself as being "same-gender attracted," distancing himself from gay culture, but he eventually returned to simply identifying himself as "gay." He would say, "I'm a conservative, evangelical, Baptist, gay youth pastor married to a bisexual woman." He seemed to take great delight in watching people's heads explode as he rattled this off (in fairly conservative parts of the Christian community). Brian was always careful to point out that his story was *his* story and that people should not apply it to others. "People take my story and then tell the gay men in their lives that they just have to go find a nice lesbian to marry," he would say with a great deal of frustration. In his particular case, he had built a deep friendship with his wife long before he realized that he wanted to date her. And when he first asked her out, she said, "What part of lesbian do you not understand?" What was, in the end, significant for both of them was the deep companionship they shared and their desire to wake up in the morning beside one another. In light of their convictions about sex, they didn't have sexual relations prior to marriage and honestly went into marriage not really knowing if the whole sex thing was going to work out for them. But they went into it with their eyes open and with a deep commitment to one another, to remaining faithful to one another, and to continuing to be honest and open with one another. Their premarital counselor joked that if all couples took marriage preparation as seriously as they did, the divorce rate would plummet. As it turns out, sex has worked out in a unique and personal way for them and is a part of their married life together. But most important for them is that they have each married their best friend and get to experience the intimacy of covenant relationship together. Some people could find things to criticize about this marriage, perhaps afraid that it reinforces opposition to gay marriage by illustrating an alternative. But who wants their life politicized in that manner? This is one unique story of two unique people finding love in a manner that is life-giving for them and consistent with their Christian beliefs and values. Interestingly enough,

Brian has more recently articulated a much more open and generous stance toward his gay friends who are partnered or married. At the same time, he is as committed as ever to the vows he made to his wife.

In my years of ministry, I have seen different kinds of disclosure in mixed-orientation marriages at different times and for different reasons. I have seen relationships that have survived and gone on to thrive, and relationships that have broken down and ended in divorce. It may be important for spouses in a mixed-orientation marriage where there is a new disclosure to begin to work with an experienced therapist who can help them process the many complex layers of response and future decision making. To achieve a positive outcome, it is critical that spouses move forward with a commitment to honesty, integrity, and extending love and respect to the other, whether the marriage continues or dissolves.

The reality is that from a hundred people you will hear a hundred stories. People tell stories of same-sex sexual involvement where there isn't necessarily an experience of same-sex orientation. People tell stories that point to some experience of sexual fluidity. People tell stories of mixed-orientation marriages. People tell stories of being gay, then not being gay, then being gay again (otherwise known as ex-gay survivor stories). In these many diverse stories, I encourage followers of Christ to listen attentively, both to the person who is sharing and to the Holy Spirit. The best perspective we can hold as we encounter different stories is to be alert to see and hear where God is at work in that person's life—and to encourage them to initiate or to continue to pursue a relationship with Christ.

5

Coming-Out and the Church

When you have been taught your whole life that being gay is not what God desires for you; when you have prayed every day for years for God to take such desires away; when you believe, though you might not articulate such a belief in words, that your acceptability to God hinges on your healing; when you have been vigilant your whole life to keep your same-sex attraction hidden and compartmentalized—a loathed part of yourself; when you have done everything you know to do to work through your emotional and psychological issues, strengthen your will, and walk in obedience, and then you are confronted with the possibility that your goal may not be attainable, and in fact it may not have been the right goal in the first place, you can be shattered.

At this point, there are a number of responses. Some just walk away. They walk away from a system of belief that let them down. After years of avoiding or suppressing their same-sex attractions, they now embark on the journey of coming-out as gay and post-Christian. This dual coming-out process can be exhausting and overwhelming. The reactions and responses of those around the individual quickly separate those who will be a source of support and encouragement from those who will not. When Christians encounter an individual in such a process and fail to appreciate his or her incredible courage and yearning for authenticity, there is the potential for damaging words to be said and doors to be closed. In that place of vulnerability, so many opportunities are lost as people focus their energies on anxious proselytizing rather than on unconditional support and love. It has been both challenging and enriching for me to have conversations and build relationships with post-Christian gay people. What I often encounter are lives that model virtues consistent with the way of Jesus: concern for neighbors, commitment to work for social justice, generosity, kindness, fidelity in relationships. Though they reject a specific system of beliefs, the residue of Jesus seems to linger in their lives. At the same time, there can be varying degrees of bitterness toward institutional Christianity. The scars and wounds remain. Post-Christian gay people can feel a lack of closure, despite their termination of involvement with the church. The Barna Group (a Christian research and polling company) found that over 70 percent of gay adults identify some connection with the Christian faith. And 58 percent indicate a personal relationship with Christ that is still important to them. But 42 percent were unchurched, which is significantly higher than heterosexual respondents (28 percent were unchurched).[1] It has been said that the gay community is full of evangelical Christians who have been shown the back door of fellowship by the church.

Others, after realizing that their hope of orientation change may not materialize, and after a period of wrestling, come to a place of acceptance where their faith in Christ remains intact. Often this will also result in investigating a coming-out process. This can be very painful and anxiety producing for the individual whose entire support system continues to believe in and support a paradigm that says identifying as gay is a problem, is antithetical to a Christian life, and is opening the door to idolatry and temptation. It can be very exhausting for an individual to face their own anxiety as well as the anxieties of all those around them. At this vulnerable point in the journey, an individual who has to explain to others why he or she desires to be honest and authentic may become overwhelmed—and abort the coming-out process. At such times, friends and family members may assume the individual has returned to the "right" path. In actuality, the individual has shut down the healthy process of accepting and coming to terms with their orientation.

High profile Christian leaders continue to say condemning things about sexual orientation. Albert Mohler, president of Southern Baptist Theological Seminary, writes, "Actually, the Bible speaks rather directly to the sinfulness of the homosexual orientation—defined as a pattern of sexual attraction to a person of the same sex. . . . A close look at this passage [Rom. 1:24–27] reveals that Paul identifies the sinful sexual passion as a major concern—not just the behavior."[2] This kind of message can "tie up heavy, cumbersome loads and put them on other people's shoulders, but [the teachers and leaders] themselves are not willing to lift a finger to move them."[3] Gay people who have done everything they know—including prayer, therapy, support groups, exorcisms, and brute determination to shift the direction and/or intensity of their attractions—without much tangible result, and who know instinctively that they need to speak honestly and authentically, are torpedoed by the kind of message that says, "the very fact that you experience same-sex attraction is sinful."

One of the messages in the ex-gay community is that personally identifying as "gay" will lead to a connection with aspects of gay culture that are inconsistent with what is presumed appropriate for a follower of Jesus. Another message is that identifying as gay implies that a person is making sexuality an unhealthy priority in life—perhaps even prioritizing it over the primary identity as a child of God. Others worry that naming an identity other than our identity in Christ will give our sexual orientation power and access into our lives. Here the comparison is often made with alcoholism and the admonition to never say, "I'm an alcoholic," but rather to articulate something like, "I'm a child of God and have had victory over alcohol for six months."

Different Christians from different traditions will have different views. In my experience, the challenge for the individual who experiences ongoing, persistent same-sex attraction is that they need to find a way to talk about it in an honest way that invites understanding and acceptance. Hiding one's sexual attraction becomes a toxic secret that erodes energy, confidence, self-esteem, and the ability to be a fully contributing member of a community. Those individuals who do come out can feel that a weight has been lifted off their shoulders. They no longer need to hide. Their sexuality no longer needs to consume so much of their energy. In my experience, coming-out can actually put same-sex attraction in a much healthier place in a person's life, where it is a *part* of them but not the overarching, all-consuming issue it once was. For the Christian who finally comes out as gay after having pursued an ex-gay route for a season, most often the biggest change is simply the opportunity to be honest. If, however, an individual encounters rejection and confrontation from fellow Christians at this vulnerable point of coming-out, it can be especially devastating.

It seems to me that some of the motivation behind the messages not to identify as gay come from those who formerly identified as gay and who now consider their experience of gay life as negative. This may be because they lived as gay persons prior to coming to Christ; or because they lived in unstable, immature, or out of control ways; or because they were deeply involved in activism that they now disagree with. The difficulty with this is one individual projecting his or her own negative experience onto another's potential experience. An individual should be allowed the opportunity to explore his or her own journey as openly gay, a journey that may not include any of those negative or questionable experiences.

For example, I have known middle-aged Christians who have come out as gay as an expression of their own honest authenticity. This coming-out process brought a light to their eyes I hadn't seen before and a spring in their steps. They felt a freedom to connect with other gay Christians, to simply be with those who were like them, with whom they could share experiences and stories, with whom they could be themselves. Sometimes they explored various experiences that had previously been off-limits: going to their first gay bar ("just to see what it was like"), going to a Pride parade for the first time, or checking out community activities facilitated by LGBT organizations. For the individuals I have known, these experiences were new and novel and interesting but took a second place to their already well-established sense of community with their local congregations, their circles of friends, and their sense of vocation in both work and service. When mature, single Christians come out, I have not seen them dropping everything and fully immersing themselves in the "gay community." The times I have seen this kind of radical life change are when Christians who were married (heterosexually) leave their spouses and immerse themselves in an entirely different life. In cases like this, the gay person has often been involved in a "double life" prior to coming-out, and the coming-out process is not simply about honesty and authenticity but rather is complicated by infidelity and the possibility of sexual addiction.

The Youth Room Has a Closet

Another coming-out experience is that of a young person, eighteen years old or younger. Over my years in ministry, I have observed students coming-out at younger ages and with a greater sense of confidence. A challenge for students coming-out in middle school is that it is very common for individuals at this age to question and experiment in the area of sexuality. So the question I often get from parents is, "How can they know? How can they be so sure?" Parents can want to delay their child coming-out so that he or she will keep his or her sense of identity open during this critical developmental stage. While I think there is wisdom in keeping one's options open, I also think this is very difficult to enforce externally. No one can tell you what your orientation is—only you can determine that for yourself. And no one can tell you when you will know for sure—only you can. Because heterosexuality is normative in our society, many adults didn't think too much about the development of their sexual orientation or identity. Most straight adults don't remember when they first knew they were heterosexual—but it was likely at an age far younger than puberty.

A study from more than twenty years ago discovered that questioning one's sexual identity is fairly common. The University of Minnesota in 1992 surveyed over 30,000 adolescents (grades 7 through 12). They found that 25 percent of twelve-year-olds were unsure of their sexual orientation. The number of students who were uncertain steadily declined through adolescence, and only 5 percent of eighteen-year-olds felt unsure.[4] It would be interesting to see where the percentages would fall today. Today there are students who question their sense of sexuality for a whole host of reasons. Students who are questioning would do well to give themselves some time and space before making a concrete declaration about their sense of sexual identity. Rushing to a conclusion as an attempt to resolve uncertainty may end up creating more difficulty. We have had students email us to describe their dilemma about coming-out as gay but who now feel increasing uncertainty; they describe the challenge of maintaining credibility among their peers as they try to determine a sense of identity that really fits them. Coming-out too soon and then changing your mind isn't the worst thing and is more common today than even just a few years ago, but it doesn't come without an emotional cost. Let's face it; adolescence is hard enough without the added pressure of trying to rescind a coming-out process.

"I think I am gay."

When encountering youth who are questioning their sexuality, it is important to check your assumptions at the door. If a young person tells you that they *think* they are gay, it may be appropriate to explore with them why they think that. You can simply say, "I'm here to listen if you want to share more about that." They may indeed be questioning their sexual identity and feeling unsure. They may have had an experience that was confusing to them or one that they are having trouble making sense of.

We typically hear from male students who feel anxious because they experienced an erection in the presence of other guys. Listen to their experience and pay careful attention to the emotions they are expressing as they tell the story. Perhaps they simply need the assurance that when you're fourteen, you don't really need a reason to have an erection; sometimes erections just happen, and it really doesn't tell you anything about your sexual orientation. But be careful not to reassure too quickly or without really listening to their experiences. Rushed reassurance can communicate that you don't have the time or interest to listen to them. Superficial listening could also cause you to miss some underlying issues they are hinting at but are having trouble telling you about. So listen carefully.

Young female students may share experiences about fixating on one particular girl. This experience may cause them to wonder if they might be gay. It may be helpful to invite the young woman to tell you a bit more about the feelings she experiences when she thinks of this other girl. You might have a conversation about the difference between attraction and admiration, which is the desire to be like another girl perceived to be more popular, talented, or pretty.

Listen for patterns of emotional dependency that may emerge as the student talks about her friendships with other girls, particularly girls whom she seems to have an inordinate attachment to. Emotional dependency is commonly marked by exclusive and intense connection in a friendship, feelings of jealousy, desire to care for or protect the other person, obsessive thoughts and fantasy about the other person, feeling defensive when asked about the relationship, inordinate physical affection, and centering one's life around the friendship. While emotionally dependent relationships can lead to same-sex sexual behavior, this behavior is not necessarily the outworking of a same-sex sexual orientation but rather a manifestation of crossing boundaries within an unhealthy friendship. While some same-sex relationships may display some of these characteristics, this is not inherently a same-sex issue. It is a relationship issue. Plenty of heterosexual relationships, including marriages, can be codependent.

Another thing to listen for is the revelation of same-sex experimentation. The student may tell you this up front or hint at it in a manner that invites you to let them know it is safe to confide in you. Sexual experimentation can be a very confusing experience for young people. Our bodies were designed to experience pleasure when stimulated. So if a young person has experimented with someone of the same sex, it may well have been a pleasurable experience. This may cause the student to wonder if that means they're gay. It can be really helpful to simply explain the difference between experiencing pleasure at a physical level and the multifaceted emotional, spiritual, (ongoing) physical attractions that make up one's sexual orientation. It is also important to inform the student that ongoing experimentation or fantasy or same-sex porn use, for example, can stimulate habits and patterns that can become entrenched over time. So while experimentation alone doesn't create or even reveal the direction of one's orientation, experimentation can open doors that become difficult to shut.

Your role in engaging this young student is not to play detective or to try to get to the bottom of what they're experiencing. Rather, your role is to provide a safe and supportive place for them to share honestly. Just being able to share what they've been experiencing may help them make sense of their experiences.

If a young person experiences same-sex attraction, nothing you can say will change that experience. However, what you say can impact whether or not that student feels safe with you and whether or not they will be willing to share their story with you.

Perhaps this student really does experience persistent same-sex attraction but may be frightened or ashamed or lacking in clear and objective information about sexual orientation. If the young person is a Christian, they may have been taught that you can't be gay and Christian—so they aren't sure how to make sense of the attractions they are experiencing. Perhaps they have heard from other people that this is just a phase; but they've been waiting for the phase to pass, and it doesn't seem to be going away. And so when they tell you they think they might be gay, they are looking for someone who will tell them it is okay. Not that they are necessarily looking for permission to date a person of the same sex but simply that it is okay to experience same-sex attraction. Understanding that same-sex sexual orientation is not a choice and may be caused by a complex combination of biological and environmental factors may help the student let go of some of the internal anxiety they may be feeling. Differentiating between the experience of same-sex attraction, over which the student may have very little control, and the choices they will need to make regarding sexual behavior may help reassure the student that their experiences can be broken down into manageable parts. Simply acknowledging that Christians with same-sex attraction navigate their journeys in different ways can encourage this student that there are options to choose from. Reminding them that God not only knows their need for love and belonging and relationship but also created them to long for those things can communicate to this student that it is God's heart that they will experience these things in their life. Encourage this student to remember that, regardless of the direction of their sexual attractions, they will do well to guard their heart and sense of worth and not give themselves away sexually too quickly or easily. These things can build a foundation from which this student gains the confidence needed to discover the ways God is calling them to integrate their experience of sexuality with their faith.

"I am gay."

When a young person tells you that they *are* gay, don't jump to conclusions about what this will mean in their life. All they are telling you in this moment is that they experience same-sex attraction. They haven't yet told you what their beliefs and values are. They haven't told you whether they have been or hope to be involved in a same-sex relationship. They are simply telling you that same-sex attraction is part of their reality. They may be able to describe in great personal detail their journey of discovery of same-sex attraction that began at a very young age (age three to five). Although their language and understanding of sexual attraction didn't develop until later, at a very young age they knew something different about themselves. And by the time they hit middle school, somewhere between age twelve to fifteen, they put the pieces of the puzzle together and intrinsically knew that this has been a persistent part of their life.

Because same-sex attraction is not just about sexual behavior, consider that this student's awareness of sexual orientation influences multiple levels of how he or she processes experiences of the world, people, and relationships. So when you say to a student, "You couldn't possibly know that you're gay at this age. You're just confused; you need to give yourself more time," what you are really saying is that you know them better than they know themselves. The fact is that if you are not gay, you have very little understanding of what it is like to experience

85

this developmental process. A straight adult can communicate a message that so profoundly minimizes the student's experience that trust is deeply damaged.

If a student, perhaps your own child, confides in you that they are gay, there are some important things to consider. First, realize they are extending to you a tremendous gift of trust. Second, they are demonstrating tremendous courage. While visibility and acceptance of gay persons has been growing in the last number of years, there is still the very real and tangible risk of rejection when coming-out. This is particularly true in the faith community. In affirmation of this trust and courage, tell this student that you are honored that they have confided in you and you are proud of the courage they are showing.

The next best thing to do is simply ask them to tell you more about their experiences. Giving a student a safe place to tell their story is very important. Many students we hear from are simply looking for that. They want someone to listen and to acknowledge their stories. Many Christians in this situation will feel compelled to state their convictions about what the Bible says. Unless you have been overtly gay affirming, this student will likely assume that if you are a Christian you don't approve of same-sex sexual behavior. Now is not the time to state your position. It will be best if you let them take the lead in telling you where they are in sorting through how they hope to integrate their faith and their sexuality. Your job is to simply listen and try to reflect their feelings, confirming that you hear them: "It sounds as if you've really done your homework and some good thinking about this." "It sounds as if you're really struggling to know what to believe and value." "It sounds as if you're pretty overwhelmed with lots of unanswered questions." "It sounds as if you are feeling pretty confident about what your next steps are."

One of the most important things to communicate is that you are open to engage with them as this journey continues. Affirming your unconditional love and acceptance of them cannot be overstated. Unconditional acceptance doesn't mean that you and this student will see eye-to-eye on everything. It does mean that no matter what they think or do, you want to have an open, trusting, and loving relationship with them. This doesn't mean that you don't have a position or opinion about what are appropriate things to believe and do. It simply means that you are committed to being a safe and caring person in their life, unconditionally.

This is also a good time to assure them that you will keep in confidence all that they share with you. A quick and devastating way to break trust is to "out" someone who has confided in you. Even if that student says, "Oh, I don't care who you tell," it is important for you to keep this confidence as a demonstration of your trustworthiness. If the young person is not your own child, you may feel that you need to speak with their parents. It is of utmost importance that you first have a conversation with the student about this. Simply ask, "Have you talked with your parents about this?" If they have, you may inquire about how it went. If they have not spoken with them, ask them how they're feeling about that. They may be frightened to speak with them. The closer someone is to us, the higher the stakes are if we're rejected. It is estimated that over 40 percent of the kids on the street have left home or been thrown out over issues of sexual or gender identity. If the student asks you not to speak to their parents, I urge you to honor this request. You may consider telling the student that you want to work with them toward the goal of disclosing to their parents—but that you will not take that matter into your own hands.

It may be helpful to ask them about their coming-out process more generally: Who have they told to this point? How was it received? How are they feeling about people's responses? A simple request is, "Tell me what that was like for you." Every time you ask them this you have the opportunity to build rapport and trust and create a more spacious place for the student to share the depth of their experience.

In future conversations, continue to foster an ethos of trust, openness, and mutual respect. These qualities can help the relationship weather differing perspectives, beliefs, or values, and help protect the relationship from manipulation, fear, and control.

It is critical that you intentionally release the student into God's care after they disclose their experience of same-sex attraction. The truth is that you do not have every answer to every question they have. You cannot fix whatever you may perceive to be broken or problematic in the situation. You cannot control or be responsible for the outcomes. Those are God's responsibilities in this student's life. You can certainly pray often and fervently for this student, but be careful to not simply pray as a spiritualized form of control. God can be trusted with this young person. God must be trusted with this young person. Letting go is one of the most difficult things to do, especially for a parent. But working through your own anxiety and worry will be extremely important. You may find yourself at odds and unable to approve of beliefs or behaviors your child experiments with or embraces, but that ought not change your acceptance and love for them.

Limiting Scripts and Life-Giving Stories

Many young people in our churches will have a certain script in their head when it comes to questions of sexual identity. These scripts will have formed, over time, from a combination of things they've heard at home, school, and church; attitudes they have encountered; and their own perceptions about the climate of their community on these matters. The scripts aren't necessarily an accurate representation of the environment around them, but scripts nonetheless carry significant weight in how young people process their own attitudes and beliefs.

The most common script we encounter is, "You have to choose between being gay and being a Christian." This false dichotomy perpetuates an unhelpful sense of "us and them," where a student who experiences same-sex attraction feels immediately marginalized and under pressure. This kind of script needs to be replaced with the life-giving story of God's gift of adoption and our identity as the beloved of God. Students need to hear that no matter what they are struggling with or having questions or doubts about, they can "take God with them." God wants to share the journey with us.

Another common script is, "If I'm gay and choose to follow Jesus, I'll never get to have sex, and I'm going to be lonely and miserable the rest of my life." Imagine being in your teens, hormones raging, endless sexual energy, and having this script haunt you day after day. God's life-giving story reminds us that he created us to be in relationship and to experience love and belonging. God created us as sexual beings, and he knows our needs. Students need the gift of generous spaciousness to wrestle with God for themselves and to explore all the options in front of them. Without this space, a young person may seem to have internalized your belief system, but such internalization may lack sustainability or may simply perpetuate a people-pleasing, striving motif that will ultimately produce a very shallow personal faith.

Some Christian students wrestle with this script, "If I'm gay, there is no place for me in the church." The life-giving story that we all need to hear is that the church is not a place for perfect people. God gives gifts to all his children, and all are needed to fulfill what he has planned and prepared for that community. The church is impoverished when we fail to welcome all those who turn their face toward Christ.

"If I'm gay and date or have a same-sex partner, people will assume that I don't care about my faith or the Bible." Given the potential of this script, it is incumbent on any Christian, regardless of their own convictions about committed same-sex unions, to examine their own attitude, language, and posture toward partnered or married gay Christians. Would there be a place in your congregation for a young gay person who was dating to explore and grow in faith in Jesus Christ?

Consider these life-giving stories that could be part of the thought and heart process of the students in our congregations who are navigating their faith and sexuality:

- "My family, pastor, and church support me in being honest about my confusion, questions, and experiences of sexual identity."
- "As a gay person, I have options to explore as I decide how to live my life in congruence with my beliefs and values."
- "I know that people in my family and church will love me and welcome me in the future—even if we have differences in our perspectives and ideas about homosexuality."
- "I can be open to whatever God will do in my life and be confident that I will have the opportunity to love and be loved."

The Importance of Self-Acceptance

Gay people may need to do the difficult work of addressing an internalized sense of shame or self-loathing in relation to their sexual difference. Because they did not choose to experience same-sex attraction, they should feel free to accept this difference as a morally neutral part of their lives. If an individual has grown up in a context that negatively caricatured gay people, self-acceptance may be very difficult to embrace. Sometimes past choices that reinforced or intensified their sense of sexual difference, including fantasies, pornography, or sexual activity outside of covenantal relationship, can be a hook for accusation or shame.

A gay person is best positioned to consider the lordship of Christ over their sexuality from a place of self-acceptance. The person who is able to identify, process, and root out any internalized sense of shame will better encounter God's self-revelation because he or she is approaching God from a sense of love rather than fear. I'm not speaking here about a candy-coated self-esteem that minimizes the very real issue of our sinful nature. Rather, I am referring to the deep grounding in our value as image bearers of God no matter what difference or challenge we experience. I'm speaking about being able to stand fully in the light, leaving denial or repression behind, and with honesty saying, "This is the real me, and I am no less loved and valued by God than any other human being."

I know that race and sexual identity are separate subjects—and my intention is not to equate them—but I think there are profound lessons to learn from the systemic perpetuation of racial inequality, the lie that some people are less than others. Consider this story:

> Dr. Johannes Capitein was sold into slavery at the age of eight at the Dutch controlled slave castle El Mina in present day Ghana. He was taken by a trader to Holland as an "adopted son." He attended Leyden University as a theology student and wrote a celebrated and bestselling thesis in 1742 entitled, *De servitude, liberati christianae non contraria . . .* (How slavery is not in conflict with Christian liberty). Notwithstanding that historic achievement of becoming perhaps the first "Black minister" in Holland, and perhaps the first African to write a dissertation in

Europe, he returned shortly afterward to El Mina to serve as "a Black minister" and tragically died at the young age of 30, an outcast of both Ghanaian and Dutch society.[5]

What struck me about the story of Johannes is the glaring picture it paints of an individual who internalized inequity so deeply that he embodied it in a manner that oppressed his brothers and sisters. I see a similar picture in some parts of the ex-gay community where people so lack self-acceptance and have such internalized homophobia that they speak very harshly about openly gay people. This internalized self-loathing was highlighted recently when a Protestant pastor, who is an outspoken opponent of civil liberties for gay people, was discovered attending the Catholic support group Courage to deal with his own experience of same-sex attraction. In the blogosphere, there were very different responses to this case. Some people felt that confidentiality had been compromised (an undercover reporter had participated in the Courage group), and the pastor's outing was inappropriate despite his antigay position. Others felt that his position of authority and influence as a pastor justified the outing. Some seemed to have greater empathy for the experience of internalized homophobia than others.

I think it would be helpful, at this stage, for the Christian community (including those in ex-gay ministries who experience ongoing persistent same-sex attraction) to accept the common usage of the term "gay." That is, it simply means, "I'm attracted to people of my own gender," and it does not mean anything about a person's behavior—past, present, or future. I believe it is important to work toward the day when people can be open and honest about their sexual identity without any fear of judgment or rejection. Christians should be able to disclose that they are gay without receiving judgment from the church because of assumed sexual behavior.

A friend talked to me about her decision-making process in coming-out to her conservative faith community. She's in a relatively mature season of life, so there are pros and cons to coming-out as gay. She believes coming-out will be liberating—and painful. Liberating, because she will be released from the weight of secrecy and the vigilance required to ensure no inadvertent clues slip out about her experience of same-sex attraction. Painful, because she will need to navigate misunderstandings and assumptions and submit to questions about intimate aspects of her experience of sexual attraction and her process of integrating this experience with her journey as a follower of Jesus.

Another friend emailed me to update me on her decision *not* to come out. For her, not identifying as gay seems to be most consistent with her head, heart, and values. She wants to honor and not overwhelm her family. She has navigated life functionally like a heterosexual for years (she is in a mature season of life), and to now identify with the gay community (in her mind) seems both foreign and uncomfortable. She is honest and open about her attractions with herself and trusted others. I respect her thoughtfulness in engaging and thinking through her journey, and I want to respond with unconditional acceptance as she chooses the place that is most life-giving for her at this time.

As a friend in these situations, I want to listen well, encourage, explore, and affirm each unique individual in accepting what is authentic, life giving, and God honoring for them at this point in their journeys. Where there is fear, I hope to be a support as they face, process, and live beyond it. Where there is lingering shame, I hope to help name it, confront it, and eradicate it. I want to help nurture generous spaciousness for them.

These ideas of self-acceptance, of coming-out, of identifying oneself as a gay individual, and of advocating for equality for those who experience sexual difference can be contentious in the Christian community. As long as they are contentious, gay people are at a distinct disadvantage when it comes to freely and confidently engaging the Scriptures for discernment and guidance for their decisions regarding relationships and intimacy. If an individual cannot stand in the light and honestly accept their own reality as they engage God's story, they will be limited in their ability to enter the story and encounter the uniquely personal ways God will reveal himself and his will to them. To suggest that the individual ought to not really engage this explorative, personal journey because "the Bible is clear" robs the individual of the richness of engaging Scripture on a personal and relational level.

Faith communities need to have the courage and openness to relate to individuals in the honesty of their reality—even when their reality is different than that of the majority. Such openness is the natural extension of the life of Christ. If Christ has come to break dividing walls, to embody reconciliation, to remove barriers, to tear the curtain in the temple, then this false notion of needing to renounce, get rid of, suppress, do away with one's same-sex attraction in order to find one's place in God's economy is tragic in the manner akin to a slave writing a dissertation supporting the slavery of his own African brothers and sisters.

6

The Journey of Discipleship

Self-Acceptance and Growth

When a follower of Jesus comes out, they may find themselves in the midst of the paradox of accepting what *is* and being open to what *may be*. On one hand, the individual needs to accept their same-sex attraction; denying, suppressing, or ignoring won't serve anyone well. The beginning of self-acceptance may sound something like this: "It is what it is. I might not have chosen this. I might not always be happy about it. But, it is what it is, and I trust that God will give me the grace that I need to live." On the other hand, every follower of Jesus is called to be open to the transforming, sanctifying work of God in their lives. How this work manifests itself in a person's life can't be fully predicted. But there are signs of maturity that any follower of Jesus can expect to receive and grow into: the fruit of the Spirit—love, joy, peace, patience, kindness, goodness, faithfulness, gentleness, and self-control—are a sure sign to look for to assess your growth in the way of Jesus (see Gal. 5:22–23).

Fruit and Virtues

Alongside the fruit of the Spirit, we cultivate virtues as our character conforms to the image of Christ. The foundational virtues are found in Paul's first letter to the Corinthians: faith, hope, and love. Additionally, there are four cardinal virtues in the Christian tradition (adapted from the work of Plato) and so named because they are considered to be the roots from which all other moral virtues stemmed. *Prudence* is the ability to discern appropriate thoughts, words, and deeds at the right time. It is wise decision making. *Justice* is navigating between self-interest and the rights and needs of others. It is essentially being able to love self and others without overemphasizing one to the detriment of the other. *Temperance* is the discipline of self-control, sobriety, abstinence, or moderation. It is the strength of will and character to fulfill life's responsibilities without hiding in any of the variety of escapes that lure us and dull us to the pain in our lives. *Courage*, sometimes called fortitude, is a persevering endurance that has the ability to confront fear, uncertainty, or intimidation. It is the embracing of a posture of fearlessness in the face of the unpredictable anxieties of life.

The fruit and virtues listed above are positive marks of sanctification and transformation in the life of any Christ follower. But are there particular ways that God will bring transformation into the life of a gay person? If an individual has grown up in a Christian community, they may have been exposed to theological paradigms that taught that God's sanctifying work in a Christian's life will reverse the effects of the original fall into sin. They may have also been taught that same-sex desires are disordered; that is, they are inconsistent with the original creation order. With this kind of teaching, an individual may feel obligated to expect that God's ongoing work in their life will affect the direction of their sexual attractions (to bring them more in line with the original creation order of opposite-sex attraction). Such expectation may cause an individual to feel pressured to be open to some degree of reorientation.

You can see, then, the paradox emerging. On one hand, the person is seeking to accept their same-sex attraction. On the other hand, they

96

feel an obligation to stay open to the possibility that God may affect some level of change in their attractions.

Some individuals try to live with this tension while inevitably leaning toward one side or the other at various points in their journey. And others will come to a point where they see this paradox as unhealthy and unnecessary, and choose to fully embrace their sexual orientation and identity as a gay person.

For the gay Christian, pursuit of growth and maturity in these virtues may provide a particularly helpful focus during times of wrestling or uncertainty regarding the specific question of committed, same-sex relationships. Many Christians (particularly those who were raised in contexts where a traditional sexual ethic was taught), after accepting their same-sex orientation, still have deep questions about what the future will hold for them in terms of love and relationship. It is not uncommon to see people change their position throughout years of wrestling. Some, even while in a loving and positive dating relationship with someone of the same sex, will continue to struggle with anxious questions like, "Am I even really gay?" "Do I really believe God blesses this relationship, or have I just tried to convince myself of that?" "Do I even believe in God?" "What do I really think about the Scriptures?" Having walked closely with those who ask such questions, I believe that they arise from a deep place where both commitment and shame reside.

A note to pastors, parents, and friends: If someone reveals this kind of uncertainty to you, rather than pouncing, it is important for you to be aware that these questions touch very deep places. For you to confront this person or call him or her to repentance at this time disregards their vulnerability and may be more about the outcome you desire. As important as repentance seems to you, the individual needs to follow their own path and not be manipulated or overpowered in times of vulnerability. God is more than able, through his Holy Spirit, to lead, guide, correct, and convict. Your role is to listen well, pray diligently, and ask open-ended questions that will help the individual better discern what God is showing them. This will not be a quick process. And sometimes, in the lifelong journey of discipleship, it may be more helpful to ask questions related to these larger issues of spiritual fruit and virtues. Sometimes people need to take a break from wrestling with the big question of whether God allows them to be open to a same-sex relationship. This question can become an all-consuming focus to the detriment of simply growing in relationship with Christ, deepening one's prayer life, and maturing in character.

This doesn't mean that we should never engage in challenging theological discussions with a gay loved one. It does mean, however, that we should be careful to walk in step with the Spirit and discern if he is leading and prompting us to speak, or if our desire to speak is coming from our own need to control the choices of our loved one. Repentance that arises from feeling shamed or overpowered in a time of fragility may prove to be quite unsustainable in the long run and may create bitterness and broken trust within a relationship. If, however, together we focus on a mutual pursuit of growing in the fruit of the Spirit and the virtues of the Christian life, we will be positioned both to be open to the conviction and correction of the Spirit and to maturing into the likeness of Christ.

Staying Alive to Hopefulness

In the midst of the journey of accepting what is and being open to what will be, it is so important that an individual stay alive to hopefulness. Living in tension and the inherent uncertainties that go along with paradox can become a drain and result in a feeling of hopelessness. It can feel as if no resolution will ever come or that this paradox will prevent experiencing the love of a life partner or negatively impact a significant relationship.

There are three things that can be very helpful in combating the seduction of hopelessness. The first is the *release of grief*. Being conscious of the losses in our lives and finding particular ways in which to personally grieve these losses will actually help us to hold on to hope. When we deny the losses we experience, or when we dwell on the losses but don't actually grieve them, we experience an unresolved mess deep in our gut. But when we find healthy outlets in which to express and release our grief, there is space in our souls to invite fresh hope. For the gay person, some of the losses they may need to grieve include: the sense that life is not turning out the way they expected; the death of dreams of following a typical life path—"the spouse, the kids, the dog, the picket fence"; the disappointment or disapproval of a parent or other family members; the injustice of fearing violence or other discrimination; unfair treatment, past or present, in school, in the workplace, or in society in general; and the sense of being marginalized in the church, excluded from opportunities to serve or be recognized. Whether perceived, anticipated, or actually experienced, these concerns cause a tangible sense of loss. Things aren't as they should be. And this necessitates the process of grieving: giving space for the anger and resentment to be articulated, heard, witnessed, and released; giving voice to the pain and fear undergirding these concerns and having this acknowledged, validated, soothed, and comforted; articulating the desire to bargain with God to even the playing field and remove the barriers, injustices, and discomforts and inviting the presence of God to compensate in the personal and unique ways that he has planned; releasing the grief through tears, screams, poetry, long runs in the early morning—whatever makes sense to that particular person so that they can begin to accept their reality with increasing serenity and peace. Acknowledging loss and releasing grief frees us to receive the new hope God has for us.

The second pathway to hopefulness is the *reception of beauty*. There is something about beauty that nourishes our soul. Beauty is not something that we can manipulate or control; we are simply faced with the choice to receive or not to receive. This is a power outside of ourselves. For the gay person wrestling with hopelessness, the reception of beauty becomes very particular. Although engaging the beauty of creation, music, poetry, visual arts, and so on can be a wonderful gift, I encourage gay individuals to consider the beauty of their sexual identity. Being a sexual minority person is a part of how they interact and perceive the world. I would ask, "How has this experience enabled you to interact in a more gracious, compassionate, sensitive, understanding way?" These are beautiful qualities. "In what ways has your sense of being different, perhaps the feeling of being on the margins, enlarged in you the

99

capacity for hospitality to those who are different?" This is a beautiful calling. "In what ways has your unique perspective on gender helped you to affirm those who don't fit neatly into preconceived notions of masculinity or femininity?" This is the ability to see beauty where others may be blinded by anxiety or presumption. "In what ways has your experience of same-sex attraction allowed you to see and offer beauty in a manner you otherwise might not have?"

It may also be helpful for the individual to contemplate the contributions of beauty that have been offered to the world by others who experienced same-sex attraction. An article in *Books & Culture* speculated on the sexual orientation of Handel, the famous composer of "The Messiah." Given the eighteenth-century context of Handel's life, projecting today's understanding of sexual orientation onto his story is not an easy fit. However, recognizing that people with same-sex orientation have existed throughout history and have made stunning contributions in the arts, philosophy, theology, and so on, can connect beauty with sexual identity in a different way. In addition, the writings of Henri Nouwen (who was posthumously outed) continue to resonate deeply with many followers of Jesus. Nouwen, in the course of his life, didn't want all of his contributions filtered through the lens of his sexuality. And my concern here is not to reduce people to their experience of sexual orientation but rather to highlight the unique and beautiful contributions made by those who have lived with same-sex attraction.

The third pathway to reviving hopefulness is the *cultivation of a positive vision for the future.* When hopelessness takes hold of us, it is very difficult to see the light at the end of the tunnel. Discouragement can give way to despair, and we can find ourselves in a very dark place. We begin to look for ways to numb or escape the pain of hopelessness; we compartmentalize our lives, deaden our emotions, and disconnect from inspiration, motivation, and empowerment. So when I suggest this third pathway, I do not intend to present it in a trivial or simplistic manner. In fact, this path of visualizing a positive future may indeed be a nearly epic spiritual battle, where we must grab hold of the tunic of the messenger of God and wrestle with him until dawn to receive the blessing of a new dream.

For the gay Christian this new dream could take a number of different shapes and perhaps even embrace multiple options. If their original dream was that God would change their attractions and that they would marry someone of the opposite sex, for some, this will evolve into a dream of fulfilling and meaningful singleness. If the script they have always told themselves is that a single life will be lonely and miserable and unfulfilling, shaping the contours of such a new dream will be difficult. Identifying the lies and untruths inherent in the messages we tell ourselves may be an important first step in allowing ourselves to be open to a new dream. Part of this may be finding positive models that are living out the new dream we are trying to nurture. A former colleague of mine often shared about an older woman in his congregation who had been single all of her life. She was a woman before her time—educated, entrepreneurial, and adventurous—and would say that she was more than any man of her day could handle. This woman had a vibrant career in which she lived out her God-given vocation. She was feisty, intelligent, confident, and mature. She embodied a life well lived. Such a model can be a tremendous asset to an individual trying to reformulate a positive vision for their future.

Others, when faced with the fact that the direction of their attractions is not shifting, may begin, perhaps tentatively, to dream of a same-sex relationship. They may need to explore this within the scope of their beliefs and values. Perhaps their convictions concerning the appropriateness of same-sex sexual behavior precludes them from dreaming of a fully consummated same-sex relationship. But perhaps they do feel free to dream of entering a companion relationship in which emotional and spiritual intimacy is shared. It is important to remember that love is love. And love is of God. There is much love to be given and received within the context of companionship or friendships, whether or not these relationships take on an exclusive or primary role in a person's life and whether or not they are consummated sexually.

Fashioning a new dream around the hope of relationship can be marked by ambiguity, tension, or uncertainty. It is important, however, to not allow such tension or uncertainty to abort the formation of a positive vision for the future. Perhaps it's best for the person to visualize a less risky dream—one that they feel confident is consistent with God's call on their life—but a positive dream nonetheless. Visualizing an encouraging support system, warm friendships, a place of belonging in community, trusted confidants, a welcome into the lives of families, special children to build relationships with, sensitive and understanding pastoral involvement, meaningful work, life-giving volunteer service. All of these things can invite new hope and energy to move forward into a life worth living.

Some gay people will begin to dream of the possibility of a same-sex marriage in their future. Where this dream is grounded in the confidence of the unconditional love and embrace of God, such a dream can be a vibrant part of a person's ongoing spiritual journey, particularly when it is based on careful study, reflection, prayer, waiting, and listening to Scripture, the Holy Spirit, and trusted mentors. Although he or she may encounter disagreement from many Christians around them, this gay person may sense God's peace, care, and leading. Cultivating such a dream may require great tenacity and courage, particularly if they find themselves in a disapproving church or family. Thinking through their values and priorities, and not devolving into daydreaming or sentimental fantasy, is a good step in nurturing a healthy dream. Aligning oneself with life-giving boundaries concerning sexual involvement outside of a consecrated relationship will help to guard one's sense of worth and value and position one to remain open to the leading and refining work of the Holy Spirit.

When navigating the challenges of accepting things that we did not choose, hopefulness is like drinking an energy drink on that last stretch of highway before you make it home. Hopefulness, in and of itself, is organic, not static. It is responsive and flexible. It moves with us, evolves with us, offers us permission and freedom. These attributes are a welcome source of energy when we're wrestling to accept difficult things.

With all of this talk about moving from struggle to acceptance, it should be noted that this is not the experience of every gay person or every gay Christian. Those who find themselves in an accepting and affirming environment may never have struggled with self-acceptance. Perhaps they have always felt completely affirmed in dreaming of finding a life partner of the same sex, raising a family, and living a very ordinary sort of life. Others, despite a context that wasn't affirming, have always had confidence to embrace their sexual identity and anticipate a positive life journey. In my experience, such individuals are quite extraordinary. Many gay people who have grown up in a Christian family and in the evangelical church struggle to come to a place of acceptance and hope for the future.

Happiness and Space to Grow

Happiness can be a confusing concept for Christians. On one hand, if we serve a good God who promises us a full and abundant life, shouldn't we be happy? On the other hand, any careful reading of the life and way of Jesus reveals a life open to suffering and self-denial. The very message of the gospel confronts the shortcuts humans take to happiness and calls those who follow Christ to a new way of life. This apparent tension has commonly become a weapon in the shouting matches between gay-affirming voices and traditional voices. The affirming voices call for the unimpeded opportunity for LGBTQ (lesbian, gay, bisexual, transgender, queer) people to experience self-fulfillment through sexual intimacy, relationship, marriage, equal status, and so on. The traditional voices point to a path of self-denial and suffering as the way to live out God's standards. For a gay Christian, when happiness and suffering are pitted against one another, this dilemma can disintegrate into a no-win situation and a source of shame.

Stanley Hauerwas and Charles Pinches challenge such a dichotomy in their book, *Christians among the Virtues*, saying, "In a time when the desire of many for happiness results in a desperate devaluing of all questions of significance, any challenge to the superficiality of our desires seems more likely right than wrong. By the same token, however, this devaluation of happiness for suffering is challenged by the same story of Jesus of Nazareth, whom God raised and who offers a new life that is full, victorious, *happy*."[1]

I experienced the pain of this dichotomy in my own life. At a vulnerable time in my teens, a pastor, whom I respected, looked me in the eye and said, "Wendy, God is not in the business of making you happy—he is in the business of transforming you into the image of his Son." This proved to be a foundational statement, one that I would return to again and again when I faced any crossroads. The problem was that at such a young age I lacked experience and discernment. I concluded, inevitably, that I should always choose what seemed to be the more miserable path because that would prove my devotion and commitment to being transformed into the image of Christ. Looking back, I realize that my mental picture of what this transformation consisted of was impoverished. It was quite far removed from the robust portrait of Christ that I learned from fearless engagement with the story of Scripture. I simply assumed that to be transformed into the image of Christ meant that I, as a person, needed to cease to exist. Though I didn't consciously articulate it, I felt that the goal was to become an empty shell through which this mystery of Christ flowed. Such self-annihilation seemed to be the only way to transformation. Any other choice seemed tied to a cheap, humanistic happiness, which would usher me into the Cadillac of deception on the highway to hell. This misunderstanding of the call of Christ led me on a path of self-loathing, fear, and (much to my shame) many secret escapes. In my life, these escapes manifested in an ongoing struggle with bulimic tendencies of binging and purging, mindless television viewing, and unnecessary shopping (which I attempted to justify by shopping at thrift stores rather than retail). These secrets and my sense of shame about them insulated and isolated me. My path was one of depression, loneliness, and inconsistency in virtue—the very antithesis of what marked a Christlike life.

Hauerwas and Pinches remind us that happiness, the life of virtue, and friendship are like the parts of the three-strand chord of which the writer of Ecclesiastes speaks, "A cord of three strands is not quickly broken" (4:12). They write, "We cannot understand the kind of happiness we should desire without understanding the life of virtue. But the life of virtue properly understood requires an account of friendship, for true virtue is not something we have or do alone."[2]

104

Consider this reflection from Jeremy, who remains married and committed to his wife despite his honest acceptance of his same-sex orientation. After years of ex-gay type ministry, he says,

> It was intoxicating fantasy to live in a world where, as long as we acted *biblically* and trusted in him, God more or less guaranteed success in everything. We believed that our struggles with same-sex attraction were at last going to count for something. We had steadfastly refused to follow the way of the world and felt we could stand with our heads up high, confident that we had a place in God's new kingdom. In reality, the long-term consequences for many who took part in our discipleship programmes were pretty depressing—near-disastrous for some. The long-term damage to all of us has been incalculable. A strategy that had largely been inspired by hyped-up charismatic expectations of change proved spiritually catastrophic. Many people gave up their faith altogether.[3]

When we read accounts of gay, celibate Christians, deeply committed to the self-denial such commitment entails, and stories of gay Christians who are affirming of gay relationships, it can cause a great deal of confusion. Inevitably, we may find ourselves asking, "Who is *really* committed to Christ?" But this kind of convenient external analysis perpetuates a system of striving and pressure that negatively impacts gay Christians. Imagine if we created such a system around issues of finances. Some Christians sold everything they had and went overseas to live among the poorest of the poor. Anyone who did not make this choice of stewardship and sacrifice with their finances was viewed with suspicion and judgment by other Christians as one who was just living selfishly. If a person owned two cars, their very faith was viewed as counterfeit. Many of us cannot imagine trying to serve God and neighbor in the stifling pressure of the scrutiny of our every financial decision. We cannot bear the thought of feeling judged and guilty when we look in our closet and see not only two pairs of shoes, but many pairs. Many of us do wrestle with God to grow, mature, and become more fearless and generous in the arena of our financial resources; but we all need grace and need to know that we are loved unconditionally in order to be able to take risks and make sacrifices that aren't motivated by guilt or fear.

To bring it a little closer to the topic, many people who are married know the depths of selfishness, hidden sin, resentment, and apathy that can reside within marriages. The ideal marriage, while a beautiful and worthy goal, is rarely realized in the households of Christians. Not only does our abysmal divorce rate demonstrate this, but among the couples who continue to journey together there is (barely hidden) pain and tension under many smiling faces.

The point is not to call for a watered-down discipleship. The point is that we all need generous spaciousness in our walk with Christ. We all need room to live in the tension of the call to virtue and the longing for happiness. And we all need to find safety and grace in our friendships and community so that we don't have to try to figure this out alone. The truth is, different people with different personalities, backgrounds, experiences, and capacities will navigate this paradox differently. The amazing good news of the gospel is that God is rich in grace and lavish in mercy. He knows us by name, he counts the hairs on our head, he knows our weaknesses and our strengths, he knows our frame and that we are dust, and he knows our heart. In him we are set free from striving, set free from being motivated by fear, guilt, and shame. In him we can find rest.

I was visiting with a friend who used to serve with me at New Direction. She is now working at a ministry overseas that holds a clear position on sexual intimacy—it is to be reserved for the marriage between one man and one woman. She experiences same-sex attraction and is committed to living a chaste, single life. She attends a church that is very diverse and includes several gay couples. Initially, she found it very difficult to be in the same close-knit faith community with partnered gay Christians. It was threatening to her and made it harder for her to stay true to her convictions. She spoke to her pastor, and he wisely suggested that she meet with one of the lesbian couples. Over dinner together, they all had a chance to share their stories. My friend told me that they were a lovely couple and that their faith in God was very evident and genuine. After the meeting, she felt confused for a time. But then God confirmed to her in a very beautiful and personal way that he wanted to be her husband. As my friend told me all of this with tears in her

106

eyes, she said it was still hard at times. Sometimes she wondered why this couple could enjoy something that she felt convicted she was not to enjoy. But as she twisted the wedding ring on her hand—a symbol that God, her bridegroom, would provide for her needs—she was able to say that God had enlarged her heart. She had grown to make room for the gay couples in her church, able to see their faith and love for Christ, even as she continues to pursue alignment with her own convictions as a person living a single life. Her journey isn't easy—but she is at peace with God. And she has allowed God to teach her and humble her such that she is not an obstacle to the gay couples in her church. This is, I believe, a beautiful example of generous spaciousness. There is room for each unique person to "work out [their] salvation with fear and trembling, for it is God who works in [them] to will and to act in order to fulfill his good purpose" (Phil. 2:12–13).

If gay Christians can model this kind of generous spaciousness with one another, then who are straight Christians to make judgment calls on a person's commitment to Christ? If those of us who do not experience same-sex attraction will have the humility to recognize that followers of Christ who do experience same-sex attraction are navigating their journeys in different ways, we can be part of nurturing the kind of spacious environment that we all need to press into intimate relationship with Christ.

7

Understanding Holistic Sexuality

There is an irony in how Christians talk about and understand sexuality. Christians often lament the world's reductionism of sex to genital interaction and raw physical pleasures, but then they typically reduce a gay person's sexuality to just that. Let's look deeper at a holistic understanding of sexuality and how this understanding should be applied to all people. Christian leaders call us to rediscover a more robust, holistic understanding of our sexuality as a multifaceted and fully integrative part of our humanity.

Consider these statements from the church:

- "The experience of people today supported by contemporary behavioral and theological sciences understands sexuality much more broadly. Sex is seen as a force that permeates, influences, and affects every act of a person's being at every moment of existence."[1]

- "Human sexuality includes all that we are as human beings. Sexuality at the very least is biological, psychological, cultural, social, and spiritual. It is as much of the mind as of the body, of the community as of the person. To be a person is to be a sexual being."[2]

- "Sexuality belongs to the mystery of personhood and the mystery of the image of God."[3]
- "Sexuality is our drive to overcome our aloneness."[4]

The idea that sexuality is our drive to overcome our aloneness is particularly helpful in the ongoing debates about the essential nature of sexuality. As sexual beings, we seek to connect with others through generosity, creativity, humor, and faithful love.

In discussions about sexuality, however, the focus is often on our understanding of the roles our biological sex and our sense of gender play on our sexuality as embodied persons. Different scholars view the link between biological sex and a person's sense of sexuality differently. Stanley Grenz writes, "There is simply no other way to be created a human, to exist as a human being, except as an embodied person. And embodiment means existence as a sexual being, male or female."[5] James Brownson, in his book, *Bible, Gender, Sexuality: Reframing the Church's Debate on Same-Sex Relationships*, argues that the use of gender complementarity by those with traditional views is not as clearly supported as often assumed. He points out that "the focus in Genesis 2 is not on the complementarity of male and female, but on the similarity of male and female."[6] He goes on to say, "The fact that male and female are both created in the divine image is intended to convey the value, dominion, and relationality shared by both men and women, but not the idea that the complementarity of the genders is somehow necessary to fully express or embody the divine image."[7] And he concludes by saying, "The 'one-flesh' union spoken of in Genesis 2:24 connotes, not physical complementarity, but a kinship bond."[8]

In the midst of these debates, however, stand our intersex brothers and sisters (people who cannot be biologically identified as either male or female). The occurrence of intersex individuals is relatively low, though perhaps higher than most people expect. It is suggested that as many as one in two hundred people experience some degree of biologically based ambiguity in their biological sex. Does that mean this person is not a sexual being? Of course not. Do they have a drive to overcome their aloneness? Of course they do. Is this drive more complex than most people's experience? Perhaps. Is their sexuality intrinsically tied to their biological sex? It would appear that it transcends the ambiguity of their biological sex as many, whether living with the knowledge of a diagnosis or not, go on to find a life partner. Tying our sexuality so completely to our biological sex seems to divorce sexuality from our experience as persons beyond being biologically male or female or our experience of socially constructed gender. Our transgender brothers and sisters will attest to this. Each human bears God's image regardless of the concreteness, ambiguity, conclusiveness, or fluidity of their biological sex, gender, or sexual orientation.

We rightly defend that we are embodied beings (rather than a separate body and soul), but to tie such embodiment solely to an individual's biological sex seems to reduce the mystery of intimate relationships to one dimension. Regardless of biological sex or sense of gender, human beings (as image bearers of their creator) fulfill the drive to overcome their aloneness in a variety of creative, relational ways. As relational beings, they have the opportunity to experience various levels of intimacy (including emotional, spiritual, and physical) manifested in a variety of relationships: a monogamous covenant relationship, long-term friendships, a member in a community, a member in an extended family, and so on.

Sexuality Is Relational

I would submit that human sexuality is, fundamentally, relational. The key to our sexuality is not our biological sex; the key to our sexuality is that we are created to be in relationship. Our experiences of relationship, particularly covenanted and consummated ones, are impacted by biological sex and gender. However, to make biological sex the foundation of all understanding of sexuality reduces our image bearing of God to a construct that does not describe our Triune God. Is God's essence connected primarily to maleness or femaleness, masculinity

111

or femininity? Or is God's essence love—relational, self-giving love? If it is the latter, then that ought to be the foundation from which we understand human sexuality as image bearers of God.

While holistic understanding of human sexuality is often promoted and defended by the church, it is not applied to gay followers of Jesus. Instead, it is all too common to encounter depersonalized reductionism. It would seem at times, in the church, that a person's entire spiritual formation is reduced where they land on the question of sexually consummated same-sex relationships. Rather than seeing the integrative beauty of our sexuality as part of our interaction with God, others, and creation, some Christians compartmentalize gay persons' sexuality as disordered, undesirable, and something to be mastered. While same-sex attraction may not be viewed as inherently sinful, it tends to be seen as overwhelmingly negative.

Sexual Brokenness

The reality is, however, that human sexuality reveals both our immense value and pervasive imperfection. This is true whether the attractions one experiences are toward the same sex or the opposite sex. Our experience of sexuality is both beautiful and broken. Across the board, our sexuality retains a connection to the goodness of creation and the devastation of the fall. But, more often than not, those in the sexual majority are unable to see the fallenness of their own sexuality. This is illustrated by an experience I had one Sunday morning some years ago.

I was preaching in a Pentecostal church about how coming to Jesus doesn't take away every challenge and struggle we face. I asked the congregation, "How many of you experienced brokenness before you came to Jesus?" Pretty much everyone raised their hand. "And how many of you were a hundred percent free of that brokenness the moment you came to Jesus?" No one put up a hand. Later in the message, when I was talking about the ground being level at the foot of the cross, I asked, "How many of us experience brokenness in our sexuality?" I was the only one who put up my hand.

112

Telling isn't it? Granted, the lack of raised hands may have simply been due to embarrassment. Nonetheless, it reveals the disconnect many Christians feel when confronted with the brokenness of sexuality. For most, a definition of sexual brokenness would be a checklist of particular moral indiscretions, such as having an affair or being involved with pornography. But *none* of us overcomes our aloneness perfectly, without shortcuts, escapes, or selfishness. Nothing completely escapes being tainted. And nothing escapes the "setting things right" action of our redeeming God.

One of my gay friends now identifies as post-Christian, despite being raised in the church and serving in ex-gay ministry for a time. One of the first conversations we had was about this concept of sexual brokenness. For her, hearing this phrase always triggered a deep sense of accusation. She said, "Wendy, you say that all people are broken and even that all people are sexually broken, and I'll even give you the benefit of the doubt that you really believe that. But when you or others say that, what I hear is, 'But you're more broken than me.'" Her experience of being categorized as sexually broken because of her same-sex attraction, while the rest of the church failed to admit their own sexual brokenness, ran so deep that no amount of explanation or qualification could redeem that language for her. This really affected me. I was so accustomed to framing my understanding of the world through the lens of creation-fall-redemption that when confronted with the challenge of rearticulating things in order to find common and neutral ground, I realized how much I assumed with this worldview. While this is a worldview that I continue to find value in, I can't expect that I will be able to communicate clearly or well with someone who finds this language oppressive and unjust. My friend and I did some exploring but didn't come up with better language per se. In the end, her foundational premise of the essential goodness of humanity and my understanding of the impact of the fall made for two different worldviews. But in that particular encounter, it was less about coming up with a conclusive solution and more about really listening to her concerns and dialoguing about finding a better way to connect and communicate. In the end, it wasn't so much about us sharing the same worldview as it was about experiencing empathy and understanding, and extending respect to one another in the midst of our different frames of reference.

For the Christians who shape their understanding of the world as created good, broken by the fall, and being made right, it is important to understand how this impacts our sexuality so that we truly can embody the equality we have before God—opposite-sex attracted or same-sex-attracted. In each human, regardless of the direction of their sexual attractions, there is the vibrant and beautiful potential that comes from being created in the image of God. This means that no matter the influence of our desires and longings in shaping how we encounter the world of people and relationships, we are primarily called and enabled to engage with God and others as relational beings in the same manner that God engages within the Trinity and with the people he has made. No matter the direction of the attractions you experience, you have the capacity and are called to embody the love, faithfulness, fruitfulness, and justice of God's character in how you build relationships.

When filming our DVD *Bridging the Gap*, one of the panelists named Ron shared this story:

An experience I had was in a men's prayer group in college. One time I couldn't make it to the group, and apparently the guys were talking about how they could pat themselves on the back for being friendly towards this broken gay person [me] and that it was a stretch to reach out and include someone like that. But the staff leader jumped in and said, "All of you guys keep coming to the group with your 'whoopsies' about your girlfriends. Ron's the only guy in the group that hasn't been crossing those lines or getting into trouble. But you're so into this assumption that gay people are great sinners that your narrative for how to relate to Ron [is] that he is the prodigal son, and you're the older brothers who are much more responsible. And you think you're being generous to welcome Ron and should be patted on the back for this." I really appreciated the fact that he could see and point out that double standard to them because I'd felt this self-righteousness, but it's hard for me to say, "Yeah, but what about you?" I think it was very helpful for creating a safer space for me in dealing with those prejudices.[9]

114

Deconstructing a false hierarchy in the way sexuality is viewed is essential. By seeing sexuality as relational rather than strictly and essentially about gender complementarity, we can expose the privilege that has been attributed to the majority.

The expression of our sexuality may bring us great pleasure, including physical pleasure, but it should never be reduced to the experience of stimulation and release. Yet in the Christian community, the sexuality of gay individuals is often reduced to erotic sexual acts. A gay person's sense of sexuality ought to be viewed through the same robust lens of holistic sexuality. Connecting our relational image bearing to our sexuality invites us to consider creativity, humor, communion, and the like as expressions of our sexuality. All of these aspects of our personhood are connected to the reality that we are sexual beings.

When we suggest that a same-sex-oriented individual ought not to identify as "gay" but should find their primary identity in Christ, it begs the question of why we don't simply give that message to every person who follows Christ. We don't say to heterosexual individuals, "Figure out a way to separate your sense of being attracted to the opposite sex from the way you view people, from the ways you express yourself creatively, from the way you offer yourself in friendship, from the ways you contribute to and experience family." But we do say all those things to gay people. We might not really mean that. What we might mean to say is, "Don't identify as a gay person because that will position you to see yourself as defined by your sexuality and eventually will make you vulnerable to being involved in erotic sexual acts with someone of the same sex." But if that is what we mean, then we have capitulated to a grossly reductionist view of sexuality.

An individual trying to suppress same-sex attraction will often feel frustrated and guilty. Many who do attempt such compartmentalization begin to experience a shutting down of desire. Since our sexuality is much more than genital-based experiences, this shutting down might cause an individual not only to feel asexual but also to experience an alarming loss of creativity, desire for connection with others, and overall depression. If this is motivated by a sense of fear and threat of disapproval or loss of belonging, this shutting down can become pervasive.

Surely this is not God's *shalom* in a person's life. And surely this must be differentiated from the invitation to grow in the discipline of self-control in the area of our sexual appetites.

We all face the temptation to use and objectify others for selfish ends. We all face the lure of escaping into addictive patterns. And we all need to grow in mastery in these areas, so that we can live lives that are consistent with the values we hold regarding God's best intentions for our sexuality. In this sense, no person ought to allow their sexuality to define them—but that is just as much an issue for straight people as for gay people.

A holistic understanding of our sexuality helps us to recognize that the rampant use of the cliché "love the sinner, hate the sin" is an un-helpful attempt to communicate acceptance without approval. When gay people have tried to explain why such a statement communicates a sense of total rejection, they often receive a judgmental response: "Don't define yourself by your sexuality."

Similarly, the phrase "homosexuality is a sin" illustrates a reductionist view of same-sex sexuality. What exactly is a sin? Is experiencing non-volitional same-sex desires a sin? Is viewing the world of people and relationships through the lens of same-sex sexuality a sin? Is creativity or humor that has been imprinted by a same-sex sexual identity a sin? Indeed, an individual making such a statement may specifically mean that erotic sex acts between partners of the same sex are sinful; in which case, the individual should articulate that (by perhaps clearly stating that they believe, "gay sex is a sin"). Or perhaps they have never really thought through what they are trying to communicate, in which case such disregard for another's personhood fails to model God's faithful and personal love.

Some may say, "It sounds as if you are equating same-sex sexuality with heterosexuality. But same-sex attractions are disordered. They are inconsistent with God's original creation order. Heterosexual at-traction is not fundamentally disordered." In my experience, an argu-ment about whether same-sex attractions are fundamentally disordered whether or not is inevitably a win-lose situation. Someone might win the argument, but in the end the relationship loses. I think it may be

116

more helpful to focus on the good news that God takes all of our ordered and disordered parts and works them out for the good of those who love him—whether they are opposite-sex attracted or same-sex-attracted. There are no favorites in God's economy. We are all equally valued and equally in need of redemption. For the person who insists on categorizing same-sex attraction as disordered, it may be appropriate to ask why he or she perpetuates this inequity between persons. This isn't just a theoretical distinction about a set of desires. Rather these desires are part of real people's experiences. And as people of God, we stand equal before God. We are equally called to submit to the lordship of Christ. We are equally, yet personally, called to walk in step with the Holy Spirit and discern our decisions and commitments in light of our formational reading of Scripture.

8

Our Image of God

To search for God's heart toward gay people, we must consider the way we see God. At the outset, humility compels us to confess that our ideas about God will always fall short. Despite books and sermons and preachers and teachers telling us how to know God, how to experience God, how to understand God—and despite our heart's longing to be more intimate with God—the most profound impact of sin is our inability to take off the dark lens through which we view God. But when we question our assumptions about God, we sometimes experience a significant step on our spiritual journey. This is really the heart of repentance—having the courage to change our minds and reconsider our perceptions and assumptions. Baxter Kruger, in his book *Jesus and the Undoing of Adam*, says, "Forcing our own ideas upon Jesus is a singular disaster, for it is only in knowing the staggering truth about Jesus—who he is and what he has done for and with and to the human race—that we are set free from the bondage of our profound and debilitating anxiety into the freedom to live."[1] Jesus said, "I have come that they may have life, and that they may have it more abundantly."[2] I think that the ideas many Christians have about God actually hinder their ability to live abundant lives.

In my own journey, I have wrestled (as Jacob wrestled all night for the blessing) with my own doubts, insecurities, hurts, and fears in order to see God in a manner that is actually life-giving. Even as a child I had paradoxical experiences of God. On one hand, the God I met in my church services and activities, my Christian school, and my supper time family devotions was, for the most part, distant, confusing, and impersonal. Growing up, I certainly learned a lot about God, and I absorbed the message that I had better keep in line with all I was being taught, or else. The idea that God loved me was some abstract, intellectual knowledge, while my fear of God, that I would fail, fall short, or disappoint him was tangible and real. God was the judge with unquenchable wrath that could be requited only by the cruel and horrific death of his only Son. God was the sovereign chess player who chose some people for eternal life and others for eternal damnation. God was pissed off for what seemed like two thirds of the Old Testament, and because I was told that he never changes, part of me assumed he was still up there shaking his angry fist. Fear and dread marked much of my intellectual understanding of what God was like.

But I also had childhood experiences full of wonder, awe, even ecstasy. I was a melancholy child, prone to feeling overwhelmed by sadness and self-pity, so my experiences of God's grandeur nourished my soul and offered a portal out of my daily sense of being unaccepted and misunderstood. One day at school, I simply didn't return to my classroom after the lunch break. I stayed outside, walking through the long grass at the end of the playground, glorying in this mysterious experience of being seen, known, lifted. It seemed a little like what Martin Luther meant when he said, "If one could understand a single grain of wheat, one would die for wonder."[3] These spiritual experiences didn't seem to connect to the God I was learning so much about. I think I instinctively sought to protect these experiences from the systematic theology my community was so steeped in.

This paradox has baffled me (at best) and haunted me (at worst) through much of my spiritual journey. I was confounded by, on one hand, a system of belief that required me to do convoluted spiritual gymnastics in order to believe (truly believe) that God loved me in spite of his wrath and my depravity. On the other hand, I had experiences that I gradually realized were of the Spirit, connecting me to the presence of the God who saw me, knew me, and loved me. At times I wondered if my mystical experiences were even God at all because there wasn't much in the framework I was taught to help me understand or affirm them. At low points, I even wondered if they were deceptions from the enemy to lead me astray into some strange, threatening, and scary New Age falsehood. But there was tenacity in my spirit to stay alive to the hope that these soul-sustaining experiences were truly of God and truly an expression of his great love for me. Brennan Manning said that he believed Jesus will ask just one question of us on judgment day, "Did you believe that I loved you?" He suggested that those who truly know God would be able to reply, "Yes, Jesus, I believed that you loved me, and I tried to shape my life as a response to it."[4]

Scripture tells us that God is love. "Everyone who loves has been born of God and knows God. Whoever does not love does not know God, because God is love. This is how God showed his love among us: He sent his one and only Son into the world that we might live through him."[5]

So we know that God is love, and yet what does this love mean? What does it mean when one is faced with a crisis of faith? What does it mean for gay persons faced with the dilemma of engaging Scripture in light of their core desire for love and family? "If God is love, and if he loves me, why am I faced with these agonizing questions and challenges?" And so the questions, "Who is God, and what does he want from us? What does he want from *me*?" are at the heart of the matter for those who deeply and desperately want to experience the fullness of life of which Jesus speaks.

Fear: The Barrier to Love

It can be a tremendous struggle to live in the truth of God's love. I believe that the biggest barrier to staying present to God's love is not wrong belief, not insufficient spiritual disciplines, not unconfessed sin, but rather fear. The apostle John reminds us, "There is no fear in love. But perfect love drives out fear, because fear has to do with punishment. The one who fears is not made perfect in love."[6] How many of us can truly say that we live fear-free lives? Who among us is truly fearless?

For those for whom the questions concerning homosexuality are personally critical—not mere theoretical abstractions, but real, heart-wrenching dilemmas—this question of fear must be faced head-on. If, indeed, fear is the enemy of love, then fear keeps us from truly seeing God as he is. When questions of homosexuality come up, so much of the conversation retreats into a convenient reductionism that can be summed up by the phrase on a bumper sticker, "God said it. I believe it. That settles it."

In one of his earlier works, Henri Nouwen said this of fear:

> When we consider how much our educational, political, religious, and even social lives are geared to finding answers to questions born of fear, it is not hard to understand why a message of love has little chance of being heard. Fearful questions never lead to love-filled answers. . . . Once I believe that God is out to get me for my bad behavior, complicated moral schemes start to occupy my mind. . . . Thus, fear engenders fear. Fear never gives birth to love.[7]

As I have talked with gay people who have grown up in Christian families and churches, it seems that many of the questions that drive their choices and decisions are born of fear. My friend David has said that one of the deepest questions he asked was whether he was lovable. When a gay person grows up in an environment that views gay people with fear, distrust, and disgust, he or she will internalize this from a very young age. If such emotions toward gay people are communicated by the spiritual leaders and authorities in the system in which they grow up, young people experiencing same-sex attraction will project those experiences onto their understanding of God and what God must think of them.

One day during Christian family camp, my twelve-year-old son told me what had happened that morning in chapel. He said that the leader had talked about the concubine from the book of Judges. (If you recall, this story is about the men of a village demanding an old man to allow them to sexually violate a [male] stranger who was visiting him. Rather than complying with the demand to send a man out to experience such violation, the two men sent out the man's concubine. She is gang raped all night, crawls to the door in the morning, collapses, and dies on the threshold.) As you might imagine, I was horrified. Apparently, this youth pastor had talked about accounts of sin throughout the Old Testament, beginning with Adam and Eve and particularly highlighting the stories of Sodom and Gomorrah, and the concubine. My son said the leader talked about how he never dreamed when he was a kid that there would be a time when homosexuality would be accepted—but now it was. He used that as the example to demonstrate how rampant sin was in our culture to try to motivate the kids toward holy living. My son was quite upset and confused. I asked my son how a gay youth might have felt, and he said, "I think they would have walked out." Sadly, I think they would have been too scared to walk out and would have instead stayed and internalized the negative message.

I made an appointment to meet with this leader. I encountered a well-experienced youth pastor with teenaged children of his own. He meant well. He wanted to encourage the kids to pursue holiness. And he felt that this was a topic that was too often ignored by the church. But I talked to him about the twelve-year-old kid who might be sitting there questioning his own sexuality (with whom this leader would have no ongoing relationship or contact) who internalizes a message that says, "I've got to fear God, I've got to be holy, or I'm going to hell." I talked to him about that kid who may struggle for years to know that God loves him as he is, the kid who may feel disqualified from pursuing an intimate relationship with God. Then I talked to him about that twelve-year-old kid who might be sitting there who is homophobic and walks away feeling justified in his attitudes because "clearly those people don't fear God." I talked to him about that student sitting there who has gay friends who now feels torn and confused about whether loving their friends would make God angry. I talked to him about the inappropriateness of using Sodom and Gomorrah and the concubine story in Judges 19 as examples of homosexuality, given that they tell stories of violence and violation of strangers, and are from a completely different cultural context. He told me that he thought the core of the gospel was holiness; I told him that I thought the core of the gospel was God's unconditional love. God extends an unconditional welcome to all, and unless people know they are loved they can never pursue holiness from any other place than fear. I told him that I was available to talk with any students who had further questions about this topic. My son told me that on the second-to-last day of camp, they made the announcement about New Direction and of my availability. No kids came to see me. No big surprise there. The damage may well have already been done. Hearing about this experience, one of my gay friends said, "Thank you for speaking to that pastor; I have been that kid sitting in many a church and chapel service, feeling confused, guilty, and sad over the things church leaders said."

When one of the biggest fear-based questions is whether or not God could truly love me and whether or not my experience of same-sex-attraction makes me despicable in his sight, it is poignantly clear how hard it is for a message of love—without fear—to break through. And when gay Christians that are confident in the love of God are demonized, accused of destroying the church, labeled as not being true Christians, it is even more understandable how the same-sex-attracted person within a traditional context finds it nearly impossible to find a spacious place in which to see and encounter the God who accepts and loves them as they are.

Will God Meet My Needs?

Another huge question facing gay Christians is whether or not God can be truly trusted to meet them at their point of need. The evangelical context, in particular, is one that often emphasizes God meeting our needs. This can range from those who essentially see God as a cosmic Santa Claus showering his faithful people with blessings to those who advocate embracing such radical self-denial that all one's needs must be met only within one's personal relationship with Christ. Gay persons in such a context may spend a lot of spiritual energy trying to figure out where they are supposed to be on this wide-ranging spectrum. But because fear is behind the question, they may constantly doubt themselves, assuming that they should always be moving toward the self-denial end of the spectrum. One way this manifests itself is the overspiritualization of personal needs. So when the gay person looks at a future lifetime with no significant, exclusive companion, fear may compel them to spiritualize that longing and say: "I don't really need companionship—I just need more of Jesus." Every time this longing arises, shame is right there to whisper, "If you were closer to Jesus, you wouldn't have these longings." Please don't misunderstand me. I believe that God is the source and the sustainer of our life. But over-spiritualizing and denying particular needs because we are vulnerable to a voice of accusation and shame is not the way God intends for us to find our life in him.

Is God Fair?

The question of justice and fairness can be another thorny area for those seeking to faithfully integrate their faith and their sexuality. They may ask: "Why would God allow me to continue to experience such desire, despite my repeated prayers for him to take these feelings away, and provide essentially no outlet for me to express them?" "Even before sin entered the world, God said that it was not good for man to be alone, then why must I be resigned to a life that is alone on the basis of something I did not choose or want?" "If the apostle Paul recognized that it was better for people to marry than to burn with desire, why doesn't that apply to me?" When these queries are overshadowed by the deep fear of God's wrath, it can be very threatening to even privately ask such questions. To keep such questioners in-line, authorities may point to God's holiness, that his ways are higher than our ways, that our hearts are deceptively wicked, that we don't trust enough, that we're selfish—and who are we to question God?

But what if unquestioning, blind obedience to the assumed truth is not what God is seeking from his children? Consider that the truth of any religious system is incomplete. No system, no theology, no interpretive grid, no amount of scholarship guarantees absolute access to absolute truth. Our best ideas about God are incomplete and flawed. To say otherwise is simply idolatrous. To presume that our understanding of God is perfectly right makes that very understanding an idol, an image of God. It may not be carved from stone or wood, but it is indeed an idol of our own creation.

Prophetic and Poetic Voices

Perhaps today's prophetic and poetic voices include those voices of ordinary believers faced with a sexual identity that does not fit the norm. These voices are decrying our idolatry of a God we can contemplate, categorize, rationalize, and reduce to a series of dos and don'ts in order to assuage our great need for certainty and security. Might it be that our gay sisters and brothers (out of utter desperation to encounter a God who doesn't hate them and who doesn't want to snuff out their sense of self) become the poets and artists and prophets among us who dare to question and doubt and step into a transformative encounter with the living God? It would seem that in the tradition of God's people throughout history, our reaction to such prophets who speak a word that upsets our comfort, certainty, and security is to become angry and stone them. When Jonah prophesied to the Ninevites, they were willing to rend their garments and put ashes on their heads in repentance. But we don't see ourselves that way. We see ourselves as holding the truth already, and our job is to guard that truth. In this light, we feel perfectly justified (and more often than not, divinely called) to crucify the false prophets who dare to challenge the coffin in which we contain our god.

Might it be that the voice of truth can come from the suffering soul who has wrestled with God over mysteries and paradoxes? Might the voice of truth be the one that in wisdom and humility says, "I don't know"?

There is a story of a group of monks in the desert who served with an old and wise Abba (father). One day a young monk came to visit. He had a question about the interpretation of a particular text and hoped that the Abba would be able to tell him the answer. He posed his question, and the Abba silently nodded his head, then picked up his broom and began to sweep. The younger monks each took turns offering their response to this hermeneutical dilemma. After lunch, the monks debated among themselves and wrestled to come to a resolution. As the afternoon grew long, the visiting monk realized it would soon be time to leave. He turned to the Abba, who had been quietly working during all the discussion and debate, and said, "Abba, you have been listening to us and you know we have not come to a resolution. You are the wisest among us. Please tell me, what is the true interpretation of this text?" The old man looked up from his work, glanced toward the heavens as if in a moment of prayer, and said simply, "I know not," and then returned to his sweeping.

The one who willingly says, "I know not," and yet lives in the transformative reality of the gospel (with a liberty and freedom that could only have come from encountering the loving presence of God) is a model for us. Apprehending the truth of God becomes incarnational: God with us, the very action of his presence, not just some idea about his presence. Nouwen writes,

> Here God is presented neither as reducible to the status of other objects, nor as outside the world and eternally distant from it, but rather as one who is received by us without ever being directly conceived by us. Here the mystery of God is revealed as an incarnated mystery, that is, the mystery of God is revealed in the midst of God's presence. . . . God is here revealed as one who is made present through the acts of love and liberation rather than through the categories of human understanding.[8]

The poet soul of the gay disciple then is one that has wrestled through the systemic violence perpetrated, in the name of God, against his or her sense of being in the world and has come through with a sense of God's presence and blessing on his or her life.

This poet soul isn't reduced to the disciple who has embraced one particular (and assumed correct) position on gay relationships. Just as there are those with very conservative convictions who may, through fear and control, create their own idol of God, there are also those who hold a gay-affirmative perspective with the rigid certainty that can foster a similar kind of idolatry through its constrained picture of God. One encounters this poetic soul not in the outcome of the wrestling but in the midst of it. It is not the destination but the journey that defines one who has embraced the mysterious poet song. It is those who resist a violent certainty who must convert the other. It is those who can embody receptivity to the presence of God, the blessing of God, in a way that sings a new song. This song is a prophetic call for those seeking God in the midst of this particular minefield. But it is also a clarion call to a church mired in a system of its own making, a system that has little room for the wildness of the God who eludes definition.

A friend, who lives and works in an extremely conservative area of the United States, embodies such a poetic soul. He speaks of navigating his same-sex attraction, his need to be closeted in his community and Christian workplace, and his choice to embrace a spiritual life that is filled with adventure, risk, and exploration. Written under a pseudonym, his book, *Superheroes, Saviors and Sinners without Secrets*, tells the story of a quest. This quest is for an authentic journey with God, despite the limitations of a faith community that doesn't value such honest searching. He writes, "Instead of compassion and encouragement to pursue my passions for same-sex relationships, or even counsel to turn away from my desires, pray and stay straight, I need reminders to honor God and live a life without regret."[9]

Our rational notions of God keep us locked into a small and fearful world. That which we cannot explain we cannot control, and that which we cannot control threatens to overwhelm and undo us. And we cannot have that. And so those who hold on to rigid, fear-driven positions concerning homosexuality may resist listening to a poetic voice because it sounds dangerous. Typically, this resistance takes a very rational form: arguments are picked apart and dissected; every point that doesn't stand up under objective scrutiny is exposed; every gap in logic is isolated, rebutted, and summarily dismissed.

The casualty in all of this is our capacity to extend hospitality and grace to one another in the midst of our differences. It is far less threatening to band together with those who think and believe and practice as we do. It is our natural inclination to proselytize those who differ from us. Such proselytizing, however, reduces people to projects. It objectifies them, dehumanizes them, and devalues their experiences and journey. It breaks and fragments the sense of common ground we share as humans, created in the image of God, called to care for one another, welcome one another, and work toward *shalom* in our communities.

When we lose touch with the reverence that acknowledges the mysterious limitations on our understanding of God, we are free to treat a fellow image bearer of God in an irreverent manner. The result is that our churches become gatherings that are rigid in ethos and expression. This is the very antithesis of a generous spaciousness that fearlessly extends room to others to explore and grow in faith. Generous spaciousness is decidedly relational. It isn't a theoretical concept to argue about but an interpersonal reality to be lived. Generous spaciousness sees generosity in God's heart; it sees spaciousness in God's patience with his creatures; it sees love as the energy motivating all that God does and says.

9

The Role of Scripture

In conversations about faith and sexuality, Scripture usually takes a pivotal role. The text of Scripture invites both the individual and the community of faith into the story of God. The invitation is to come into a spacious place where God is revealing himself personally, relationally, and with increasing depth. The plot of this story is redemption, and its main character is Jesus.

But this invitation into the story of Scripture can also cause us to hesitate. Perhaps this hesitancy is motivated by past experiences when Scripture was used to wound us or when it provoked fear or shame, resentment or defiance. Tim Keel, in his book *Intuitive Leadership*, says,

> Unfortunately, rather than living deeply within scriptural stories in a way that shapes our imagination, we use them in a way that kills it. We reduce these stories to prescriptions for how churches in all times ought to respond regardless of context. In my experience, leading in this manner does not take hard work and dependence on the Holy Spirit. Systems of control and structures of belief that do not reflect the witness of engagement and incarnation found in Scripture rarely do.[1]

The question to ask is: do we view Scripture as stories to imaginatively live into or do we view Scripture as prescriptions for how to live?

Reading Scripture Formationally

In the project *Eat this Book: A Conversation in the Art of Spiritual Reading*, Eugene Peterson reminds us that we are called to encounter, read, and engage Scripture formationally.[2] Our spiritual lives are formed through the Holy Spirit in response to the text of Scripture. We are called to be participants in the revelation of God and to find ourselves in the story of God. This calls us into the dance of obedience—the kind of obedience that positions us to fully live the life God intends.

Peterson differentiates this formational reading of Scripture from the ways we make Scripture utilitarian. He suggests three primary ways we use Scripture where *we* are in control rather than allowing *Scripture* to form us. This utilitarian approach to Scripture dominates many of the discussions about homosexuality.

The first is when we use Scripture to tell us how to live. The Bible becomes a self-help guide to successful living. In and of itself, living right and living as optimally as possible is not a bad thing. But if this is our primary approach to Scripture, we will have failed to allow Scripture to form us.

The second way we use the text is for inspiration. In this case, we pick and choose the passages that comfort, encourage, or motivate us. This emphasis also fails to allow Scripture, in its entirety, to form us.

The third way we use Scripture in a utilitarian way is for intellectual challenge. We see this when people excel at scholarship but potentially fail to allow the Spirit and text to call them into submission to the Scriptures.

Peterson observes that anyone who interacts with the Bible inevitably finds themselves using Scripture in one of these ways at one time or another. But he reminds us that such utilitarian engagement with the Bible avoids its relational aspects and actually interferes with our receptivity to what God personally wants to form and shape in us. These utilitarian approaches disregard how God wants to transform us by his self-revelation.

In addition to the depersonalized, utilitarian approach to Scripture, Peterson suggests we overly personalize our interaction with Scripture because of our needs, wants, and feelings. No one is immune to doing this. However, this very thing prevents us from finding our true place in God's story and being transformed by his self-revelation. Like the utilitarian approach, the personalized approach puts us in the place of control over Scripture rather than putting us in a posture of receptivity and submission.

Much of the evangelical church is concerned about usurping Scripture's authority and making our own experience the text by which we live our lives. While I think disregarding Scripture's authority does have the potential to derail the Christian life, I have often observed people presumptuously accusing gay Christians of this. The assumption is that the gay person who chooses to *wrestle* with Scripture rather than simply following the principles taught by their church—or the gay Christian who concludes that God invites them to have a same-sex relationship—has put their experience, needs, wants, and feelings ahead of submission to the text. Often such an assumption goes without challenge in the evangelical community. It seems that much of the energy of the church is concerned with orthodoxy (right thinking) or orthopraxy (right doing). Another possibility, however, is to consider *orthoparadoxy*, which is "living rightly in the tension and mystery of the mysterious and revealed God of the Scriptures."[3] Orthoparadoxy requires radical dependence on the Spirit of God living in and working through God's people as they wrestle and search his heart for their lives.

The assumption that sexual minorities engage Scripture governed by their feelings and desires fails to listen to the journey of gay Christians and the ways they have or have not allowed Scripture to form and shape them. Such an assumption also seems to reduce the story of God's revelation and its entire influence in our formation to six or seven texts. In other words, when it is assumed that experience or personal desires have shaped a gay person's approach to Scripture, this assumption is really looking at only one specific decision individuals make in terms of their openness to sexual intimacy in a same-sex relationship.

Peterson says, "We are fond of saying that the Bible has all the answers. And that is certainly correct. The text of the Bible sets us in a
reality that is congruent with who we are as created beings in God's
image and what we are destined for in the purposes of Christ. But the
Bible also has all the questions, many of them that we would just as
soon were never asked of us, and some of which we will spend the rest
of our lives doing our best to dodge."[4]

A trusting openness to Scripture inevitably introduces us to the inherent paradoxes and mysteries that are woven throughout the texts of
our Bibles. While we recognize the ultimate author of Scripture (God),
we are also cognizant of the multiple human authors who wrote within
their various contexts. Peterson, in responding to a question after a
lecture, encouraged his listeners to live with the tensions between the
divine nature of the biblical story and its earthiness. To focus on the
divine nature of the text without acknowledging the human element is
to make the words of Scripture belong to some disconnected, angelic
voice. To focus too much on the human authors and historical context
will miss the glorious ways that heaven meets earth in the text. This
is, of course, the mystery of the incarnation. The meeting of heaven
and earth. The integration of the human and divine. A mystery that
we will not fully apprehend this side of heaven, but a mystery we are
called to enter, to find ourselves in, and to be willing to feel and be
present to its tension.

When I consider how so much of the Christian community deals
with the question of faithful discipleship and same-sex sexuality, I see
little willingness or spaciousness in which to live in such mystery and
with such tensions. More often than not, Scripture is used precisely in
the ways Peterson encourages us to avoid. He says, "But nothing in our
Bibles is one-dimensional, systematized, or theologized. Everything in
the text is intimately and organically linked to lived reality."[5]

As I have journeyed with gay Christians, I have seen a number of
threads of God's story that are particularly challenging. These threads
often have an internal sense of paradox and tension. To put a new spin on
an illustration used by Corrie ten Boom, Scripture can be like a tapestry.
On the underside are many different colors, knots, and tangles amongst

the threads. But when turned to the right side, the chaos transforms into a beautiful image. In the case of Scripture, this image is not the image of us living our lives with perfect morality. It is the image of the living God. Out of the mystery of the paradox of threads and themes running throughout Scripture emerges a beautiful revelation of God. In order to fully receive this revelation, we must be willing to enter the living story, complete with tension, paradox, and questions.

Our human nature, however, wants to avoid tension. We want to resolve paradox. Rarely do we willingly live in the midst of it.

Embracing Suffering vs. "It Is Not Good to Be Alone"

Suffering is a normal part of the Christian life. It is a vehicle through which many of us experience growth. Consider how suffering is expressed in 2 Corinthians 4:7–12:

> But we have this treasure in jars of clay to show that this all-surpassing power is from God and not from us. We are hard pressed on every side, but not crushed; perplexed, but not in despair; persecuted, but not abandoned; struck down, but not destroyed. We always carry around in our body the death of Jesus, so that the life of Jesus may also be revealed in our body. For we who are alive are always being given over to death for Jesus' sake, so that his life may be revealed in our mortal body. So then, death is at work in us, but life is at work in you.

Embracing a willingness to suffer is seen as a sign of allowing Scripture to form and shape our characters and refine us to be more like Christ. It is a tangible way to avoid using Scripture to meet our needs, fulfill our wants, or cater to our feelings. In contrast to a triumphalistic expectation that following Christ will cause you to prosper in every way, embracing a robust theology of suffering postures the disciple to follow in the footsteps of the Lord, the apostles, and the early church. A robust theology of suffering is not a place of hopelessness or resignation. Rather, it is a space in which self-giving love and maturity flourish as one grows in dependence on God's grace in our weakness. It is a place of radical trust.

The underbelly of embracing suffering can be seen when suffering becomes an idol. Choosing the way of suffering can become so important to an individual that he or she is unable to take risks to experience new opportunities for love, for purpose, or for fulfillment. Another pitfall is when an individual who has embraced suffering looks on the different choices of others (which seem to entail less suffering) with judgment or pride.

This can be particularly challenging for a gay person who has committed to living a single, chaste life and who encounters another gay Christian who has a partner or spouse and is living in a committed covenant relationship. I was speaking to a group where I knew there were a few same-sex-attracted people who were pursuing the possibility of marriage to an opposite gender spouse but who were currently single. In this same group, there were people who were open to having a gay partner, and one gay person who was currently dating. I was there to talk about how they might bridge some of the gaps within their own group, how they could foster a place of honesty and authenticity, how they could support one another with integrity, and how they could move forward with their eyes fixed on Christ, as individuals and as a group. One man, who was pursuing an ex-gay path, said, "At first I felt really jealous, like why could they have this and I couldn't. God and I did a lot of talking about it. In the end, I've accepted that this is what God has asked of me and that he has a purpose in it, and that I need to find what I need from knowing that I am living in the way I feel God has asked me to." This young man had embraced the reality of suffering, self-denial, and sense of vocation and calling in his singleness (since he was well aware that his dream of being heterosexually married might never happen). He had worked through his initial feelings of jealousy and judgment toward other gay Christians who were pursuing a different path. And this set him free to live a life that was consistent with his own convictions and to be a loving friend to others. This small group was able to cast down any idols of suffering or superiority, and commit together to do their best to keep their eyes on Christ and to encourage and support one another in growing in their faith and sense of calling. They were choosing to nurture generous spaciousness in their relational and spiritual commitments to one another.

Embracing suffering as a gay Christian committed (but not necessarily gifted) to celibacy might seem to be in tension with the biblical idea that "it is not good to be alone." This idea begins with God seeing something not good in his perfect, sinless creation. It was not good that the man he had made was alone. God himself exists in the relationship of Father, Son, and Holy Spirit. God is thoroughly relational. Out of the overflow of love in the relationship of the Trinity, the world was created. God's calling us into relationship is clearly more than only sexually consummated relationships. And yet, there is something unique and special about finding someone who will be your life partner.

Physical affection and sexual consummation flow out of a loving, committed relationship in which we overcome our aloneness. It is an opportunity to offer ourselves fully and intimately to another, to serve them with self-giving love. For the gay person, this part of the story—that God sees our aloneness and makes a way for us to know another and be known—can be a powerful chapter. The idea that their particular sexual orientation excludes them from this invitation to not be alone can feel arbitrary and unlike the God who sees and knows his children and who, when asked for a piece of bread, does not give a stone.

Since these themes seem paradoxical, the temptation may be to choose one path over the other, to either choose the way of suffering or to claim God's desire to not be alone. Any follower of Jesus, regardless of the direction of their attractions, will do well to situate themselves in the midst of the tensions of these realities: to both embrace a robust theology of suffering and welcome the invitation to God-honoring intimacy, even when that may be initially complicated by uncertainty or fear.

Singleness as Vocation vs. the Desire for Marriage and Family

The themes of singleness as vocation and the desire for family are easily connected to questions around suffering and our longing for relationship. In the history of the church, singleness and the celibate state were elevated in ways that we Protestants are particularly disconnected from today. The combination of a focus on martyrdom (with its accompanying discouragement of entanglement with worldly pleasures) and an overemphasis on Paul's judgment that it is better to not marry (1 Cor. 7), encouraged early church leaders like Origen to prioritize celibacy over marriage. Jerome is credited with saying, "Marriage populates the earth, virginity populates heaven."[6] After the Reformation, however, marriage was reclaimed as a normative way to bear God's image. In contemporary expressions of the evangelical Christian community, this emphasis continues with a prioritized focus on the nuclear family.

A balanced view, mutually honoring to both those who are single and those who are married, is not often actualized in our churches. Many single people express feeling like second-class citizens in their church communities where life revolves around marriage and family. In this context, a gay person often encounters the expectation that they will commit to a single life. Where there is open discussion of this, Christians may encourage gay people to see this commitment as part of their vocation in service to God. And yet there is often little affirmation or support to sustain this decision in life-giving ways.

One gay woman said of her singleness, "With believers I express it in terms of being faithful to the One I love more than anyone on earth, as the goal is intimacy with the One who loves me, and anything less than fidelity to that relationship just won't do. Framing it in these terms also places singleness in proper context with marriage; namely it defines both in terms of fidelity in a relationship of love, faithfulness, and trust." This woman, and many like her, have articulated a sense of meaning and vocation in their lives as single persons.

In her book, *Real Sex*, Lauren Winner articulates a deep sense of purpose for the single person. She writes, "The unmarried Christian who practices chastity refrains from sex in order to remember that God desires your person, your body, more than any man or woman ever will."[7]

In a similar manner, Rob Bell in his book, *Sex God*, writes,

Some of the most sexual people I know are celibate. They sleep alone. They have chosen to give themselves to lots of people, to serve and give and connect their lives with beautiful worthy causes. You can be having sex with many, and yet you're alone. And the more sex you have, the more alone you are. And it's possible to be sleeping alone, and celibate, and to be very sexual. Connected with many.[8]

We are encouraged to recognize that marriage and singleness equally image the divine intent for our sexual lives. It is critical, however, that local fellowships intentionally evaluate whether their life as community is actualizing this mutually honoring posture. Regardless of the reason a person is single, and whether this is a long-term commitment or an unchosen and hoped-to-be temporary state, the faith community loves well when it honors and validates finding meaning, purpose, and serenity in the single life. Where this is lived out, gay persons who believe the single life is most congruent with their beliefs and convictions will be better positioned to experience the value of their singleness as vocation.

For many gay people, the idea of lifelong singleness is not only overwhelming but devastating. This ought not to be assumed to be due to an overactive sex drive. In my conversations with gay Christians, this has much more to do with the fundamental longing for the love and companionship of marriage and the capacity to parent children. Particularly in the Old Testament narratives, such longing is heard and validated. We remember the stories of Sarah, Rachel, and Hannah with their longing for children. Psalm 113:9 says, "He settles the childless woman in her home / as a happy mother of children." And Psalm 68:6, "God sets the lonely in families."

In Paul's writings, when he is discussing the merits of celibacy and marriage, he says, "I am saying this for your benefit, not to place restrictions on you. I want you to do whatever will help you serve the Lord best, with as few distractions as possible."[9]

Such emphasis can present gay persons with a dilemma. They don't feel called to singleness, and feel they will be unable to faithfully live a single life. If they try to commit to singleness, it could have two results: one, most of their emotional and spiritual energy will be spent trying to maintain chastity in singleness, which renders them not very engaged in life, community, or service; and two, the likelihood of moments of weakness resulting in indiscretion is increased. This leaves them with the question, "What is better? To faithfully commit to a same-sex partner, be free to grow in self-giving love, experience sexual expression within the boundaries of covenant, and be able to look beyond myself in service to others. Or to strive to be single, risk the guilt, shame, and hurt of sexual expression outside of covenant, and experience limited usefulness to others because my striving is taking up all my energy." Mark Tidd, pastor at Highlands Church, an affirming church in Denver, says, "I think all the people that are wrestling to exegete the seven passages and develop a new hermeneutic ought to take a vow of celibacy until they come to resolution and see if that doesn't speed up the process." Indeed, it seems rather convenient for straight, married leaders to pronounce clear calls to celibacy or to drag their feet in making any accommodation of grace for Christians who are gay and partnered. These leaders need to consider that while they have an opportunity for relational and sexual fulfillment, their theology denies it to others.

This tension in the Scriptures between the calling of singleness as vocation and the affirmation of marriage and family is a real and complex challenge for gay followers of Jesus. Such tension needs to be entered, experienced, and lived through Scripture, in prayer, and may entail tears and struggle and pain. It is not a dilemma the follower of Jesus seeks to resolve outside of Scripture but rather in the very midst of the biblical story. It is not resolved by proof-texts but lived through the unfolding story. And like any story, we encounter different layers and different insights at different points in engaging the story. This is true for gay Christians who seek to allow Scripture to form and shape their lives while at the same time living day to day, making choices, experiencing relationships, encountering desire and emotion. The church ought not short-circuit this process with demands and simplistic expectations but rather cultivate an environment of generous spaciousness that gives the individual room to navigate the journey.

A Personal God vs. the Call to Community

The individual and particular nature of each person's relationship with God and the call to be submitted to and centered in community can also present tension.

It is a powerful realization, when a person truly embraces and connects with living faith: to know that the God who created the universe knows your name, counts the hairs on your head, has good plans for you, and will bring his good work to completion in you, uniquely you. Psalm 139 reminds us,

> You have searched me, LORD,
>   and you know me.
> You know when I sit and when I rise;
>   you perceive my thoughts from afar.
> You discern my going out and my lying down;
>   you are familiar with all my ways.
> Before a word is on my tongue
>   you, LORD, know it completely.
> You hem me in—behind and before,
>   and you lay your hand upon me. (vv. 1–6)

In a world of franchise, mass production, cheap imitations, and big-box shopping, it is dazzlingly outrageous to ponder that God created you like no one else. It is astonishing to encounter the self-revelatory God through words in Scripture, the beauty of creation, a song, a picture, a dream. To grasp that you have access, limited as it may be, to this holy, all-powerful God, and to know his good thoughts toward you is life-changing. Many Christians never forget the first time they read a portion of Scripture and experienced, as John Wesley once said, their hearts strangely warmed. That experience changes everything.

For the gay person, it is profoundly important to encounter such a personal God. They need to know without a doubt that God knows them, understands them, extends grace and mercy to them, is patient with them, is kind to them, finds them delightful, smiles and sings over them, and wraps them in his unconditional love. Confidence in these truths will form a solid foundation from which they can ask questions, tackle paradoxes, deal with doubt, make wise sacrifices, and ultimately find serenity in submitting to the lordship of the Christ who personally knows and cares for them.

But these profound truths can unfortunately transform into a "me and Jesus" mentality that fails to find itself in the story of God's people, the beloved community. Where our personal relationship with Jesus becomes privatized, where we take the profound truth that God knows us intimately and use it to lock the door to mutual submission and accountability in community, we have failed to see the fullness of God's heart. In far too much of the church, we have capitulated to the idolatry of autonomy. Our delight in being known by God becomes a defense against needing to be known by the community.

The corrective is to truly engage in the life of the community. If we are profoundly and personally known by God, then God calls us to share that with fellow disciples. Allowing oneself to grow through loving others when it is difficult, to submit to others when our pride would just as soon stalk off and do our own thing, to open our engagement with the Scriptures to the minds and hearts of other disciples when their insights might challenge us in ways we don't want to be challenged—this is the stuff that forms us to be like Christ. Without community, we are impoverished in our experience of the Christian faith.

Law vs. Justice

Another significant area of Scripture that must be engaged by gay Christians seeking to be formed and shaped by the divine intent is the question of the place of the law in their quest to understand God's will for them.

It is not uncommon to encounter those who use Leviticus 20:13 as a simplistic response: "If a man lies with a man as one lies with a woman, both of them have done what is detestable. They must be put to death; their blood will be on their own heads" (NIV 1984). In the battle over gay marriage in California, this text was written on a placard with an image showing two rope nooses side by side, mimicking the same-sex symbol. To most Christians, such a threat of death is inconsistent with the new covenant experienced in Christ (even if the protestors believe the Leviticus prohibition of same-sex sexual behavior is binding). You can still encounter literal injunctions of this Levitical passage today; we see this with stark clarity in Africa where some pastors have advocated for the death penalty for gay people. Still other Christians claim that Leviticus ought not be used against gay Christians in light of Christ's summary of the law found in Matthew 22:37–40, "'Love the Lord your God with all your heart and with all your soul and with all your mind.' This is the first and greatest commandment. And the second is like it: 'Love your neighbor as yourself.' All the Law and the Prophets hang on these two commandments" (NIV 1984). But just a few chapters earlier, Jesus says, "Do not think that I have come to abolish the Law or the Prophets; I have not come to abolish them but to fulfill them. For truly I tell you, until heaven and earth disappear, not the smallest letter, not the least stroke of a pen, will by any means disappear from the Law until everything is accomplished."[10]

These questions are exacerbated by the glaringly inconsistent application of the Levitical law in the lives of contemporary Christians. We Christians are known for the ways we pick and choose which laws we will apply today and which we will conveniently ignore as culturally bound or insignificant. And it can seem so much clearer to hold as timeless those injunctions that have absolutely no bearing on one's own personal life.

The Pauline Epistles offer much to consider on this question of the law. Paul says in Galatians 3:10–14,

All who rely on observing the law are under a curse, for it is written: "Cursed is everyone who does not continue to do everything written in the Book of the Law." Clearly no one is justified before God by the law, because, "The righteous will live by faith." The law is not based on faith; on the contrary, "The man who does these things will live by them." Christ redeemed us from the curse of the law by becoming a curse for us, for it is written: "Cursed is everyone who is hung on a tree." He redeemed us in order that the blessing given to Abraham might come to the Gentiles through Christ Jesus, so that by faith we might receive the promise of the Spirit. (NIV 1984)

Paul also says, "Let no debt remain outstanding, except the continuing debt to love one another, for whoever loves others has fulfilled the law. The commandments, 'You shall not commit adultery,' 'You shall not murder,' 'You shall not steal,' 'You shall not covet,' and whatever other command there may be, are summed up in this one command:

'Love your neighbor as yourself.' Love does no harm to its neighbor. Therefore love is the fulfillment of the law."[11]

Given these seemingly conflicting perspectives, gay persons need to wrestle with the larger story of Scripture to understand and accept its implications for their lives. Such a process may mean exploration beyond the accepted position of their particular church, family, or community. This can be incredibly difficult and result in feelings of anxiety and uncertainty about wrestling with Scripture in a way that places too much emphasis on their own needs, wants, and feelings. In addition, there can be fear from daring to question the accepted perspectives of the church and not wanting to be perceived as betraying the community they love, not wanting to be labeled a rebel, a heretic, or one who compromises. Some individuals may never ask the hard questions because of these fears.

Others come to a place of prioritizing the ethic of not harming their neighbor as the basis for their reflections on the law as it relates to the question of same-sex relations. Justin Lee, executive director of the Gay Christian Network, in his essay "The Great Debate," says,

> We could literally go through every single one of God's commandments and show that each one of them is simply an extension of this basic principle to live a life of servant love. ("Love" here of course doesn't mean romantic love; it means the deep, abiding, unconditional love that comes from God.)

> But wait—the very definition of the Traditional View says that *even when two relationships are equally loving*—even when they're motivated by the exact same selfless desires and the exact same servant hearts—that one of them can be ruled sinful just because of a person's gender. Traditionalists say that this command is from God. But if it's from God, then why does it contradict the rule Paul gives us here—a rule that applies to *every other commandment?*[12]

When one begins to struggle with the impact of the law in faith formation, there is often a simultaneous wrestling with the implications of God's emphasis on justice. Biblical justice ensures that everyone gets what they need to live. It breaks down inequality and exclusion. It cares for the weak and the needy. Biblical justice, with over nine hundred references throughout Scripture, stands in stark contrast to the laws that exclude people on the basis of disability, ethnicity, and status. Consider this well-known text from Micah 6:8: "He has showed you, O man, what is good. And what does the LORD require of you? To act justly and to love mercy and to walk humbly with your God" (NIV 1984). Jesus says something very similar when he reflects the prophet Hosea's words in both Matthew 9:13 and 12:7, "I desire mercy, not sacrifice."

What do such justice and mercy look like for a gay person? For some, this challenges the primary assumption that they are excluded from marital intimacy on the basis of gender. For others, this means the right to a safe environment where they can be honest and up front about their same-sex orientation as they wrestle to know and follow God's will for them. For others, this mercy means a supportive environment as they walk out their commitment to chaste singleness. Marvin Ellison, a Christian ethicist, pushes this issue further when he says, "Relational justice, if it is to take firm root in this religious tradition, requires more: a positive revaluation of sexuality, including appreciation for the goodness of gay (and nongay) sex; the dismantling of the prevailing sex/gender paradigm that privileges heterosexuality; and conscientious efforts to provide the social, economic, and cultural conditions so that all persons, whether partnered or not and whether heterosexual or not, may flourish and be honored within their communities, including their faith communities."[13] Despite Christians disagreeing on the implications of justice for the gay person, there is no doubt that this concept is one that must be engaged in the journey to understand how to integrate the experience of same-sex attraction and the Christian faith. Considering the implications of justice is an essential part of nurturing generous spaciousness.

Embodied Temples vs. Dualism

The emphasis in Scripture on our being embodied has significant implications for those who are gay. Unlike the separation of body and soul in a dualistic view of humanity, the Judeo-Christian tradition has held that humans are unified, embodied beings. Our physical bodies matter. They are beautiful, in all their shapes and sizes. They are valued. Therefore, what we do with our bodies matters deeply. The apostle Paul emphasizes this when he says, "Don't you know that you yourselves are God's temple and that God's Spirit lives in you? If anyone destroys God's temple, God will destroy him; for God's temple is sacred, and you are that temple."[14] He later says, "Flee from sexual immorality. All other sins a man commits are outside his body, but he who sins sexually sins against his own body. Do you not know that your body is a temple of the Holy Spirit, who is in you, whom you have received from God? You are not your own; you were bought at a price. Therefore honor God with your body."[15]

For those outside the heterosexual mainstream, being able to affirm the goodness of their bodies and sexuality may involve a long process. This will be especially true if they have internalized a sense of self-loathing and poor body image. But as they accept the reality of their orientation, they may also come to love, value, and appreciate their unique physicality.

How might intersex people, who have ambiguous sexual characteristics, hear and internalize God's affirmation that he formed and shaped them in their mother's womb? How might a person who has experienced profound gender dysphoria (feeling disconnection between one's biological sex and one's gender) or body dysmorphia (feeling disconnected from and critical of a part of one's body) for as long as they can remember internalize this message? These realities are part of being embodied. Are they not part of God's wonderful work in creating them and knowing all the days ordained for them before they were even born?

Being embodied also reminds us of the inherent boundaries we are called to honor. The clearest expressions of these boundaries have to do with love and faithfulness. Boundaries set limits that prevent coercing or objectifying others. But some Christians also consider the creation order and complementarity of male and female bodies (both in terms of "fit" and capacity for procreation) to be one of the essential and inherent

146

boundaries on our physical bodies. The practical outworking of this understanding is the preclusion of any physical, sexual interaction that fails to express this complementarity, regardless of love, faithfulness, mutuality, or orientation.

One aspect of this understanding of complementarity is the connection of heterosexual marriage as a symbol of Christ and the church. An example of this is articulated by Peter Ould (who has personally experienced same-sex attraction): "If husband and wife in their biological distinctiveness signifies Christ and the Church, then the lack of that biological distinctiveness in homosexual sex means that such a relationship cannot represent the saving work of Jesus. Male and male would signify Christ and Christ, the clear interpretation of which is that Christ is not interested in saving the Church. Female and female sex (Church and Church) signifies that humans don't need Jesus to save them."[16]

Scholar N. T. Wright, in an article written for the *Times*, sums it up this way, "Our supposedly selfish genes crave a variety of sexual possibilities. But Jewish, Christian and Muslim teachers have always insisted that lifelong man-plus-woman marriage is the proper context for sexual intercourse. This is not (as is frequently suggested) an arbitrary rule, dualistic in overtone and killjoy in intention. It is a deep structural reflection of the belief in a creator God who has entered into covenant both with his creation and with his people (who carry forward his purposes for that creation)."[17]

Others would argue that gender complementarity, while the experience of the majority, is not the only experience that can be pleasing to God. One gay Christian articulates it this way,

> It's certainly true that God designed our bodies with heterosexuality in mind; that's how new human beings come into the world. I don't think anyone can deny that heterosexual sex is the way our bodies were built to function. But does that mean that using our bodies in any other way is sinful? The argument that "you shouldn't do that because that wasn't God's design" is really more of an excuse than a real argument. If anything becomes sinful just because it wasn't part of the original design of creation, we'd have to condemn wheelchairs, makeup, open-heart surgery, bicycles, acrobatics, pre-packaged foods . . . well, you get the idea.[18]

On this question of the implications of being embodied, there are different questions, different emphases, and different conclusions. Regardless of how one settles this question, it is one that gay people of faith must wrestle with.

In all of these themes and resulting tensions, many gay Christians rigorously wrestle with Scripture. In contrast to the common assumption that a gay Christian who dares to question traditional perspectives doesn't care about Scripture, it is precisely because they care so deeply about God's Word that these tensions cause such struggle. This will become even more apparent as we consider the complexities of the interpretive task in the next chapter.

10

The Challenge of Interpretation

Interpretation is the vehicle through which we engage Scripture. It doesn't take long to find great diversity in the way different Christians tackle the interpretive task. For the gay Christian it can be a challenging journey spiritually and emotionally to evaluate the system of interpretation inherited from their family and church of origin.

Many gay Christians may experience not only fear but a voice of accusation as they struggle to make sense of their experience of same-sex attraction and the authoritative text of Scripture. For example, if a gay Christian starts to wonder if the Bible really does say that same-sex relationships are sinful, others can accuse them of acting like the serpent in the creation story who questions God's commands. In the book of Genesis, the serpent says to Eve, "Did God really say, 'You must not eat from any tree in the garden'?"[1]

This text can be used to manipulate, shame, instill fear, and control. It is like playing the ultimate power card: "If you question, then you obviously do not love God as much as I do; you obviously don't care about the Scriptures as I do; you obviously just want to do what you want to do."

While there may be Christians who twist Scripture to justify how they want to live, assuming this about someone at the beginning of a discussion leads to a no-win situation.

A Hermeneutic of Trust

It can be convenient and comfortable for Christians to have great certainty and conviction over the question of Scripture's admonitions regarding sexual behavior for gay people, given that this question doesn't apply to them personally. It is no wonder that Christians are perceived as inconsistent and arbitrary when they accuse gay people of reading Scripture incorrectly while rarely challenging their own escapes, comforts, and luxuries, which they embrace in largely privatized lives.

But alongside those of us who selectively follow the texts that don't shake up our world too much are those honestly trying to wrestle with God, to glimpse more of his character through the story of Scripture, to discern the way forward to follow him and to experience his best for their lives. If we fail to listen to these stories, if we fail to see their pilgrim spirit, if we simply presume a selfish agenda, I fear we fail to honor the biblical legacy of people of faith wrestling with God. The biblical story tells of people who encounter the God who welcomes their questions and invites them to struggle with him.

Many of the gay followers of Jesus I know have wrestled with God through prayer and through asking questions of the biblical text. I often see people shift back and forth between a more traditional understanding that precludes same-sex sexual behavior and a more gay-affirming perspective that views covenanted gay partnerships as an expression of God's grace. This back-and-forth journey is not because the issues are trivial to them. Rather it is precisely because of the depth of their commitment to be faithful to Christ and to honor the authority of Scripture that many continue to wrestle. I have also heard these individuals testify that this uncertainty has drawn them into a deeper, more trusting, and dependent relationship with Christ. Those who have come to a conclusion on this question often have arrived at their conclusion after much study, prayer, and a desire to submit to God's will. Indeed, I know gay Christians who have pursued studies in the original languages of Greek, Hebrew, and Aramaic just so they could better engage the particular texts that pertain to same-sex sexual behavior. And, of those who studied the original languages, some now affirm a traditional call to celibacy for gay Christians and others affirm the invitation to experience love in consummated covenant relationship. Given this diversity, one won't agree with every conclusion reached by these searching individuals but, I hope, will extend respect for the intentional and disciplined journey that has brought them to where they are. Over the years, I have grown in respect for those who continue to seriously wrestle with the interpretive challenges of the biblical text, and I recognize that it may result in different conclusions for different individuals.

But when people misuse a text with "Did God really say . . . ?" to shut down someone's honest wrestling with God, they betray what seems to be their own lack of faith and humility. We ought not to be threatened by someone's searching. We ought not to try to control the outcomes in another's journey. We ought not to resort to using shame or fear or guilt to ensure others share our certainties. God can be trusted to lead those who question and struggle through prayer, his Word, their minds, and their experiences. Let's focus on encouraging one another rather than accusing and condemning one another. In such a spacious place, I believe more people will have the opportunity to discover the truth of Jeremiah 29:13: "You will seek me and find me when you seek me with all your heart."

Priorities in Theological Reflection

In addition to Scripture, key sources to consider in theological reflection are experience, tradition, and reason.

Experience

Experience can be viewed suspiciously by some Christians given its subjectivity and our human propensity for self-deception and manipulation.

But experience is a critical aspect of all the other sources. We interpret and consider Scripture, tradition, and reason through the filter of our experiences. What is most effective in determining the truthfulness of an interpretation of Scripture (a theological concept) is its lived reality. When we consider the role of experience in the questions around covenanted same-sex relationships, there are a few categories to consider.

First of all, there is the experience of gay Christians. As we have seen in earlier chapters, among these stories is a significant amount of diversity. Some people experience mastery and stewardship in the area of attraction, such that they find it manageable to refrain from same-sex sexual behavior. This may be experienced in the context of being committed in marriage to an opposite-gender spouse or as a single person. Others had negative experiences in trying to suppress or change their same-sex attractions. Despite spiritual discipline, commitment to work through various personal issues, and submission to others for support and accountability, their same-sex attractions persist or increase in intensity. Some gay Christians have journeyed along the path toward accepting their orientation. Some identify as gay, some choose not to; some disclose widely, and some disclose very selectively. Each choice carries with it a different experience. People may experience acceptance and authenticity as a single person, as a married person in a mixed-orientation marriage (i.e., married to an opposite-gender spouse), or in partnership/marriage with someone of the same sex. There are also differences in experience for an individual who has grown up in a faith community or has come to faith later in life (potentially after having come out or establishing a long-term same-sex partnership). There is a great deal of complexity in the variety of experiences a gay follower of Jesus may have.

Within the context of these different experiences, there is variety in the ways that faith in Christ is expressed, and a variety of levels of growth and maturity. Faith journeys are further influenced by personality, life experience, models, mentors, teaching, training, and motivation, just to name a few.

Then there are the experiences of those within the heterosexual mainstream as they encounter the subject of homosexuality. Straight

Christians are individually influenced by the teaching, ideology, and social and family systems they engage. They are also influenced by the diverse stories of gay people they encounter, including both Christian and non-Christian gay people, as well as their actual experiences of personal friendships with gay people.

In many of the debates around homosexuality in the Christian community, minimal attention is given to the tremendous diversity in experience that people bring to the table. Such experience affects our ability to be objective when exploring a topic that tends to be so emotionally charged. Rather than attempting to push experience to the background, it is much more honest to be able to acknowledge the variety of experiences and to have conversations about the ways such experience influences our ability to reflect and discern God's best way forward for gay people.

For example, if one Christian has gay Christian friends who are partnered and who demonstrate strong faith in Christ, commitment to worship, prayer, service, mission, and justice, they will have a very different sense of experience than the Christian who does not personally know any gay people, let alone a gay Christian. I hosted a screening of a film that profiled the lives of over twenty young, gay Christians, and afterward an elderly man in the audience admitted that prior to seeing the film he did not realize there were young people who were solid in their faith and commitment to Jesus who also experience same-sex attraction. This may sound ludicrous to some, but the limitations of this man's experience made him susceptible to caricatures and stereotypes about gay people.

It is not uncommon to hear lament in the church about the overemphasis on the role of experience in our current theological reflections. While this may be a legitimate concern, it is clear that if we are committed to listening to one another in the exploration of how to find unity in our diversity by nurturing generous spaciousness, then we must take the time to humbly consider which experiences influence the ways we reflect on these theological questions. The process of discerning how our experiences should be applied is guided by the presence of the Holy Spirit.

Tradition

It is a common statement to hear that one can't argue with two thousand years of church tradition that has consistently banned same-sex sexual behavior. A high profile evangelical leader with whom I recently had lunch has often pointed to church tradition as an authority. As we were eating, he said he had discovered that throughout church history there isn't nearly as much written about homosexuality as he thought.

Nonetheless, concrete citations from church history are nearly unanimous in their negative appraisal of same-sex sexual behavior. For example, Saint John Chrysostom, in the fourth century, explicitly referenced same-sex sexual behavior and indicated that it was worse than murder.[2] In the Middle Ages, influential voices like Thomas Aquinas explicitly wrote of the danger and sinfulness of same-sex sexual behavior.[3] In the Reformation era, Martin Luther had stark things to say: "The vice of the Sodomites is an unparalleled enormity. It departs from the natural passion and desire, planted into nature by God, according to which the male has a passionate desire for the female. Sodomy craves what is entirely contrary to nature. Whence comes this perversion? Without a doubt it comes from the devil. After a man has once turned aside from the fear of God, the devil puts such great pressure upon his nature that he extinguishes the fire of natural desire and stirs up another, which is contrary to nature."[4]

John Boswell, a Yale professor and committed Catholic, published *Christianity, Social Tolerance and Homosexuality* in 1980. In this book, Boswell presents the thesis that the church, up until the twelfth century, paid little attention to same-sex sexuality and even had cases of celebrating same-sex loving relationships. His research came under fire from both the gay community, who insisted that Boswell was too easily letting the church off the hook for centuries of oppression of sexual minorities, and the church, many of whom simply dismissed what they considered a radical misinterpretation of the church's tradition. Today, Boswell's work has been essentially eclipsed by researchers who have benefited from the refutations of his work. However, the legacy of his work is that he challenged the assumption that church tradition delivered a uniformly prohibitive response to the question of covenanted same-sex unions.

Tradition does not, however, point only to theologians, doctrine, and dogma from the past. Rather, tradition encompasses *current* theological influences as well as the *current* beliefs and values of one's family and church community. Tradition therefore could be highly diverse, depending on which podcasts you listen to, which blogs you read, which radio and television speakers you follow, which books you read, and so on. Feminist, liberation, queer, and eco-theologies all bring diverse perspectives to consider. The role of tradition may simply reinforce what one already thinks, broaden and challenge the sense of tradition one has held, or be so diverse as to foster tension, confusion, and profound questions. When we nurture generous spaciousness, we aren't afraid to read widely and engage different aspects of the Christian tradition with the confident trust that the Spirit will continue to guide and help us to discern what is helpful and best.

Reason

Reason plays an important role in our reflections on Scripture. Typically, reason considers the resources of disciplines such as biology, psychology, philosophy, anthropology, and sociology. Our ability to use these resources with critical thinking offers a way of evaluating and perhaps challenging the assumptions of church tradition. Again, people apply the resources of reason in different ways, depending on their affinity for black-and-white (vs. gray), their talents, their modes of processing, their educational level, and so on.

It is very hard for most of us to think outside of the paradigm that we believe is the right one. Therefore, the ways we think are often limited by the boundaries of what we already believe to be true. My friend David Hayward, who blogs at nakedpastor.com says it this way, "The very lens we use to understand the truth is prescribed to perceive the truth we already believe. What is required is a radical revolutionary thinking outside the box. The lens itself, somehow, must be removed. Of course at first [the new way of thinking] will be rejected because it doesn't fit the paradigm. But eventually, as the evidence mounts, the new paradigm will have to crash in upon us."[5] What this reminds us of is the inevitable tension that exists between those who have an affinity to think outside their own paradigm and those who naturally resist such exploration. In the midst of these tensions, generous spaciousness calls us to humbly listen to and engage with one another, seeking to lay our anxieties aside.

Considering these sources of experience, tradition, and reason helps us describe the complex and diverse factors that affect how people engage the question of faithful discipleship for gay people. There are certainly those who simply don't engage the question, assuming that they know the truth. However, in this determination, they have inevitably (though perhaps unconsciously) also been influenced by their view of homosexuality, their approach to Scripture, their experiences, their interaction with tradition, and their interaction with the resources of reason.

Principles of Interpretive Practice

The following insights about good interpretive practice may be helpful to put us in a place of humility as we encounter those whose interpretations differ from ours (or who may not yet have a definitive interpretation).

Interpretation must function in dependence on the leading, guiding, and quickened discernment of the Holy Spirit. Those who wish to take seriously the message of the text must learn the disciplines of walking in step with the Spirit. Interpretation, while rigorous and demanding our best thinking, is not primarily an intellectual pursuit or a culmination of our best talents, abilities, and expertise. First, we humble ourselves in dependence on the life of the Spirit within us guiding us into all truth. We do this even as we recognize that we see through a glass dimly, are prone to self-deception, and will not engage the Spirit with perfect clarity.

Interpretation of any portion of the text must find its focus in the person of Christ. God's story points to and climaxes in the incarnation, death, and resurrection of Jesus Christ. This grand mystery energizes our Spirit-led imagination to ask of any text, "Where is Christ seen?" Martin Luther said, "If you will interpret well and securely, take Christ with you, for He is the man whom everything concerns."[6] This presupposes, of course, that we have steeped ourselves in relationship with Jesus—his birth, life, death, resurrection, words, ministry, commands. That's why when people say, "Jesus said nothing about homosexuality," intense emotions flare up on all sides. If people say that this demonstrates that homosexuality was not a priority issue for Jesus, this should not be viewed as a weak attempt to say, "This is no big deal." Rather, this individual may be truly seeking to ground themselves in the central focus of God's story—the incarnated, reconciling Redeemer. Their conclusion may be that if it was not a high priority for Jesus, we ought not to be making it such a significant litmus test today. Alternatively, when others react to this statement with a seemingly ferocious defense that Jesus obviously knew and maintained consistency with the Levitical admonishments about male same-sex behavior, this ought not be seen merely as an inability to consider the weight of Jesus's silence on the matter for gay people. Rather, consider that this individual may be attempting to protect Jesus from what seems to them to be a misuse of his silence on a significant question.

Jesus's silence alone, however, is clearly not the only issue in tension. In the ministry of Jesus we see a Savior who reaches, intentionally and consistently, to the margins. He talks and eats and heals and experiences solidarity with all the "wrong" people. His ministry, seen from this perspective, is all about inclusion. And surprisingly enough, sometimes that inclusion carries very little (or no) instruction about right living or avoiding sin or even the need for confession or repentance.

Consider the story of the ten lepers found in Luke 17. Jesus encounters the lepers, who cry out for his mercy, and he tells them to go show themselves to the priest. This was the traditional way in which an individual with a skin disease could be proclaimed clean and be reintegrated into the life of the community. On the way to the priest they are cleansed. The one leper, with no hope of reintegration into community, no matter how clean his skin, returns to Jesus. He is a Samaritan. Samaritans were not allowed to enter the temple. He realizes that his only hope is to return to the One who mysteriously has the power to physically heal him. He seems to intrinsically know that his best hope at a new life is to return to Jesus. Jesus says to the leper, "Rise and go; your faith has made you well" (v. 19). Imagine that. I would have felt obliged to instruct him. If this were the only time I had with him, I would have done my best to give him a crash course on living a God-honoring life. I would have said something about sin, confession, holiness, prayer, reading the Scriptures, the coming of the Spirit to help him, the importance of being with a worshiping community, the need to get a good mentor or spiritual director, and the importance of justice, service, and love. But Jesus doesn't do this. He simply sends him on his way with an affirmation of his faith—knowing that he will tell his story and represent Jesus to the people in his community. In other encounters, Jesus offers a little more instruction. Jesus tells the woman caught in adultery to "go and sin no more." He tells the man let down through the roof by his friends that "your sins are forgiven." He tells the Samaritan woman that "a time is coming and has now come when the true worshipers will worship the Father in the Spirit and truth, for they are the kind of worshipers the Father seeks."[7] These four people— the leper, the woman caught in adultery, the paralyzed man, and the Samaritan woman—are all people on the margins of their society, and Jesus had very few words of instruction for them (while he had plenty of instruction for the religious leaders of the day).

When we are caught up in the story, we can worry less about dotting every "i" and crossing every "t" in terms of what Jesus's formula for reconciliation is, and we engage our own sense of personal reconciliation with God as actualized in our faith in Christ and experience of the Holy Spirit. This frees us to rejoice and anticipate the reconciliation of those on the margins in our current context.

A great comfort in the interpretive quest (particularly for those who may feel limited in their training or understanding) is the accessibility of the Bible's central message. The Bible tells a story of a God who reconciles people into life-giving relationship with himself and is about the work of making all things marred by sin and brokenness right. This is understood to be the "perspicuity of Scripture." This means that anyone who reads the Bible can understand its good news. The invitation of redemption is plain to see regardless of how much one understands or has studied how to best interpret the Bible. The challenge is when people take this idea of perspicuity and apply it much more broadly than the central message of redemption to include specific complex contextual questions. The result is the expectation that a plain, literal reading of the Scriptures will offer a clear answer to any question confronting a Christ-follower. This can be seen in the myriad of huffy blog comments left by Christians who insist, "The Bible is clear" and who therefore refuse to listen, engage, or extend respect, care, and sensitivity to the Christian who questions this presumed clarity. A comment left this morning on one of our video clips featuring a gay Christian who is currently single but open to having a partner demonstrates this. The commenter writes, "You are a reprobate! you have one foot in hell! you are not a christian! a real christian will shun you! it is a grave sin to even debate this. the bible is super clear on this! you Lots wives will all burn in hell forever! that is where this begins and ends! no debate none! None!"

This expectation of perspicuity on all moral and ethical matters can be a cover for refusing to engage the threatening process of confronting one's assumptions or the ways the text is used to exert power over others. It can cause panic to think of questioning the system that holds our faith and confidence together. But such panic fails to see beyond oneself and is ultimately narcissistic.

It is necessary in interpretation to consider the context of the text. Each text is part of the full counsel of God (all of Scripture), the particular book in which it is found, the grammatical meaning of specific words, and the historical context of the author and intended audience. Attention to context will prevent pulling specific phrases out of the larger frame of reference, as is so often seen in proof-texting. It will also ensure that texts that are understood to reference homosexual behavior will be considered in light of the redeeming, reconciling message of Scripture, the exegetical challenges of interpreting key words in their original languages, and the cultural backdrop of the author and audience. Careful consideration of contextual issues will quickly highlight diverse perspectives promoted by different scholars, practitioners, pastors, and gay followers of Jesus.

Of the texts that refer to same-sex sexual behavior, there are Old Testament narrative texts that tell stories of the threat of gang rape;

there are Levitical texts from Old Testament law; there are New Testament vice lists; and there is a more theological text in Romans 1. These different genres of Scripture arise from different contexts. In the narrative texts, the context of violence is a significant consideration. We have already raised some of the questions about discerning the implication of old covenant law. The vice lists contain dispositions and behaviors that nearly every Christian struggles with, such as greed, but for which we extend much grace. The Romans text arose from a context in which idolatry was rampant in the expression of same-sex sexual behavior. All of these contextual factors are hotly debated and provide many sources of disagreement.

Language and Translation Issues

The fine points of exegesis require looking at the language and translation issues, where there is potential for ambiguity. Consider these examples that highlight how contentious questions of language and translation can be:

- In the Levitical texts (18:22; 20:13), the word *to'evah* is used and commonly translated "abomination." Some scholars suggest that this term is used primarily for purity violations rather than a moral violation where the term *zimmah* is more likely to be used.

- In Romans 1:24, the word *atimia* is used and can be translated as "degrading." Because of how this word is used in other places, there are questions about whether this indicates social disapproval or an ethical or moral violation.

- In Romans 1:27, we also find the word *aschemosyne*, which can be translated as "indecent." This same word is found in the well-known text from 1 Corinthians 13:5, "love does not act unbecomingly" (NASB).

- Again from Romans 1:26–27 is the phrase *para physis*, which is normally translated as "unnatural." Some suggest that this cannot mean "immoral" because Paul uses this word to describe God's act of including gentiles in Romans 11:24. Paul

160

also uses the same wording in 1 Corinthians 11:14–15 to state that long hair on men is against nature. This raises the question of whether it is inherently immoral (that is, for all times and all places) or a statement for that culture.

- And then, in 1 Corinthians 6:9 and Timothy 1:9–10, we find the word *arsenokoitai*, which is a composite term of "male" and "bed" not found in Greek writing prior to Paul. This word is very hard to translate. Both Clement of Alexandria and John Chrysostom, who were both vigorously opposed to homosexuality, did not use *arsenokoitai* in their writings, even though they used thirteen other words to describe homosexual persons and homosexual behavior. In the vice list texts, some suggest that *arsenokoitai* refers to pederasty (sex between a man and a boy) or anal sex between husband and wife. Others say that "homosexual person" is the best translation.

- Also in these vice list texts we find the word *malakoi*, which is currently translated as "homosexual offender" in most Bible versions found in use in our churches. This same word, however, is used by Jesus to describe a fine cloth in Matthew 11:8. The connection here seems to be the connotation of softness. Paul could have used the word *truphe*, which means "effeminate" but didn't. Some wonder if *malakoi* should be understood to mean "weak willed." Others feel it refers to male prostitutes. And others feel it should be applied to any gay person.[8]

This very brief overview simply reminds us that issues of language are complex and in great dispute when it comes to seven specific Bible passages on same-sex sexual behavior. Translation questions continue to make these matters challenging for gay Christians, pastors, leaders, and church members who are seeking to be discerning and wise.

Historical and Cultural Issues

Historical and cultural issues also fill entire books. This brief treatment will again highlight the complexity and contentiousness regarding these issues.

161

In Israelite culture some key factors affected the view of sexuality and gender.

- Women were viewed as property, first of their fathers and then of their husbands.
- Male children were considered more valuable than female children.
- A barren woman experienced great shame.
- A woman who bore only daughters was a disgrace.
- In procreation, it was understood that the man's semen was the carrier of the child and the woman's body provided only the womb in which the child could develop.
- Male temple prostitutes (who offered sex to other men) were seen as a despicable problem within other nations that could never be tolerated in Israel.

The low view of women meant that any man who behaved in what was perceived to be the female role in sexual coupling would be disrespected by the community. This was considered *anathema* (something detested or loathed). The mistaken understanding of the role of semen in procreation created the assumption that any semen that was spilled was akin to the murder of unborn children. In male same-sex activity, semen was clearly not being stewarded toward the propagation of children and the preservation of the community.

In the New Testament culture in which the apostles lived, the awareness of same-sex realities was likely most influenced by the pederasty that was common in Greek culture and the plethora of male temple prostitutes. For example, these prostitutes would have been highly visible at the temple of Aphrodite in Corinth, the city where Paul lived when he wrote his letter to the Romans. It is argued that there was at this time a social awareness of long-term, adult male same-sex relationships as well, though evidence of such relationships is not as clear as the common reality of pederasty and male prostitution.

In the first century after the crucifixion, the surrounding Roman culture essentially saw four reasons to condemn same-sex behavior. First, it was believed anyone engaging in same-sex behavior was willfully

162

overriding their natural desire for the opposite sex. Second, it was believed that same-sex sexual behavior resulted from an uncontrollable sexual appetite. Third, it required one partner to behave in a way only suitable for the opposite sex—which no male citizen should ever be subjected to. Finally, it was feared that homosexuality would cause extinction of the human race because it was believed it made men sterile. With all that we have learned about same-sex orientation today, we can see the limitations and misconceptions in these views.

In the general context of the biblical story, there is no understanding of a different sexual orientation than heterosexuality. The social construction of a homosexual orientation is a much more recent development. The biblical context is highly affected by the cultural understanding of gender roles. Feminist theology has particularly helped us understand patriarchy and its impact on the biblical story. Some would suggest that gay-affirming theology helps us see a false elevation of heterosexuality. Others see the complementarity of male and female to be an intrinsic part of the image of God and his intentions for the human race that transcend any concern for patriarchy or privilege.

As I encounter people in the church engaging the question of gay partnerships, my general observation is that those who are open to or affirming of them may give significant weight to the historical/cultural context. Those who maintain a traditional understanding of heteronormative sexual intimacy, generally speaking, seem to view the application of cultural considerations as clearly secondary to what seems to them to be a clear reading of Scripture. They may also view such historical/cultural research as untrustworthy and disregard it, believing it to be used as an excuse to discount the prohibition.

Personal Limitations in the Interpretive Quest

Any serious interpreter of the Bible will be well-acquainted with his or her own limitations. This means several things. First, we must recognize that any appeal to the authority of Scripture has the potential to be colored by the limitations of our ability to interpret rightly the very authority we seek to call upon. It can become very easy to talk past one another when the assumption is, "I care about the authority of Scripture and you don't." It can be unhelpful to wax eloquent about the inerrancy of Scripture without an accompanying acknowledgment that, while Scripture may be inerrant, there are no inerrant interpreters of Scripture. We do well to remind ourselves that we see through a glass dimly and that no one has a perfect pipeline to the mind of God.

Second, it is important to maintain openness to engage with other traditions that may function with a different hermeneutic. No one tradition within the Christian community holds the monopoly on correct interpretation on every question. To engage only scholars and thinkers who agree with the presuppositions you bring to the text will, in the end, lead to an impoverished interpretive task and result. When this hermeneutical quest is confronting questions as personal and intimate as the ones facing a gay person, it is no small emotional or spiritual matter to explore the insights of different traditions and perspectives. The courage and maturity required to engage the questions with a spirit of surrender, willingness, and submission to God's direction is significant.

The reality is that a young gay person may be facing questions and decisions in life (for example, regarding same-sex relationships, a life partner, and building a family) before they have had the time to develop the spiritual and emotional maturity that will help guide them in discerning God's direction for them. In other words, they may make decisions that others can easily critique. There is little control that can be externally exerted by parents, church leaders, or friends without the potential of emotional, spiritual, or personal violence. I use the word *violence* because I have seen the painful fallout of coercive attempts to bring people in line with certain positions.

The comfort and grace, for us as individuals and for those in caring relationships, are that our lives are about the journey of receiving and accepting the fullness of God's redemptive work and living in a manner that emerges from our grateful response. Nothing we think, believe, or do at any point in the journey will change the love of God for us or the accomplished work of Christ. What can and does change through the course of our lives is our receptivity and actualization of this grace. Some journeys follow a trajectory of increasing openness, maturity, and capacity to live in the reality of all that Christ offers us with accompanying demonstrations of faith. Other journeys are a bit more like the picture on our family's GPS as we drove through the mountains from Palm Springs to San Diego. One of my children looked at the GPS image and exclaimed that it looked like someone's large intestine. It was a winding pathway that seemed to turn back on itself more often than not. Still, it was a road that eventually brought us to our destination. The scenic route, affording the opportunity to explore nooks and crannies that a more efficient and expeditious road might have missed, is also a path that can induce "stomach in the throat" moments of nausea and unpredictability. Such a path ought not be glamorized or romanticized. But it also shouldn't be avoided at all cost. If this is the path of your journey or the journey of a loved one, then God will meet you in it. Your calling in the midst of a winding path is to keep your eyes fixed on Christ, to more fully trust in his sufficiency and love, and to grow in the capacity to trust and respond in obedience to his leading.

Such winding paths look different for different individuals. A gay person might initially choose to remain celibate but along the way discover that this choice is driven and motivated by fear and striving and eventually emerge with the robust confidence in the love of God that allows them to explore the potential of a relationship. Another individual starts out searching for a partner, settles for a series of relationships, and concludes that their soul has been searching in the wrong places. This individual may come to a place of serenity with living a single, chaste life and experience life as full and robust as they find themselves connected in community, serving others, and experiencing intimacy in friendship. Sometimes, such an individual will go on to meet and experience a relationship with a partner after a fruitful season of singleness. Sometimes it looks different. Such winding paths are fertile soil for God's grace.

One woman describes her winding journey this way:

I've taken biblical courses at a secular university, a Christian college, and also through a local church divinity school (hermeneutics, reformed theology, etc.). So, for me, it's been ingrained that, basically, one CAN-NOT get to know God/know God's will/grow spiritually . . . apart from Scripture. And there are many ways you can approach Scripture: historically, scholastically, devotionally, culturally, etc. When it came to my first attempts to trying to integrate my faith and my sexuality—I felt I had to step away from Scripture because I wasn't feeling FREE . . . free to discern for myself what God reveals about himself and his interactions with his creation, etc. in Scripture . . . because I had always relied on others' teachings to tell me what it means. Once I admitted to myself that I do, in fact, have a same-sex orientation (for whatever reason/cause—I'm no longer trying to answer the "why"), I was able to return to Scripture devotionally, and I continue to do so, with the added overarching theme of the redemption of mankind and with the understanding that God (as Triune) had an original plan and purpose before the Fall. . . . He desires a Bride, a House, a Body, and a Family, with whom He could share in community and fellowship, like that which exists between the Godhead. This "thread" of themes is revealed in Scripture. So, if I cannot integrate/line-up what I discern was his "original" intention for me/us as mankind (via what I "see" in Scripture), then I will choose/am choosing NOT to go with it . . . no matter how I "feel" or react emotionally or even physiologically (i.e. the desire for sexual pleasures). My thinking is that, even if I allow myself the "freedom" to embrace a same-sex relationship and "go with it," in the end, when it's all said and done, and I'm on my death-bed, I will regret that I chose that path because what I'm discerning these days is that same-gender sexual relationships were not part of his original intention . . . and I don't want anything that is "second best," or "lesser than," even if his grace is there to "cover it," and salvation is still assured. I'm still open to "not landing," but, alas, I keep finding my heart/conscience . . . having landed.

The third limitation we are called to explore is the way our own status and privilege may obscure the selfish and power-maintaining version we hold of God's story. Richard Middleton and Brian Walsh make the observation that postmodern critics of the biblical metanarrative (overarching story) tend to see it as a human construct that is the "legitimation of the vested interests of those who have the power and authority to make such universal pronouncements."[9]

For those of us who find ourselves a part of the heterosexual main-stream, we must reflect on the potential influence our hetero-normative assumptions may bring to the text. Jenell Williams Paris, in her book, *The End of Sexual Identity*, says, "Because sexuality has moved center stage in defining human identity, heterocentrist theology constructs a hierarchy of persons. Even humble heterosexual Christians who make every effort to be kind and gracious toward homosexuals are not really reaching out; they're reaching down from a place of moral elevation."[10] I often encounter ministry leaders who try to engage their reflections and subsequent position and policy statements by asking themselves how they would approach the subject if one of their children were gay. Even closer to home is asking the question, "What if I were gay?" "If I were same-sex-attracted, how would I wrestle with the text? How would I live in the tension of my own drive for love and intimacy and my desire to live in fidelity to the authority of Scripture as it reveals God's character to me?" At the end of the day, those of us who navigate life's journey in the comfort of the dominant experience of sexual identity will never fully know how we would answer that question. That ought to remind us to engage this conversation of interpretation of Scripture with a spirit of humility and a willingness to listen well.

Even as we have been discussing important aspects of the interpretive quest, we must always remember that our engagement with Scripture is to be lived communally with a commitment to mutual submission and honoring of one another as we collectively listen, relate, discern, and wrestle with the implications of the text for our daily lives. If individuals of differing perspectives are to find a way to listen well, extend respect, and embody the priority of peace-making over proselytizing, we will need to recognize the potential within our interpretive lenses for diversity. And we will need to refrain from automatically assuming that someone whose perspective differs from our own is failing to honor the authority of Scripture or submit to the lordship of Christ. Generous spaciousness humbly acknowledges our limitations and intentionally chooses a posture of listening and learning. It recognizes that among those who identify as followers of Jesus and have a high regard for Scripture, there are diverse perspectives on many different questions (including but not limited to the matter of same-sex sexuality) in regard to how to live as a faithful disciple of Christ. Despite these differences, generous spaciousness makes room for us to join in conversation together in a shared quest for a deeper and more robust relationship with Christ.

11

A Disputable Matter?

I grew up in a denomination that did not ordain women into ministry offices until 1995. The hottest years of the debate happened during my teens and early twenties. I remember poignantly how painful it felt to hear the back and forth, the characterizations of one side by the other, the agonized fear that this would split or destroy the church, the weariness, the anger, the hurt. I remember the waiting. And I remember feeling that I was somehow partly responsible for this pain I saw my church wrestling through—because I was one of those women who felt called into ministry.

After many stops and starts, the final decision came down, and it was rather consternating. The governing body of our denomination chose to recognize that two different conclusions on this question could be biblically faithful. With this controversial decision, they sought to honor and respect the consciences of people holding positions across the spectrum. The decision allowed geographical groups of churches to either open the way for women to be ordained or not to. Additionally, the governing body precluded women from the highest levels of leadership within denominational governance and declared that this decision could not be revisited for the next few years. In 2009, for the first time, women were seated as delegates at our binational synod. And in 2010, I sat as not only a delegate, but an officer of synod. As a popular commercial used to say, "We've come a long way baby." But it certainly wasn't without pain. When these decisions were made, churches left our denomination. I personally know of families who were torn apart because of their differences on the appropriateness of women in the offices of pastor, elder, and deacon. Even now, eighteen years after the ordination of the first woman, overtures come to our synod related to these questions. It has not been a smooth or easy ride for our tribe to live in the tension of viewing this as a disputable matter. That is, our denomination chose to see this issue as one we can disagree on while still being unified; it is not an essential matter of the faith but one that each individual, church, and region of churches needs to wrestle with and discern how they will proceed.

As a relatively young person at the time of the decision, I remember wrestling with the question, "How can two different positions both be biblically faithful?" I found myself feeling uncertain and anxious about the whole notion of truth and how we apprehend it. I felt, at the time, that too many things were left up in the air. Even though I felt called into ministry, I was very uncomfortable with this lack of resolution. I wanted the church to proclaim the truth once and for all. I didn't want to have to endure the uncertainty of hearing one person extol the role of women and then the next person exhort us to repent and "get back to the Bible." Having grown up questioning if I was actually hearing from God, I just wanted to be sure. I didn't want to have to deal with any more insecurity about my calling.

Over the years, however, I have experienced and witnessed the ways that this decision in our church has caused us to grow. We've had to learn to live with one another, respect one another despite differences, and experience one another's faith and spiritual gifts. We've had to learn to listen well. We've been humbled, I believe, by choosing to live in this tension. And we've grown, I trust, in extending hospitality to those who differ from us. And after more than fifteen years, I believe God has blessed our denomination as we have experienced freedom from

170

endless debate on the question and have focused energies on questions of mission, diversity, and justice.

I share this background because I recognize that it is an important factor in my wrestling with the questions around the application of "disputable matter" principles regarding gay marriage. I have spent a lot of time pondering the question of whether gay marriage is a disputable matter. Is it a matter that we as a body can disagree on and still remain unified? Is it a matter where two different conclusions can both be biblically faithful? And whether or not both sides can be biblically faithful, how do we deal with the fact that there is dispute in the church over this matter?

The concept of "disputable matter" arises primarily from texts attributed to the apostle Paul and applies to issues around which Christians in the early church disagreed with each other. Romans 14 describes such a dilemma. (Another lengthy passage discussing these types of dilemmas is 1 Cor. 8–10.)

Paul begins Romans 14:1 by saying, "Welcome with open arms fellow believers who don't see things the way you do. And don't jump all over them every time they do or say something you don't agree with—even when it seems that they are strong on opinions but weak in the faith department. Remember, they have their own history to deal with. Treat them gently" (Message).

After describing two scenarios, one pertaining to eating meat sacrificed to idols and the other to Sabbath regulations, Paul says, "There are good reasons either way. So, each person is free to follow the convictions of conscience" (v. 5 Message). He then offers encouraging guidelines for how to navigate being in community together in the midst of disagreement (vv. 7–23 Message):

> None of us are permitted to insist on our own way in these matters. It's God we are answerable to—all the way from life to death and everything in between—not each other. That's why Jesus lived and died and then lived again: so that he could be our Master across the entire range of life and death, and free us from the petty tyrannies of each other.
>
> So where does that leave you when you criticize a brother? And where does that leave you when you condescend to a sister? I'd say it leaves

you looking pretty silly—or worse. Eventually, we're all going to end up kneeling side by side in the place of judgment, facing God. Your critical and condescending ways aren't going to improve your position there one bit. Read it for yourself in Scripture:

> "As I live and breathe," God says,
> "every knee will bow before me;
> Every tongue will tell the honest truth
> that I and only I am God."

So tend to your knitting. You've got your hands full just taking care of your own life before God.

Forget about deciding what's right for each other. Here's what you need to be concerned about: that you don't get in the way of someone else, making life more difficult than it already is. I'm convinced—Jesus convinced me!—that everything as it is in itself is holy. We, of course, by the way we treat it or talk about it, can contaminate it.

If you confuse others by making a big issue over what they eat or don't eat, you're no longer a companion with them in love, are you? These, remember, are persons for whom Christ died. Would you risk sending them to hell over an item in their diet? Don't you dare let a piece of God-blessed food become an occasion of soul-poisoning!

God's kingdom isn't a matter of what you put in your stomach, for goodness' sake. It's what God does with your life as he sets it right, puts it together, and completes it with joy. Your task is to single-mindedly serve Christ. Do that and you'll kill two birds with one stone: pleasing the God above you and proving your worth to the people around you.

So let's agree to use all our energy in getting along with each other. Help others with encouraging words; don't drag them down by finding fault. You're certainly not going to permit an argument over what is served or not served at supper to wreck God's work among you, are you? I said it before and I'll say it again: All food is good, but it can turn bad if you use it badly, if you use it to trip others up and send them sprawling. When you sit down to a meal, your primary concern should not be to feed your own face but to share the life of Jesus. So be sensitive and courteous to the others who are eating. Don't eat or say or do things that might interfere with the free exchange of love.

Cultivate your own relationship with God, but don't impose it on others. You're fortunate if your behavior and your belief are coherent. But if you're not sure, if you notice that you are acting in ways inconsistent with what you believe—some days trying to impose your opinions on others, other days just trying to please them—then you know that you're out of line. If the way you live isn't consistent with what you believe, then it's wrong.

This passage ought to help us talk about whether a particular topic might be viewed as a disputable matter. But simply raising this question is enough to get some people's blood boiling. I remember a seminar in which I raised the question of whether gay relationships are a topic sincere Christians could disagree on. A pastor got up into my face and declared that it most certainly was *not* a disputable matter. Wiping the spittle off my cheeks from the intensity of his reply, I got the clear message that this was not a safe place to raise the question. But given the diverse perspectives in the church on gay marriage, I believe the disputable-matter conversation is essential.

There is debate whether or not Paul would have been familiar with lifelong, committed same-sex relationships. N. T. Wright has said that Paul was familiar with the practice (and therefore condemned it in his passages on homosexuality), "In particular, a point which is often missed, [the Greeks and Romans] knew a great deal about what people today would regard as longer-term, reasonably stable relations between two people of the same gender. This is not a modern invention, it's already there in Plato."[1] Others say that sexual *orientation*, socially constructed as we understand it today, would not have been understood at the time of Paul's writings. So while Paul may have been aware of long-term same-sex relationships, he would not have had an understanding of sexual orientation as a context for such a relationship. (And therefore Paul's writings against homosexual behavior did not take into account a person's sexual orientation.)

Reasons to Discuss Disputable Matters

Considering if this subject is a matter that Christians can disagree on ought to be motivated by the desire for love and unity in the body of

Christ. As the oft-quoted saying about unity in diversity reminds us, "In essentials unity, in non-essentials liberty, in all things love."[2] After many years of navigating the tremendous differences in the Christian community in relation to this question of intimate relationships for gay people, I am more convinced than ever that it is inherently spiritually formational to willingly enter the tensions of diversity. Rather than fleeing the discomfort of disagreement, I believe we are called to submit ourselves to the Spirit's work of increasing our humility, graciousness, and generosity. To sequester ourselves in a community of uniformity stunts our growth in learning to love those with whom we disagree. Jesus put it this way,

> You're familiar with the old written law, "Love your friend," and its unwritten companion, "Hate your enemy." I'm challenging that. I'm telling you to love your enemies. Let them bring out the best in you, not the worst. When someone gives you a hard time, respond with the energies of prayer, for then you are working out of your true selves, your God-created selves. . . . In a word, what I'm saying is, *Grow up*. You're kingdom subjects. Now live like it. Live out your God-created identity. Live generously and graciously toward others, the way God lives toward you.[3]

Engaging these matters is about learning to be the body of Christ together in our diversity. We are reminded that we serve a Savior who said that he would leave ninety-nine sheep in the pen to search for the one who is lost. God's heart is for each individual. He cares about their struggles and burdens. He knows their needs. He longs for them to know wholeness through intimacy with him and others through healthy, self-giving, loving relationships. Even if this matter were only about those who are gay in the church, I believe God would still challenge us to engage it. As it is, these questions are much larger. They are essentially the question of, "How now shall we live together?" and "What does it really mean to be the church?"

Ultimately, I have to wonder if our preoccupation with either preventing or celebrating two gay adults in a covenanted relationship has missed the priority of God's heart for unity in the church. I well know it is not so simple. I know that larger questions of biblical authority, God's holiness, and the tensions around truth and relativism make the matter a complex one. But in the great debates about slippery slopes and rigid legalism, I can't help but think we miss the forest for the trees. By making homosexuality the litmus test in these larger questions, the needed spaciousness is closed off for gay individuals to authentically search for truth for their lives. This particular litmus test is convenient for the majority, who see this as a merely theoretical and theological issue—not a real-life, heart-crushing question of love and family.

But this is not just an internal problem for the church. It is also an external one, because a lack of internal love and unity has drastic external ramifications. Our infighting and refusal to consider the consciences and beliefs of one another within the church on questions around covenanted same-sex unions has tarnished our witness to those who increasingly find themselves in a post-Christian context. To those outside the church, the battles over gay marriage in the church seem completely incompatible with the idea that Christianity is about serving the God of love. Their perception of the church using the Bible to exclude or deprive a group of people of love and family is a stench rather than a beautiful fragrance of Christ. One has to consider that when 91 percent of 16- to 29-year-olds perceive Christians to be antigay, our ability to reach this generation with the good news of the gospel is significantly hindered.[4]

The Global Church

At the same time, I'm aware that the global South perceives that the gay-affirming church approves and celebrates something their cultural mores strongly reject. Discernment has to be exercised when considering the impact of the disputable-matter conversation on the global church and its ability to be a witness in its own context. However, after speaking with Henry Orombi, the Archbishop of Uganda, I came away from the meeting thinking that too much emphasis was being given to protecting local culture regarding this question and not enough emphasis was on nurturing justice and respect for sexual minorities. I have felt similar reservations after speaking with Christian leaders from the Caribbean. Nonetheless, such leaders are seeking to be wise and strategic in influencing their particular cultures. Europeans and North Americans ought to prayerfully (and with repentance) consider that one result of having sown a modernity and Western-shaped Christianity in these postcolonial countries is (at least in part) this current harvest of the churches insisting on absolutes and voicing clear-cut responses to such complex matters.

Despite the significant differences in context between the church of the global South and the church of North America, it is crucial that we find our center in the gospel of Jesus Christ when deciding if this subject is a disputable matter. While cultural context is an important factor, it must be secondary to deeply redemptive and imaginative reflection on God's self-revelation throughout Scripture.

If we refuse to consider that gay marriage might be disputable, we inevitably put ourselves in a position of discounting those with whom we disagree, despite their profession of faith in Christ and regard for the Scriptures. This is no small matter. Today one cannot simply write off as a small, rebellious, renegade group of liberal revisionists those who view covenanted same-sex relationships as a faithful option for followers of Jesus. Rather, one is likely to find people holding this position in nearly every expression of the Christian church from Catholic to mainline to evangelical. And certainly, one will find many people who feel uncertainty and tension in trying to sort out what they believe on this question. These are people who love Jesus, people who believe the Bible is authoritative for their lives, people who care about missions and sharing the gospel, people who value worship and spiritual disciplines, people who deeply wrestle with how to live out their own faithful discipleship in a complex and challenging world. It seems incredibly audacious to me that anyone would consider sitting in the seat of judgment regarding the authenticity of faith of those who demonstrate good fruit in their lives. If we can't have a conversation about this as a disputable matter, we are judging our brothers and sisters and casting stones at them.

Exploring the question of whether Christians can faithfully come to different conclusions on gay marriage is not the same as giving up the convictions we hold to be true about same-sex relationships. Exploring the questions means holding our convictions in a manner that acknowledges that others in the body of Christ come to a different set of convictions based on their best wrestling with Scripture. We are not saying our convictions are incorrect or inconsequential. We are simply acknowledging the mystery and paradox that come when different people, with different experiences, and different emphases in tradition and hermeneutics discern their convictions about a challenging topic differently. In doing so, we intentionally choose a humble posture.

The challenge is holding our beliefs with true conviction and fervor while humbly acknowledging the limitations of our ability to interpret Scripture perfectly. One pastor, when confronted with the disputable-matter question, said of those with a different position, "At worst they are deeply deceived by the enemy, and at best they are deeply mistaken." What I didn't hear him say is that *he* might be deceived by the enemy or mistaken. To contribute to a conversation on disputable matters is to acknowledge that, despite having done your best to discern correctly and despite deeply holding your convictions, you too could be the one who is wrong, but you will move forward in congruence with your conscience with the kind of humility and grace that Paul advocates. This ability to temporarily suspend your deep convictions in order to enter dialogue is a hallmark of nurturing generous spaciousness.

Unity and Diversity

We are reminded in 1 Corinthians 12 that for the body of Christ to function faithfully and well, we need to embrace the different parts of the body. We are not all the same. We don't all play the same role. We don't all offer the same contribution:

> The eye cannot say to the hand, "I don't need you!" And the head cannot say to the feet, "I don't need you!" On the contrary, those parts of the body that seem to be weaker are indispensable, and the parts that we think are less honorable we treat with special honor. And the parts that are unpresentable are treated with special modesty, while our presentable

parts need no special treatment. But God has put the body together, giving greater honor to the parts that lacked it, so that there should be no division in the body, but that its parts should have equal concern for each other. (vv. 21–25)

Are we really prepared to say that those who have different views on homosexuality, different processes for theological reflection, different approaches to Scripture and tradition, and different types of experiences are not part of the body of Christ? If these brothers and sisters confess Jesus as Lord, how can we cast them out? Consider these words, "If you declare with your mouth, 'Jesus is Lord,' and believe in your heart that God raised him from the dead, you will be saved."[5] If brothers and sisters share in the essentials of our faith—believing in Father, Son, and Holy Spirit; the life, death, resurrection, and ascension of Jesus Christ; and his atonement for us to be reconciled—who are we to say they are not part of the body?

Other Disputable Matters

The issues that Paul raises—the matter of eating meat previously sacrificed to idols or the appropriate day for worship—can seem to be fairly benign issues to us today, while the question of gay marriage can seem to be a much more significant matter. This can cause a knee-jerk reaction: "Of course gay marriage is not a disputable matter." But for Paul's readers, particularly those who were of Jewish background, the food you put in your mouth was directly tied to your commitment of faith. The Jewish Christians had grown up keeping kosher—butchering in just the right way, observing dietary restrictions associated with feasts and festivals, fasting regularly, and so on. And they had grown up hearing the stories of the Old Testament Scriptures that make no small matter of avoiding idolatry. There are no positive references in Scripture of association with idolatry. The Jewish people had endured extreme punishment through exile and the destruction of the temple because they embraced idolatry. The idea of eating meat that was not kosher and likely associated with idol worship was huge. On the flip side, the gentile believers likely had limited ability to understand what the big deal was for their Jewish comrades. Jesus had set them free from the law—Peter had the vision, the church council in Jerusalem had told them to simply stay away from sexual immorality and eating meat with blood in it, and this meat was well roasted with no blood to be seen. What was the problem? There were very distinct differences in backgrounds, expectations, and experiences.

But on these weighty matters, notice that Paul's concern is not with the questions, "What is the right interpretation? What is the clear answer?" Rather, Paul's focus is acknowledging the diversity and asking a new question, "How now shall we live together?" Paul doesn't even attempt to pull them together into a uniform position on the matter. However, he wants them to prayerfully consider how they will relate to one another, how they will nurture an environment in which each person could make decisions according to his or her own conscience. His biggest concern is to help the believers *find a way to experience unity in their diversity*.

Typically, in contemporary experiences of disputable matters, there are two common realities. First, there are prohibitive biblical texts as well as positive biblical texts addressing aspects of the issue. Second, the issue personally impacts the majority of people in the community. We see this with the role of women in ministry, the use of our financial resources, the consumption of alcohol, or observance of the Sabbath. The challenge with this particular question of covenanted same-sex relationships is that there doesn't seem to be any positive textual references to such relationships. Additionally, this issue does not personally impact the majority of people. Rather, the majority of people have very strong opinions about a question that personally impacts only a minority of us.

Some people look at close and intimate same-sex relationships in the narratives of Scripture (such as David and Jonathon, Naomi and Ruth, or the Roman centurion and his servant) as a positive reflection of the love that can be shared in a same-sex context. But such an inference of sexual innuendo can be offensive to those who see these stories as reflecting friendship and nothing more. What may be more helpful than arguing the unanswerable question of whether there was any physical or sexual intimacy shared in these relationships is the consideration that these stories do illustrate that deep and intimate love between people of the same sex is not only *not* inherently abhorrent to God but also seems to be pleasing to God. The weight of this comes when we consider that for gay people, their longing for a covenanted relationship is much more multifaceted than a focus on erotic behavior. Gay people feel that they would be completed and complemented by someone of their own gender in all areas: spiritual, emotional, psychological, and physical (practical) support and care. Genital sexual activity is not likely to be the sole or highest priority in the relationship, any more than it is in a heterosexual relationship.

When people are asked to explain *why* they believe what they do regarding what Scripture says about covenanted same-sex relationships, many stammer and struggle to articulate their reasons. A good number will simply say, "The Bible is clear," or "This is what I've always been taught," or "I just know it's wrong," or inversely, "I just know it's right." It is not uncommon to encounter people with very strong views who really haven't done their homework to wrestle with Scripture and the variety of thought found in the Christian community.

Any deviation from the hetero-normative tradition is automatically suspect for some. For example, Albert Mohler, in referring to an interview of megachurch pastor Joel Osteen (by Piers Morgan), wrote on his blog, "To his credit, Osteen did answer [Morgan's] question [if he believed homosexuality was sinful], and by staking his position on the Bible's teaching that homosexual acts are sinful, he took the only road available to anyone with any substantial commitment to the truthfulness of the Bible."[6] The assumption Mohler makes is that anyone who disagrees with his position lacks a "substantial commitment to the truthfulness of the Bible." Not only is this an audacious statement to make, it also completely discounts the testimonies of faith of anyone holding a different position.

It can be very hard to risk wrestling with these questions knowing that you may be labeled as one who has compromised, watered down the truth, and will lead people astray. One of the commenters on a blog that quotes Mohler's article says, "The wages of ALL sin is death. This doesn't mean we go execute them. We biblically principled Christians call them to repentance and love them regardless. We don't, however, tell them that their sin is no sin at all. The delusional apostates are doing their best to make God into their own image." What this commenter fails to take into account is that those he calls "delusional apostates" are people created in God's image, deeply and profoundly loved by him, who may indeed be growing and experiencing intimate and deep relationship with God, having gratefully received reconciliation through the gift of grace given by Jesus Christ. In this kind of climate, one can feel very threatened to approach this question from a more generous posture, a posture that explores whether there may be more than one faithful way for gay believers to move forward in their journey of trust and obedience.

Rules of Engagement

Therefore, if there is going to be any fruitful conversation about whether gay relationships are a disputable matter, there needs to be a safe environment of generous spaciousness. A safe environment is built on the premise that no one in the conversation is going to be written off as not caring about the truthfulness of Scripture. Nor will the conversation be marked by an agenda-driven attempt to proselytize others by promoting one particular position. The question to be explored is not which position is correct but rather whether or not Paul's admonishments concerning disputable matters might be applied to the question of gay marriage as an expression of Christian faithfulness. Such conversation invites those from a variety of perspectives to extend the humility that says, "I could be wrong." When this attitude is mutually shared, the playing field is leveled and we can focus on actually listening to one another.

But what should we be listening for? Should we listen for whether the application of exegesis, hermeneutics, tradition, reason, or experience has been navigated with integrity? Correctly? In a way that we approve? I know both straight and gay believers who have gone on to graduate and postgraduate education to try to learn enough to develop an airtight case. The problem is, even at the highest levels of scholarship, there is disagreement. Among even the most learned the outcome is disputed. So for those of us with significantly less education and research under our belts, perhaps looking for the airtight, scholarly case won't be the most effective route.

Should we be listening for evidence that the person is being led by the Spirit? Absolutely. But how do we do that? We are all prone to self-deception. And while we seek to walk in step with the Holy Spirit, how do we rightly judge if someone else is being led by the Spirit, particularly when they are espousing thoughts and ideas with which we disagree. Let us not overestimate our ability to discern the Spirit when we are feeling particularly threatened. So, yes, we should listen for the Spirit's presence in those who hold different perspectives, but we also must admit that our ability to discern rightly, given our own personal filters, may be less than optimal.

Perhaps we look for the evidence of good fruit. Jesus said, "By their fruit you will recognize them. Do people pick grapes from thorn bushes, or figs from thistles? Likewise, every good tree bears good fruit, but a bad tree bears bad fruit. A good tree cannot bear bad fruit, and a bad tree cannot bear good fruit" (Matt. 7:16–18). What fruit is proceeding from the lives of those who hold a different perspective on this question? Do you see the fruit of the Spirit at work in them: love, joy, peace, patience, kindness, goodness, faithfulness, gentleness, self-control? Do you see the fruit of service: do they feed the hungry, give drink to the thirsty, visit the sick and those in prison, clothe the naked? Do they look after widows and orphans? Do they touch the untouchables? Do they demonstrate spiritual gifts? Do they love their neighbor as themselves? If we see good fruit in their lives, what shall we conclude? Jesus says that a bad tree cannot bear good fruit. That is not to say that everyone who bears good fruit is correct about everything, but it may be something to reflect on as you consider whether your brother or sister ought to be treated in the manner Paul describes in Romans 14 rather than as someone who "at worst is deceived by the enemy, and at best is deeply mistaken."

To recap, Paul says that when we encounter a genuine believer who disagrees with us we need to accept them, without quarreling, without viewing them with contempt, and without a judgmental attitude. He says not to put a stumbling block in a brother's or sister's way and to work toward peace and mutual edification. He challenges us to keep our convictions about disputable matters to ourselves and to live consistently with our consciences. Imagine if that actually became our posture toward one another in this contentious conversation at the intersection of faith and sexuality. Imagine if we didn't back one another into a corner demanding to know where we stand on this question of covenanted same-sex relationships as the ultimate orthodoxy test. Imagine if we did not judge the heart's motivation of those who conclude differently than we do. Imagine if we ceased showing contempt to those who disagree with us. Imagine if we stopped our quarreling. Imagine if we no longer put stumbling blocks in the way of those who were deeply wrestling with these questions and desperately needing some safe space to search out God's heart and will for them. If all those things were true, we would be experiencing the richness of generous spaciousness.

I suggest that we reframe this question of whether gay relationships are a disputable matter just a bit. I believe the answer ought to be determined by those who must make a decision about entering one. If you consider Romans 14, Paul is not speaking to those who have only theoretical ideas about eating meat sacrificed to idols. Every single person reading Paul's letter needed to eat food and therefore needed to make decisions about what they would eat and what they would refrain from eating. Paul's admonishments weren't for those who stood on the sidelines offering opinions and directives. It is very easy for a straight pastor to write a blog stating that the scriptural validity of covenanted same-sex relationships is not a disputable matter because of his belief that the Scripture is unequivocally clear. But ultimately, he is, from his theoretical perch, discounting the lives of gay Christians who are in the trenches wrestling out these questions with God, in the context of commitment to Christ, concern and care for the Scriptures, and a desire to live faithfully. And for those who are wrestling, is being taught what to think (from someone who has never had to wrestle personally with this) really the most effective way to disciple and impart wisdom for the stewardship of desires and drives?

We are called to a living, embodied faith. We are called to wrestle with the spirit of the law (which is much more challenging than wrestling with the letter of the law) as we walk in intimate relationship with a personal God revealed to us through Jesus Christ.

Gay Christians Weigh In

When we look to the community of gay Christians, we see men and women committed to Christ, committed to engaging the Scriptures as God's revelation to them, and committed to journeying as faithful disciples. Among them, we see that this is truly a disputable matter. There are those who believe that faithful discipleship means not embracing their same-sex attraction and who seek to love and serve an opposite-gender spouse. In these lives we see their courage of conviction and their discipline of stewarding desires. We see commitment to fidelity and to chastity. We see good fruit.

There are other gay Christians who also exhibit good fruit, but who have navigated their journey in a different way. These Christians sense no contradiction in Scripture to live honestly and authentically as someone who is persistently and predominantly attracted to their own gender yet who lives out their scriptural convictions through an intentional commitment to celibate singleness. Does this difference from the first group discount the good fruit of discipleship, maturity, service, and love that is in their lives?

What about our gay brothers and sisters who fully believe that God's love and grace extend to them as they offer their lives to a same-sex partner as an act of self-giving love? What about the fruit of faith that enables them to believe that God's love embraces and enfolds them as they journey with a partner? Shall we sit in the seat of God and declare that theirs is not legitimate faith? What about the ways these brothers and sisters share their faith in Christ with their friends and neighbors? Shall we count such witness as bad fruit? What about the commitment of these believers to work for justice for the poor, abused, and oppressed in our society and world? Shall we consider such efforts to be not of Christ? What about the times of prayer, the faithful worship, the engagement with Scripture, the sharing of fellowship with other believers? Shall we consider this all counterfeit so that it fits our grid of understanding?

Consider this discourse between Jesus and John in Mark chapter 9:

> "Teacher," said John, "we saw someone driving out demons in your name and we told him to stop, because he was not one of us."
>
> "Do not stop him," Jesus said. "For no one who does a miracle in my name can in the next moment say anything bad about me, for whoever is not against us is for us. Truly I tell you, anyone who gives you a cup of water in my name because you belong to the Messiah will certainly not lose their reward.
>
> "If anyone causes one of these little ones—those who believe in me—to stumble, it would be better for them if a large millstone were hung around their neck and they were thrown into the sea." (vv. 38–42)

A number of gay Christians are pursuing (and modeling) Paul's guidelines on how to live out unity with diversity. I've witnessed friendships between gay Christians with differing beliefs in which space is given to allow the other to live according to one's conscience, where judgment is withheld, where instead of a spirit of contempt there is a spirit of humility, listening and caring for one another.

Having had the opportunity to be present and worship in such gatherings of gay believers, I can attest to the beauty of such unity in diversity. There is a beauty of preferring the other. There is an awareness of the need to resist the natural pharisaical spirit that so easily arises within us. There is freedom to encourage others to stay true to their convictions—even when they differ from ours—because we most want our friends to live congruent lives in commitment to Christ. Words are spoken with care. Feelings are considered. Sensitivity is a regular discipline. In such space there is an astounding atmosphere of love and acceptance. Not because "anything goes" but rather because people understand that every individual has been on a journey of wrestling with God. And there is a unified commitment to truly not be a stumbling block to one another. There is perhaps a keen awareness to "be kind; everyone is fighting a hard battle." Until one has experienced rejection, alienation, inequity, or injustice, such a quotation may seem merely sentimental. But when, collectively, a group of people sharing similar difficult experiences gathers, there is a capacity for grace in the midst of difference because there is a keen awareness that the battle is real and difficult.

Such unity in diversity isn't a perfect or ideal experience all the time. In such a space there are inevitably those who do not think they could be wrong and who do try to proselytize others to their position. There are those who are wounded or immature who do not yet have the capacity to follow Paul's advice. There is still conflict, there are still moments when *shalom* is interrupted or broken. But even with all of this, there is a larger picture of what unity and peace and unconditional love can look like when we live out Romans 14 in the midst of our significant disagreements.

The great irony I see is that gay Christians are living out this challenging experiment while many straight Christians are unwilling to even consider it. A brief look at any Christian blog that brings up the subject of homosexuality will quickly show the many straight Christians who are certain and clear, not only in their own convictions but in their judgment of and contempt toward those who differ from them.

One has to wonder if the process of wrestling with a particular question personally is the foundation from which one can internalize Paul's teaching in Romans 14 of not getting in the way of someone else's choices and making life more difficult for them. For when you get on your knees at the side of your bed night after night pleading with God to take away your same-sex attractions, you experience solidarity with others who have had the same experience. When you do the hard work of processing fear and shame related to your sense of being different in your sexuality or sense of gender—there is that sense of solidarity with others who have done the same. When you face the potential rejection of family, friends, and church by honestly speaking about your experience of same-sex attraction, when you search through Scripture to try to understand how God truly feels about you, when you wrestle to try to make sense of the longing you feel for love and family and the story of Scripture that doesn't contain a clear model for you, you feel an empathy and closeness for whoever else has had to walk that road. And so, even if you come to different conclusions in the midst of a genuine desire to follow God and live a faithful life, there is a sense of connection, there is a sense of understanding, there is a sense of not wanting to make the other's journey any more difficult than it has already been. And out of this very real and personal place arises the kind of mutuality and preference for the other that Paul speaks of. The truth is straight people will never be able to fully enter that space—because straight people have never wrestled in those particular personal and deep places.

Disputable Matters in Community

How can we as leaders teach on an issue if we acknowledge that sincere Christians disagree about it? What would happen if one Sunday a preacher promotes the virtue of gay marriage, then the next Sunday a different speaker contradicts the first speaker, calling all gay Christians to abstinence and celibacy? How could a community possibly navigate such confusing and contradictory messages? The point Paul makes is that people need to live consistently with their conscience, and each person's conscience will engage the matter differently. So, when teaching on such a matter, my suggestion is that the primary focus should be to equip people to discern and to understand the principles of biblical interpretation, to walk in step with the Holy Spirit, to weigh how much our own experience should be a factor, to think deeply, and to discuss with others in community our discernment process. Our teaching should prepare people to wrestle with the challenges and questions through scriptural reflection, allowing Scripture to shape and form their convictions; through prayerful contemplation, inviting silence and solitude; and through an overall commitment to grow to maturity in faithfulness, obedience, worship, and service to others. Our teaching should emphasize values such as self-giving love, mutual respect, and fidelity. Teaching should empower people to move from fear to love. Teaching should encourage people to live in alignment and faithful commitment to their convictions (while interacting with those who differ from them) with the postures of humility, generosity, and graciousness as an essential part of their spiritual formation.

Teaching people how to navigate a disputable matter can be helpful, but that doesn't mean living in community where there are different convictions is easy to do. It can be exhausting and draining to extend forgiveness and grace and choose to not take offense. It can feel unfair to always have to take the high road, while the person you disagree with communicates in passive aggressive and immature ways. To be willing to live in the tensions that arise from the acceptance of a disputable matter can be costly. But the goal is to become mature followers of Christ who learn how to deeply love and prefer one another in the way of Jesus. Nothing about this is wishy-washy or weak. This isn't relativism. This is learning to live graciously with one another despite disagreements, while focusing on Christ to grow in you the fruit of his Spirit. Nurturing generous spaciousness demands courageous humility.

Barriers to Embracing a Disputable Matter

Despite the benefit of maturing as a community, there is often resistance to considering any degree of being open to covenanted gay relationships. Why is that?

Certainly, there is the fear of being disobedient and the fear of diminishing a high view of the authority of Scripture. There is the fear of opening the door to a moral relativism that will undermine a determined and disciplined pursuit of holiness. There is discomfort with the idea that the Bible potentially offers more than one appropriate way to navigate discipleship in this area. There is fear of creating a climate of confusion and chaos that will impact the vulnerable and weak. And there is fear of further instability in the nuclear family model.

While we are called to fear God in Scripture, we do well to remember that such fear is about reverence not fright. And when we look at many of the reasons we resist living in community with the understanding that gay marriage is a disputable matter, we see that there is a lot of fear behind our resistance. But in our resistance, we are withholding from

188

others the spaciousness needed to wrestle with God, and usually we are doing so from a convenient place of detached theoretical thinking.

Risking to live in the tensions of a disputable matter offers space to live consistently with your conscience—something Scripture deems to be very significant. Risking to live in the tension of a disputable matter offers the opportunity for spiritual formation and growth. In these places we become enlarged in our ability to set aside our own pride (which is often fueled by our own fears and insecurities) and embrace a new depth of humility. We become enlarged in our capacity to respond with graciousness to those with whom we disagree. We grow in learning to extend hospitality to the stranger. And we learn to extend a spirit of mutuality and honor to one another in the midst of our diversity.

What do you think smells more like Jesus: arrogant certainty or humble hospitality? A refusal to listen to the testimony of one who differs from you or an eagerness to see where God is at work, speaking through one whose journey has taken them to a different place? A tightly held control to the literal letter of interpretation or trust that the Spirit is alive and well and more than able to lead us, in our distinct contexts, into truth and righteousness in our personal lives and in our shared discipleship?

If we demand uniformity on this question, I believe we will miss the blessing God wants to extend. In the midst of this, we are each called to search the Scriptures; listen deeply to the Holy Spirit through prayer, fasting, and times of silence and solitude; and consider the good fruit in the lives of those disciples who are living in the reality of these questions. We must be consciously aware of *why* we believe what we believe. But we also need to take the time to hear why others believe what they believe. Because (mysteriously and infuriatingly) in the body of Christ there are faithful disciples who come to different conclusions and hold different convictions. And while this may threaten or anger us, we perhaps do well to remember that there are many, many differences in the body of Christ in how we understand the journey of sanctification. Individual Christians live out their sanctification very differently from one another. We all have unanswered questions. We all throw ourselves on the grace and mercy of Christ. And in the midst of our differences, we lay down our striving, knowing that it is only through grace that we have been saved through Jesus Christ our Lord.

As we nurture generous spaciousness, we help to tear down walls that divide. We tangibly begin to dismantle the negative perception that all Christians are "antigay." We foster an environment in which those who are tentative, cynical, wounded, or afraid can ask questions, explore faith, and genuinely consider the invitation of Christ. In these places of generosity, we can extend *shalom*, without reservation, within our neighborhoods to anyone who comes across our path, with the full confidence that the Holy Spirit can be trusted to lead people into all truth.

Friends, let us not miss the opportunity to be shaped and formed into the likeness of Christ in the midst of our diversity. Let us not allow fear to be the prominent motivator in our wrestling as individuals, as families, and as congregations, communities, and denominations. Let us honor the mystery of the Spirit speaking to our individual consciences and to the larger community of faith. And let us be committed to nurturing safe and spacious places where people can explore and grow in faith in Jesus Christ.

190

12

Engaging the Church

We were about two thirds of the way through the eight-hour seminar when one of the participants said (with no small amount of frustration in her voice), "Everything you're saying presumes that people hold a traditional position on homosexuality." She went on to describe the diversity of perspectives in her congregation and how her church's desire was to find a way through these differences in a manner that honored and respected one another, nurtured their unity, and prioritized their missional heart. Every resource she'd encountered seemed to focus on maintaining a conservative, traditional perspective or embracing a gay-affirming theology. Neither approach would serve their multiethnic, intergenerational congregation well.

When I first began in this area of ministry and spoke on the topic of homosexuality, I could pretty much count on fairly monolithic audiences. Based on the denominational or organizational background of the group, I could guess their degree of readiness to engage the complexities and to navigate the gray areas. There were often exceptions in the audience—that parent of a gay loved one, that individual who worked with gay colleagues, that university student studying sociology and psychology, or that person who identified as gay. These individuals, because of their personal experiences and relationships, shared a more nuanced journey and asked more penetrating questions. These conversations usually happened long after most of the audience had left.

Occasionally, I would encounter an individual who disrupted the presentation or directly confronted me. In one situation where I'd been invited to preach, a man stood up and loudly declared that I was twisting Scripture and warned the congregation not to heed this false teacher. He concluded by saying that women weren't supposed to preach and teach, and then he stormed out. I had preached from Matthew 5:43–48, the text about loving our enemies. My focus was on navigating relationships with people we disagree with. I'd challenged the congregation to engage and serve with love those whose beliefs and practices regarding homosexuality differed from their own. (After the man left and the service concluded, I was mobbed by people who apologized for his outburst and said they appreciated the relevance of my message.)

Today, most congregations are diverse. Some people are looking for me to pass their orthodoxy test, to reassure them that I am in agreement with their position, and to offer a presentation that will simply reaffirm what they already think. There are others who feel very unsure about what is an appropriate directive for gay people. They feel the tension between their understanding that the Bible precludes gay relationships and their emotional connection with gay friends in their lives. Perhaps they know gay Christians who are partnered and who love and serve God. And there may be people in the same audience who believe that committed, monogamous same-sex relationships are God's grace to gay people.

Many people within our churches are wary of perceived agendas when it comes to this topic. No one wants to be pressured to change their perspective, regardless of what that might be. In addition to being wary, many congregations are weary of this subject. They have felt the pain and intensity of disagreement—they have tried to be gracious, tried to listen, tried to be patient—and have felt like all their efforts haven't borne much fruit. Splits still happened, and people continued to ignore those they disagreed with. For them, the ideal of robust hospitality still seems a long way from the reality of their fellowship. It isn't that such folks don't care about gay people necessarily, but it may be that there aren't actually any openly gay people in their small congregation, and this discussion seems to have sucked up a whole lot of emotional and spiritual energy.

Other congregations continue in avoidance mode, ensuring this topic is given little airtime. Churches have watched as other denominations seem to have imploded over their discussions around homosexuality. There is a fear of this topic draining and dividing their own group, and so they prefer to avoid entering the fray. This can seem to be a safe, defensive strategy as long as there are no personal situations that arise to challenge the status quo. But waiting until a gay person walks through the door, or a member comes out, puts a congregation and a pastor at a great disadvantage. Seeking to work through what hospitality will look like in a congregation under the pressure of an immediate response creates additional stress and may hinder the growth that comes from engaging such a conversation. Rather, it is important to recognize that addressing questions of hospitality and creating a safe space are really just about asking what it means to be the church, called to be bearers of *shalom* in our neighborhoods, living in an increasingly diverse and pluralistic context.

Congregations should consider some of the tensions that arise for gay Christians who attend churches that have clear boundaries limiting sexual intimacy to heterosexual marriage. Remaining static isn't an effective way to address these tensions. We need to learn how to better welcome into our church communities people who are different. Different not only in terms of sexual orientation but potentially different in how they approach Scripture, how they view the character of God, how they engage mission, and what they prioritize in a worship experience. The body of Christ isn't meant to be a uniform group. It is meant to be a body with different parts, different gifts, different experiences, and different strengths. Navigating tension isn't something to avoid. As we willingly enter tension together, we have the opportunity to grow in the fruit of the Spirit—self-control, patience, and humility. We become enlarged in our capacity to be generous with one another.

Hospitality and Authenticity

Pastoring a congregation toward a mind-set of generous spaciousness can be a challenging process. We are accustomed to expectations of conformity in the church. This can be couched in language of sanctification or holiness, but sometimes it simply comes down to "We will be most comfortable if everyone in our church acts in a certain way."

The expectation of this kind of uniform goodness can be a real breeding ground for secrets. It's hard to be honest about the gritty realities of our lives when it feels that everyone expects some godly, nice, state of perfection. However, if we fixate on the gritty stuff in one another's lives, our precious sense of unity might become quickly eroded. We might discover how very difficult it is to love one another through this kind of messiness. And we might realize that our patience, grace, maturity, and humility need to be enlivened by the Spirit's presence if we are to address the deep-seated systems of shame and pride, judgment and hiding.

Many congregations have a silent system of DADT: "don't ask, don't tell." It refers to a former practice in the United States military that compelled soldiers to keep their same-sex attractions, gay identity, and same-sex relationships secret. As a pacifist-leaning Canadian who is admittedly ill-informed about US military issues, I find the whole concept of DADT to be counterintuitive. If you are asking soldiers to entrust their lives to one another, it seems to me there would be tremendous benefit in fostering an environment of authenticity and integrity. Asking a group of individuals to hide such a significant part of their sense of self perpetuates a climate of secrecy that, in my mind, erodes corporate integrity. In many ways I observe a similar expectation of DADT within the Christian community. And I think such a system erodes our corporate integrity and authenticity as the family of God.

I've had more conversations than I can count with Christians, across the spectrum of sexual orientation, who find themselves uncertain, living with ambiguity on this issue of homosexuality. I hear, as they quietly confide in me, a kaleidoscope of emotions: fear of believing the wrong thing, anxiety as they confront and critique long-held assumptions, concern to not hurt or betray the church they love, exhaustion at the

194

thought of trying to explain to their fellow church members (who are so very certain and so very clear) how and why they are at the place they are, frustration at the lack of safe spaces for them to articulate their thoughts and questions around these realities, resignation in their assessment that it is simply too costly to rock the boat given that it will likely bring limited change to people's mind-sets anyway. All of these emotions describe an environment that hinders true authenticity, courageous exploration of biblical texts, the Holy Spirit's leading, and shared discernment. They describe an environment in which control wins out over honest wrestling. It isn't necessarily that these individuals want to dramatically change the theology or policy of their churches. It can be as simple as wanting a more spacious place in which these questions can be explored without judgment, condemnation, or fear.

But DADT encourages the formation of secret clubs within a given fellowship. Lines get drawn between those who are "open-minded" and those who are not. Knowing looks when certain statements are made perpetuate invisible divides. Assumptions and judgments flourish in this kind of environment. Perceived agendas aren't actually talked about or confronted. People simply keep their distance from one another. Relationships become more superficial or overtly strained. Experience of community is compromised.

In intercultural, intergenerational, post-denominational, post-Christian contexts we encounter complex layers of diversity within our local fellowships. While this ushers in a messy, uncomfortable, and sometimes painful exercise in learning how to love one another, this also presents an exciting opportunity for growth and maturity. Experiencing such diversity is often God's way of transforming us into the character of Christ to become inviting, hospitable, not threatened, not easily offended, willing to be misunderstood. God can shape us into a church that breaks barriers, stands for justice, reaches the marginalized, refuses to play favorites, extends forgiveness, pursues reconciliation, and embodies freedom.

I have become convinced that we ought not run from such diversity, ought not try to control it or coerce it into uniformity. We ought to live in the midst of it, live in the tensions it creates, wrestle with the paradoxes that arise. We ought to face the challenge of mastering our own selfish, fearful, prideful, and easily threatened hearts.

But DADT gives us the easy way out. We don't have to face the reality of our diversity. We don't have to wrestle through the hard questions. We don't have to examine and reexamine what we believe and why we believe it, and how it is that we hold what we believe when we encounter those who think in a different way. DADT is false freedom from conflict. Behind the mask of peace lies a leprosy that eats away at authentic community. It keeps us secretly divided with a false sense of unity.

DADT obviously impacts gay people who need a safe and spacious place in which they can be honest. I see how this has shipwrecked lives due to the energy that must be spent on hiding. I've seen people fracture under the pressure and walk away not only from the church but from God. I've seen mixed-orientation marriages shatter after years of secrecy as the truth emerges with such pent-up intensity that navigating the challenges of the marriage seems inconceivable. I've sat with people as they wept over lost years—years of not being able to be known for who they truly were. I've sat with people who identify as ex-gay but who continue to struggle with same-sex attraction while everyone assumes they are "healed." I've ached to hear the incredible isolation that DADT causes real people with real lives.

When we intentionally choose to nurture generous spaciousness and welcome diversity in experience and perspective, we recognize that we all have areas of strength and areas of weakness, that we all need space and grace to grow, that we need love and acceptance extended to us in the journey, and that we are mutual and interdependent pilgrims with those who differ from us. We are positioned to take the risky steps needed to begin to experience real and authentic community with one another. In this kind of community, we can find ourselves most receptive to experiencing both the freedom and the increasing mastery that every Christ-follower needs in their walk of faith.

I think this is summed up well in the statement that is read at every worship service at Highlands Church in Denver:

> Married, divorced or single here, it's one family that mingles here.
> Conservative or liberal here, we've all gotta give a little here.
> Big or small here, there's room for us all here.

196

Doubt or believe here, we all can receive here.
Gay or straight here, there's no hate here.
Woman or man here, everyone can here.
Whatever your race here, for all of us grace here.
In imitation of the ridiculous love Almighty God has for each of us and all of us, let us live and love without labels.[1]

The conversation about nurturing generous spaciousness is really just the conversation about being a community that humbly recognizes and welcomes people who are searching for a way to embrace faith in Christ in the midst of the challenges of our lives. The conversation is about becoming friends, seeing one another's humanity, sharing meals, being in one another's homes, and praying for one another through the joys and struggles of our everyday lives.

It is quite different from a discussion aimed at figuring out when people should be removed from fellowship because of a lack of alignment with a particular set of beliefs. In our fragmented, individualistic, and isolated culture, I have often articulated that church discipline, in the spirit of working toward restoration, shouldn't be about removing people but about saying, "We're going to stick with you. You can't get rid of us unless you remove yourself because we are committed to walking with you and committed to trying to grow in faith together." This is messy and difficult. It means there will be times when we're uncomfortable with people's choices. It means we'll feel tempted to withdraw from one another and retreat back into an artificial unity and niceness. It means the pull of power plays will tempt us to focus on protecting the perceived purity of our church.

Leadership

With the kind of groaning that expresses our longing for the redemption of all things (Rom. 8), we live in the now and the not yet. Not every congregation has the capacity to work out these tensions with the maturity and grace that is required. This is especially apparent when it comes to the question of leadership positions. How, in a context where committed gay relationships might be viewed as disputable, are matters of leadership addressed? Returning to the text in Romans 14, we see that Paul indicates that those whose consciences allow them less freedom in the matter are the weaker brothers and sisters and need to be treated in a manner that honors and protects their faith. Consider verses 14–15, "I am convinced, being fully persuaded in the Lord Jesus, that nothing is unclean in itself. But if anyone regards something as unclean, then for that person it is unclean. If your brother or sister is distressed because of what you eat, you are no longer acting in love. Do not by your eating destroy someone for whom Christ died."

When it comes to the question of leadership in a congregation where there are brothers and sisters who (on the basis of conscience and conviction) cannot accept covenanted gay relationships, honoring such convictions may be especially important. Being called to submit to the leadership of someone whom your conscience tells you is not living consistently with God's direction can create a stumbling block. For those who do believe such relationships are blessed by God, their act of love is to prefer their weaker brother or sister. This concession is not about rejection or judgment. It is about submitting oneself to a community with a commitment to sacrificial love. Those who do not approve of gay relationships have the opportunity to extend sacrificial love as they humble themselves to listen for the ways God is at work in their partnered gay brothers and sisters as they worship and serve together. On the question of the offices of leadership, such as pastor or elder, those who affirm such relationships extend sacrificial love as they willingly choose to defer to the needs of those who do not. This is the pain of love at work in the midst of our diversity. It is not a mere compromise. It is a choice to cultivate sacrificial love.

In my conversations with many gay Christians, I encounter a great capacity for graciousness and generosity. There is a willingness to honor those who disagree with their convictions. They want to be a part of a worshiping community that has the spaciousness for open dialogue, respectful listening, and an ability to disagree and still love one another. And they want to use their spiritual gifts in service. They recognize that there are many opportunities to serve beyond the traditional leadership offices.

For gay Christians who do feel particularly called to ordained leadership, there are opportunities in an affirming church, where their service won't be a battleground or contradiction of conscience for other church members. In the context of an affirming church, gay Christian leaders can simply get on with offering their service to the body of Christ without the distraction and drain of constant debate.

Leadership in the church is about service and willingly laying our lives down for the church. It is not about making a political or social statement. Leadership doesn't demand authority, and it isn't about personal affirmation. Leadership is the call to self-emptying love for the community you serve.

Such limitations and concessions are challenging and in some ways very unsatisfactory responses. As a woman in ministry, there are places I am not welcome to share my gifts and calling. I can feel a sense of injustice and grief about that. But I am called, in my vocation, to love the church, despite its weaknesses. I am called to love it sacrificially. That means I don't barge in, I don't demand, I don't fight. It means I ask the Lord to enlarge patience and grace and generosity and humility in me. It means I serve where God opens a door rather than banging on a door that is locked from the inside. It means I allow these inequities to spiritually form me in the likeness of Christ, who stripped himself of all privilege, became a man of sorrows, was acquainted with grief, and was despised and rejected. This is difficult. It is painful. But it is rich. It is the way of Christ.

The difficult questions of leadership can be navigated when there is a corporate commitment to self-giving love, to humility, to honoring one another, and to embracing spiritual formation through suffering. It won't be easy. There will be clashes and conflict. We resist being incarnational people. We resist stripping ourselves of our rights and privileges. Our flesh rises up and demands recognition and affirmation. Forgiving again and again, humbling ourselves again and again is exhausting. Communities that take on these immense challenges can experience deep seasons of weariness. But in the midst of this weariness, God is at work shaping us into the likeness of his Son, Jesus. For all of the challenge of navigating a disputable matter, it is profoundly spiritually formational.

Sadly, many churches seem unwilling to struggle with what these questions mean on the ground, in the context of people's lives. Consider this email my friend Tracey sent to churches in her area:[2]

Hi There,

My name is Tracey and my wife, Peggy, and I are still fairly new to the area. We moved here in November of last year from Halifax, and we truly love it here! We have tried a few churches out here but have not felt like any of them were truly a community where we could not only learn, but serve. We recently got married in May and would love to be a part of a church community that, above all, loves Jesus but is also not scared that we are a same-sex couple.

We are both from Halifax and were involved with more evangelical churches there. I have grown up in conservative churches, while Peggy became a Christian in her teens, so our church experiences vary a little. While we love the evangelical church's zeal for Jesus, we also felt that they wouldn't be comfortable with us "as a couple," especially to be involved in any capacity, like being on the worship team or teaching Sunday school. Not only that, but we don't feel comfortable coming to a service on Sunday, wondering if this is the morning they are going to teach how wrong our lifestyles are. We truly feel God's blessing and leading on our lives, something the church as a whole has had a hard time dealing with.

We really don't want or need to convince anyone about the positive or negative issues with gay marriage, or being a gay Christian. We love Jesus, we love each other, and we just want to journey this life together with other believers.

So, I was wondering if your church would be a place for us? If you could give me any more information, that would be awesome.

Thanks for reading this, and bless you!
Tracey

Here are two responses Tracey received:

Tracey you did right in contacting us, and of course you and Peggy are welcome to come to our church. The church belongs to our Lord Jesus and, as such, He invites everyone. His church therefore cannot be [just] any kind of church; He has given us Holy Scripture to instruct us. Therefore the Bible is our textbook. To be honest and fair with you, let me quote what we believe . . . from our . . . Equipping Bases course workbook: . . . "Statement of Family: . . . We believe in both singleness and marriage as biblical lifestyles. We believe that Scripture teaches that marriage is between a man and a woman; and that the Christian is called to a life of purity in both thought and action." We are not to condemn but to instruct. I trust you will see: we must be faithful to the Scriptures. . . . See also . . . Romans 1:26–27. . . .

Pastor B.

Hello Tracey,

Thank you so much for sending an email to [us] and for inquiring about being involved in the ministry at our church. Tracey, there are two parts to the answer to your questions. First, our church is certainly a place that you and Peggy are more than welcome to attend; we love all people regardless of race, gender, age, demographic, and the like. That being said, second, our church would not be a place where either you or Peggy would be welcomed to join the ministry team. We are committed to a sexual ethic that is founded on the teachings of Scripture, and as such, individuals whose lifestyles do not align with that (regardless of whether or not they are homosexual or heterosexual) are not affirmed as leaders in the house or given the honor and responsibility that comes with that.

Love in Christ,
J. W., Pastoral Assistant

The leaders who wrote these responses probably thought they were responding in grace and truth. But to Tracey, such blunt and impersonal statements communicated a disregard for the authenticity of her faith and her desire to serve and use her gifts.

That's why I am so grateful for the examples of experimental communities that are trying to live out the hospitality of diversity by wrestling with what it means to view covenanted gay relationships as a disputable matter. I am hopeful that the church at large will be open to hearing and engaging their stories—not as a cookie-cutter template but as a glimpse of the kind of seeds that could be sown in their own churches.

One pastor, seeking to embrace these tensions, said it this way,

> We did not arrive at a consensus with respect to God's response to same-sex relationships. . . . However, in the process of engaging these dynamics, we did find that we could find consensus on other aspects of the conversation, namely a commitment to chastity, monogamy, etc. In other words, whether gay or straight, we agreed that sex is reserved for the covenant relationship of marriage. . . . We recognized that, while each of us held strong beliefs, we also acknowledged that the issues in question were not as clear cut as we had originally considered. . . . We also realized that there are many other significant aspects of theological and moral beliefs where different members of the community believed very differently. Those issues, however, did not divide us. We were willing to live with those differences—never denying or ignoring them, but never allowing them the power to divide us. Could we do the same with this reality? In the end, this is what we decided to do. . . . Let me be very clear at this point: We did NOT accept a position of moral relativism on this point. We believe that God has absolute wisdom and expectations for His people with respect to sexuality. However, we could not, with full confidence, say that we knew what that was without a fair amount of uncertainty. Further, we have, as a community, taken positions on other issues where others have chosen to leave our community as a result. In other words, this response is not simply an easy way to avoid uncomfortable confrontations. There are people in our community, even on our core leadership, who believe differently about this. While we are respectful (given that this is primarily a pastoral issue, not simply a theological one), we are also open and honest about our differing perspectives. Further, we are not blind to the complications that this raises. What if I, as the pastor, do not believe it is right? While I may be willing to worship with my gay brothers and sisters (and I should note here that we unanimously affirm they are Christians), would I be willing to perform a wedding for two members of the same sex? What about teaching on sexuality? Can we truly teach both perspectives without being hurtful and/or alienating? We are . . . not done exploring these questions. . . . Interestingly, it is the very fact that we have differing perspectives on the topic that has made our community a safe place

for some of our gay members. Why? Because they know that we do not hold our position(s) out of ideology.[3]

I have encountered some church leaders who attempt to communicate generous spaciousness by declaring that they "don't have a position on this issue." My word of caution here is that if you actually do have a position, but you are trying to hide behind saying that you don't, that will get sniffed out pretty quickly by those who are very familiar with this complex conversation. You are better off simply communicating your position and demonstrating through relationship the way that you want to be open, welcoming, and hospitable. The only real way you can say you have "no position" is if you are able to acknowledge that Christians come to different conclusions on the matter of committed gay relationships and that your church is open to journey with people regardless of their position.

Preaching and Teaching Style

The preaching/teaching style of a pastor has a significant impact on the congregation's experience of generous spaciousness. There are two typical models of teaching in the church. One common model has the leader presenting the truth while the followers try to absorb and apply it. Another style of teaching refrains from giving answers and focuses instead on raising questions and encouraging discernment. A focus on discernment invites interaction and mutuality. In an age where cynicism is high and people are leaving institutionalized religion behind, I believe this model of teaching offers hope to reengage people in the quest for faith. Those on the verge of leaving the church do not want to be told the answers. They want to be invited into the conversation of seeking what is life-giving, truthful, and consistent with the person and ministry of Jesus.

Acknowledging different perspectives and extending the invitation to search out one's conscience and convictions help to welcome people to find their place in God's story. In the process, we can trust that the Holy Spirit is more than able to guide people rightly and to correct them when needed. This kind of teaching connects to the desire for a journey that is real, that is traveled in generous and spacious places marked by unconditional love rather than fear, threats, or coercion.

It does, however, require that the teachers and preachers among us let go of a lot of the control that they may be accustomed to. If this control is relinquished as an expression of trust and dependence on the Holy Spirit, we can be confident that God will build his church through the lives of the individual disciples he loves.

Time to Transition?

Despite genuine efforts to nurture an environment of generous spaciousness, there may be times when separation is the best way to move forward. If a church does have a clear boundary related to same-sex relationships, a gay couple may journey for a time with such a church but may come to the point that they discern a need to experience greater freedom to use their spiritual gifts in service within the body. My hope is that their process of discernment will be shared with their community. My hope is that their current pastor will have built relationships with other pastors in the neighborhood in whose congregations a gay couple would be welcome to serve and grow in their gifts and calling. My hope is that if a transition seems to be the best next step, it would take place in the context of community (with both grieving and celebration of past relationships and anticipation and welcome into new relationships). And my hope is that beyond particular congregations, friendships would cross such boundaries, and people would continue to share their lives with one another and be willing to humbly learn from one another.

Outside of personal relationships, I'm not sure there will be tangible growth beyond the current polarity of this subject. Without humility, I'm not sure there will be the kind of spaciousness that is needed to move forward. Apart from entrusting one another to the leading of the Holy Spirit, I'm not sure we'll learn to embody the unity Jesus prayed for.

Because of the diversity, wariness, and weariness experienced by many congregations, I have found it very important to assure pastors and their congregations that the conversation I seek to begin is not proselytizing in nature. I am not trying to convince individuals or a congregation to adopt a particular position. Rather, my focus is to reflect on the posture and ethos of a congregation, with the focus on relational hospitality and nurturing generous spaciousness. This isn't about theoretical doctrines. This is about real people, in their churches and in their neighborhoods, who need to find safe and spacious places to explore and grow in faith in Jesus Christ. Part of that exploration and growth is the ability to be honest about the questions and values and beliefs they are wrestling with, knowing that they will be heard and honored. Listening and extending respect to another person doesn't mean you have to agree with them. It simply means that you trust that in their seeking they are turning their faces toward Christ, and you trust that the Holy Spirit will be faithful to lead them into the life-giving way of truth in their journey with God.

Tolerance vs. Hospitality

The distinction between hospitality and tolerance may be particularly important here. Tolerance often means a somewhat superficial acceptance of everyone's ideas, beliefs, values, and practice. Differences aren't really discussed. There can be a sense of coercion with the concept of tolerance, the feeling that it is being externally imposed. I encounter this when I hear the bitterness in people's voices from within the Christian community whose experience of tolerance has been feeling forced to accept a certain political correctness and being part of systems that suppress expressions of true belief and opinion. Granted, some opinions ought not be publicly expressed because of the damage and hurt they would inflict on others. Nonetheless, resentment simmers when this kind of tolerance stifles the expression of deep convictions.

Hospitality, however, creates a very different environment. Hospitality welcomes the other, the stranger, the one who is different. But inherent in this welcome is the acknowledgment of difference. Instead of difference being superficially expunged, differences can be explored. Hospitality enhances our humanity as individuals and as those called

205

into relationship with one another. Tolerance can flatten our humanity with its expectation of enforced acceptance. But such acceptance will rarely lead to embrace.

When the question is asked, pastors and church members for the most part will exuberantly claim that everyone is welcome at their church. Occasionally, I will hear a more thoughtful reply that says, "I cannot guarantee that a gay person or a transgender person will feel welcome here. I will welcome them—but I cannot vouch for every response they may encounter." We can often hide behind our insistence that we have a hospitable church. But we don't really think about what that means when someone arrives who challenges our comfort and security simply by who they are.

One Sunday night after preaching, I noticed a middle-aged man sitting quietly in the pew. A lot of people had talked with me after the service, and this man had waited a long time. His hesitancy spoke a thousand words, so I slid into the pew beside him and said hello. By this time, we were the only ones left in the sanctuary. Ian had been invited to this service by his cousin, and much to her surprise (and his), he actually came. He told me that he hadn't been in church for years but that he really liked my message. He then blurted out, "Do you think gay men will go to hell?" He was a lapsed Pentecostal, a divorced father, a gay man in great inner turmoil. Ian and I talked a long time in that quiet sanctuary. He promised to email me, and sure enough, on Monday morning there was a long message in my inbox.

Over the course of our conversations that week, Ian asked me if I would help him find a church. He thought he might be ready to give it another try. He was looking for a particular kind of church, one that would be open to the "moving and gifts of the Holy Ghost." I knew that a large church in Ian's area had had some gay and transgender folks visit their church, so I was hoping this might be a good fit for Ian. When I phoned this church, the first person I talked to was in administration and was clearly uncomfortable with the subject I raised. She didn't feel she could answer my question about whether Ian would be welcome at their church, so she referred me to one of the pastors, and I left a message on their voicemail. Two or three days later, he called me back and told me that he was referring me to a different staff person. Finally, I got through to the right person.

I said, "I have connected with a gay man in your area who is interested in returning to church, would he be welcome?"

"Of course, everyone is welcome." (Pause.) "Is he a practicing homosexual?"

"I don't know if he is partnered or not, I've just met him. He loves the Lord and wants to participate in worship that is alive and filled with the Holy Spirit. Would he feel welcome in your church?"

"Well, he would need to meet with one of our pastoral staff."

"He would need to meet with a pastoral staff member just to come to a worship service?"

"Well yes. They would want to talk with him about homosexuality, and, if he is practicing, they would need to talk with him about repentance."

"So let me get this straight, this man who loves the Lord who hasn't been to church in several years, who is tentatively considering returning to church would need to meet with a pastoral staff person to be confronted about his homosexuality prior to being able to come and experience worship with your congregation."

"Yes."

The Importance of Candid Clarity

Can your church really extend hospitality to gay people if your foundational beliefs state that marriage and sexual intimacy are reserved for the covenant relationship between one man and one woman?

First of all, I encourage you to be relationally focused in all of your discussions on these matters. Make decisions in the context of how they will impact real people. Second, prioritize unconditional hospitality. Third, take the time needed to see how God is at work in an individual or couple in your church. Take time to prayerfully listen for the Holy Spirit's guidance. Discern the timing for a conversation with this person or couple about the boundaries your church believes in. This conversation shouldn't be a blunt pronouncement of limitations. Nor should it feel like a bait and switch: "Yes, you're welcome here"; and then a year down the road, "Oh, by the way, you can't serve as a Sunday school teacher." The conversation about the policies of the church should be exactly that, a conversation. Questions should be invited, thoughts and reflections shared. Discerning and praying together about moving forward in a way that prioritizes the individual's growth as a disciple of Jesus and makes optimal use of their gifts and passions should be the focus.

It is important to be clear regarding what your doctrine and policies say and don't say. No one benefits from a lack of clarity. Consider these questions:

- Would a gay person be welcome to come into a worship service and participate?
- Would a gay couple be welcome to come into a worship service and participate?
- Would a gay person be able to become a member in your church?
- Would this membership be conditional on their agreement with the church's belief about marriage and sexual intimacy?
- Would this membership be conditional on some kind of proof of chastity?
- Would membership for a heterosexual person be conditional on their agreement with the church's belief about marriage and sexual intimacy?
- Would membership for a heterosexual person be conditional on some kind of proof of chastity?

I was consulting with a team of pastors from a multisite congregation that was missionally focused and very engaged with their community. The pastors had relationships with gay people and tried to nurture an environment in the church that was welcoming. We had a conversation with a number of gay Christians, some of whom were currently attending that church. Of the gay Christians present, some individuals were committed to celibacy and shared the church's understanding that marriage was to be reserved for one man and one woman. Others were uncertain about what they believed and were still wrestling with Scripture, tradition, reason, and their experience. Others were open to being in a gay relationship. One individual, a young woman who had grown up in a denomination that was gay affirming, said she hoped to find a partner, marry, and have a family. She understood the church's position and chose to worship there regardless. Her posture was respectful in the sense that she was not on a campaign to change the church's position. She did want to know, however, if she could be welcomed as a member. The honest answer was that she could not because she was supportive of gay marriage.

However, we learned that this was a double standard: straight people who supported gay marriage were not only allowed to be members but also served in leadership. What became clear was that as long as straight people observed an unspoken DADT (don't ask, don't tell) policy about their personal views on gay marriage, they could carry on as fully contributing members of the congregation. But if it became known that a gay person was open to dating a same-sex partner with the goal of marriage, despite currently being single, they would be prohibited from church membership and opportunities to serve.

In my conversations with gay Christians, I regularly encounter those who are open to finding a partner of the same sex who also choose to worship in a church that holds a hetero-normative view of marriage. Sometimes this is because there isn't an affirming church in their area. Sometimes these individuals simply desire to be in a church that has vibrant worship, meaningful teaching, active involvement in their communities, and concern for mission and justice; this is more important to them than an affirming stance, which may come with a more liberal theological bent on other matters. Their hope is that such a church would make space for them. In my experience, I have seen a great capacity for grace and patience in these individuals as they are willing to live in the tensions that arise from differing perspectives. This is not to guarantee that every gay individual in these situations will engage with respectful, gracious maturity. But it does seem to contrast the fear that I hear from pastors who worry about a gay member eroding clear boundaries or setting up an ultimatum. Some pastors seem to be very afraid that extending hospitality to a gay person will result in confrontation, challenge, defiance, and the demand for complete affirmation of gay marriage and ordination of partnered gay leaders. No one can guarantee that this won't happen. But I would submit that it is the exception, not the rule.

In addition, and most important, I want to remind pastors and leaders that we do not own the church—God does. We aren't called to serve the church from a place of fear with our primary focus on protecting our boundaries. We are called to fling wide the doors, to invite to the banquet those on the margins, those who will challenge our comfort and our aversion to getting our hands dirty. Announcing the kingdom is risky business. When our experience of church becomes so predictable and so controlled, one has to wonder how far we've strayed from the calling to be ambassadors of reconciliation to those far beyond the walls of the church.

My family and I have attended a Christian family camp with a group of friends since my children were small. This past summer I found that more than ever I felt like a misfit in this context. The messages in the morning and evening chapels were so certain and so clear. Everyone around me seemed so nice, so content, so glad to absorb the wonderful answers handed down from the male-dominated pulpit. It sounds a bit funny, even now as I recount it, but one particular incident topped it for me. My friend came into chapel late one morning. In his rush and attempt to settle into the flow of worship, he forgot to take his ball cap off. The usher came up the aisle and said, "Take your hat off," then walked away. This minor encounter summed up for me my sense that presumed measures of holiness trumped hospitality. When you worship with the same Christian families over generations, you can perhaps afford to ignore common courtesy and politeness, but it will be a sure way to alienate and drive away those on the margins—cynical and unsure—yet searching for spiritual meaning and connection.

After the hat incident, I wrote on my blog:

The world I live in is chaotic, uncertain, messy, complex. The world I live in will not tolerate the luxury of the theoretical where the Bible gives the principle and you just need to follow. The world I live in demands that you think and rethink and question and yes, even doubt. The world I live in rages in the face of sanitized faith and challenges foundational paradigms that used to lull me through the inevitable paradoxes of life. The world I live in has erased the lines drawn between sacred and secular, saved and lost, sinner and saint. The world I live in is composing a magnum opus to the heart-stopping, outrageously unbelievable unconditional love and acceptance of God that crushes and demolishes the vestiges of self-righteous "us and them." It's a scary world sometimes. It is a wild and risky place. It is a place that invites, yes even insists, on a free-fall into the mercy of God where there are no favorites, where the slackers get the same wage as the keeners, where dignified fathers hike up their robes and haul butt off the porch to meet excrement encrusted losers . . . with no "but" in sight. And it makes us nervous . . . because it seems too good to be true. We somehow want God to be wrathful—because that makes sense to us. We somehow want to hear the boundaries on what makes a "real Christian" because that allows us some tangible security.

And we want to know who is "in" and who is "out." We want to know who is "right" and who is "wrong." We want to know, "Are you on our team? Or aren't you?"

And I feel like I'm walking the precipice with no safety net saying, "Those are the wrong questions."

To me, the questions are, "How are you loving people?" "How are you serving people?" "How are you trusting God to do his work in people's hearts, in his time, in his way?"

So the first priority in considering how your church might engage those outside the heterosexual mainstream is that of patient, relational hospitality. And the truth is such hospitality is costly. It will cost us our comfort, it will challenge our assumptions, it will confront "the way we've always done things." Hospitality will realign us to the reality that church isn't about us. The church exists to be a blessing to those around us. The people of God, as an embodiment of the love of Christ, are to nurture *shalom* in the places and neighborhoods in which God has placed them.

I think a key issue we need to wrestle with in regard to extending hospitality is facing our own fear and our own tendency to want to protect ourselves from the perceived threat of losing our security. A

211

helpful follow-up question is to look at what we are placing our security in. Philosopher and theologian Jean Vanier says:

> When religion closes people up in their own particular group, it puts belonging to the group, and its success and growth, above love and vulnerability towards others; it no longer nourishes and opens the heart. When this happens, religion becomes an ideology, that is to say, a series of ideas that we impose on ourselves, as well as on others; it closes us up behind walls. When religion helps us to open our hearts in love and compassion to those who are not of our faith so as to help them to find the source of freedom within their own hearts and to grow in compassion and love of others, then this religion is a source of life. . . .
>
> It is not easy to strike a balance between closedness, having a clear identity that fosters growth in certain values and spirituality, and openness to those who do not live with the same values. . . . Being too open can dilute the quality of life and stunt growth to maturity and wisdom; being too closed can stifle. It requires the wisdom, maturity, and inner freedom of community members to help the community find harmony that not only preserves and deepens life and a real sense of belonging but also gives and receives life.[4]

Incarnational Living and Deconstructing Privilege

Critical in this quest to deepen a sense of robust hospitality in your congregation is to understand what it means to live as incarnational people. Ever since The Message version of the Bible was published, people love to quote its rendition of John 1:14: "The Word became flesh and blood, and moved into the neighborhood." To move into the neighborhood is to begin to understand what it means to live incarnationally.

A friend of mine is a church planter with a strong focus on local context. She takes her dog for a daily walk in their neighborhood, starting conversations, making friends. She often tells me about the gay people she meets out in her community and of the conversations that emerge. In these conversations, she doesn't say that she is a pastor and usually doesn't bring up church. Their church meets in one of the historic church buildings, and they have developed the stage, lighting,

212

and sound such that it is a hot venue for theater and concerts in their community. Often neighbors make the connection between the event, the building, and the church, and discover that she is a pastor. By this time, my friend has built rapport and trust, and her neighbors will often tell her their stories of faith and being hurt by the church. My friend is careful to never make her neighbors feel like they are a project to her—or an assignment to get another butt into the pew. She is an incarnational friend as she pastors her neighborhood while walking her dog and encountering those who may have no desire to darken the door of a church, but who nonetheless want to talk to her about their prayers, hopes, beliefs, and a yearning for God.

In Philippians 2, we encounter the well-known passage from which we base the theological concept of *kenosis*. *Kenosis* means, in its essence, "self-emptying," such that we are filled with the fullness of God, able to relate to others as God would relate to them. Paul speaks of Jesus as the perfect and complete model of *kenosis*. And he tells us that we should imitate Christ in our relationships with one another:

> Who, being in very nature God,
>   did not consider equality with God something to be used
>   to his own advantage;
> rather, he made himself nothing
>   by taking the very nature of a servant,
>   being made in human likeness.
> And being found in appearance as a man,
>   he humbled himself
>   by becoming obedient to death—
>   even death on a cross! (vv. 6–8)

In the New International Version (above), the text says that "he made himself nothing." The King James Version says, he "made himself of no reputation." In The Message, he "didn't think so much of himself that he had to cling to the advantages of that status." And in the New Living Translation, "he gave up his divine privileges."

It seems to me that this text challenges the heterosexual privilege that pervades many of the discussions in the church around homosexuality. This is something that most straight Christians never give much thought to. But when I speak to gay Christians, they are keenly aware of the ways that privilege and status color the conversations they seek to have within the church.

A common checklist for heterosexual privilege considers that on an ongoing basis as a straight person:

- I can be pretty sure that the people I encounter will be comfortable with my sexual orientation.
- If I pick up a magazine, watch television, or play music, I can be certain my sexual orientation will be represented.
- When I talk about my heterosexuality, such as in a joke or talking about a significant relationship, I will not be accused of pushing my sexual orientation onto others.
- I do not have to fear that if my family or friends find out about my sexual orientation there will be economic, emotional, physical, or psychological consequences.
- I did not grow up with games that attack my sexual orientation, such as, "fag tag" or "smear the queer."
- I am not accused of being abused by my parents, warped, or psychologically confused because of my sexual orientation.
- I can go home from most meetings, classes, and conversations without feeling excluded, fearful, attacked, isolated, outnumbered, unheard, held at a distance, stereotyped, or feared because of my sexual orientation.
- I won't be asked to speak for everyone who is heterosexual.
- People won't ask why I made my choice of sexual orientation.
- People won't ask why I made my choice to be public about my sexual orientation.
- I won't have to fear revealing my sexual orientation to friends or family. My orientation is assumed and it's accepted.
- People won't try to convince me to change my sexual orientation.
- I won't have to defend my heterosexuality.
- I can easily find a faith community that will not exclude me for being in a heterosexual relationship.

- I don't need to worry that people will harass me because of my sexual orientation.
- I won't need to qualify my straight identity.
- My masculinity or femininity won't be challenged because of my sexual orientation.
- I won't be primarily or solely identified by my sexual orientation.
- If I experience a negative encounter with others, I need not ask whether it has sexual orientation overtones.
- I am guaranteed to find people of my sexual orientation represented in my workplace.
- I can walk in public with my significant other and not have people do a double-take or stare.
- I can remain oblivious to the language and culture of sexual minority persons without feeling any penalty for such oblivion.
- I can go for months without being called "straight."
- People do not assume I have engaged in sex merely because of my sexual orientation.
- Nobody calls me "straight" with maliciousness.
- People can use terms that describe my sexual orientation and mean positive things (e.g., "straight as an arrow," "standing up straight," or "straightened out") instead of negative things (e.g., "ewww, that's gay," or "stop being so queer").
- I am not asked to think about why I am straight.
- I can be open about my sexual orientation and not worry about losing my job, getting access to housing, reserving a room at a bed and breakfast, or receiving a critical response in a health crisis.

Some people when reading this list may feel twinges of defensiveness. Perhaps many straight people have never really thought about the status, privilege, and reputation they enjoy simply because of being in the sexual majority. However, when we consider our call to imitate Jesus in our relationships with other people, we find someone who intentionally stripped himself of his status, reputation, and privilege. The divine Son of God emptied himself by becoming human; but Jesus was also

Jewish and male, and relinquished the power of those positions, too. He spoke with women and Samaritans and lepers and tax collectors and intentionally chose to hang out on the margins of society. Emptying ourselves means that those in the majority choose to step outside of the benefits afforded by that majority status.

Jenell Williams Paris, in her book *The End of Sexual Identity*, says,

> In each class I teach related to sexuality, I "come out" as no longer heterosexual. On the one hand, this is inane. I'm happily married to a man, and I'm a mother, an evangelical and Christian college professor, all of which mark me as a heterosexual. I reap the social benefits of being perceived as heterosexual in society and in Christian settings. But, as I tell students in class, I don't want to be heterosexual. I don't want to get life, secure my moral standing or gird my marriage with a social identity that privileges some and maligns others on the basis of inner desires and feelings. Heterosexuality is a concept riddled with problems. I'd even call it an abomination.[5]

Paris taps into something extremely important: if straight Christians hope to live as incarnational friends with their gay neighbors—both in and out of the church—we need to be willing to lay down benefits that we did nothing to receive in order to "move into their neighborhood" so to speak. This means choosing to relinquish majority status, choosing to be willing to be misunderstood, choosing to identify with those who seem "other." It means choosing to not take offense when your actions are misunderstood by others or when the demand is made to stop rocking the boat. Clearly, all of this comes at a cost. None of this is easy to do consistently. And when the push-back comes and the hurt and betrayal come, as they inevitably will, we need to be willing to seek God's grace and strength to persevere in living in the way of Jesus. Even Jesus himself wept in the garden and asked that the cup would be taken from him. But he concluded that he would choose God's way over his own way.

Living as incarnational people among our neighbors, including those who are very different than we are and those who are on the margins, embodies a sense of mutuality. Incarnational people don't "help" others—they identify with them. Incarnational people don't consider what others deserve—they extend dignity and respect to them simply on the basis of their being image bearers of God. Incarnational people remember the words of Desmond Tutu, "If I diminish you . . . I diminish myself." And so they live in a manner that is relationally present and open to all they come in contact with.

Miroslav Volf, in his book *Exclusion and Embrace: A Theological Exploration of Identity, Otherness, and Reconciliation*, asks, "Why should I embrace the other?" His answer:

> The others are part of my own true identity. I cannot live authentically without welcoming the others—the other gender, other person or other cultures—into the very structure of my being. For I am created to reflect the personality of the triune God. The one divine person is not that person only, but includes the other divine persons in itself; it is what it is only through the indwelling of the other. The Son is the Son because the Father and the Spirit indwell him; without this interiority of the Father and the Spirit there would be no son. Every divine person is the other persons, but he is the other person in his own particular way. Analogously, the same is true of human persons created in the image of God. Their identity as persons is conditioned by the identity of other persons in their social relations.[6]

Here we see that when we fail to live incarnationally, when we fail to strip ourselves of majority privilege, we diminish our own sense of identity, our own humanity. This deep awareness of our interconnectedness is the truth that can set us free from social constructions of orientation that elevate some and marginalize others.

Paul, well aware of the cost of living as incarnational people, makes special mention of some intrinsic motivations to spur us on in persevering and being resilient in our commitments to step outside of majority privilege. He begins the *kenosis* passage by saying, "If you have any encouragement from being united with Christ, if any comfort from his love, if any common sharing in the Spirit, if any tenderness and compassion, then make my joy complete by being like-minded, having the same love, being one in spirit and of one mind" (Phil. 2:1–2). He reminds us that we are united with Christ in this endeavor. Every resource that is his is at our disposal in our commitment to live as he did. Not only that, but we have comfort from his love. Nothing can separate us from his love. No matter how many times our best intentions fall by the wayside or we slide back into old patterns, his love is our secure resting place. And not only that, but we share in the mighty working of the Spirit within us. We cannot do this in our own strength and desire. We fail to live out our ideals. We fear the loss of our own status and reputation. We dread the hurt and pain of being cast to the side. But the Spirit is with us, helping us, restoring us, reminding us that we are the beloved of God. And in these firm foundational promises, we reconnect to our own hearts. We reconnect to our own compassion and tenderness. In our hearts, we find that longing for our fellow humans to find equal space to flourish as children of God. And finally, Paul says, remember, don't try to do this as a lone ranger. Do it together. Live this way of erasing false levels of privilege together. Female, male, poor, rich, black, white, gay, straight, transgender,[7] cisgender.[8] Be like-minded, with love for all, united in mind and heart to live this subversive way in a status-driven world.

Navigating Differences and Pursuing Peace

My priorities for engaging the church have evolved to center on core values rather than boundary maintenance. I ask more questions about how to bridge the gaps between our differences rather than trying to promote or defend one uniform position. Bridging the gaps will often require us to be open to and stay present in places of uncertainty. It requires us to be willing to be uncomfortable. It demands that we open ourselves up to change—perhaps not change in our theological perspectives but changes in our attitudes and motivations, and the way we relate to others.

Whether we like it or not, our context is changing. We can stamp our feet and behave like a three-year-old having a tantrum, but that will not change the paradigms of thought around sexuality that are changing and, frankly, changing quite rapidly. In a time of transition, in which we now find both the church and culture, we need a sense of synergy among our diverse responses. In the culture wars of the last generation, we saw plenty of evidence of disunity in diversity. But increasingly the next generation is impatient with this lack of synergy. Not all young people are stereotypically liberal in their theology of sexual ethics, but many are unwilling to perpetuate a sense of enmity among diverse responses.

When I interviewed Tony Campolo for our *Bridging the Gap* DVD series, he said,

> There is a multiplicity of answers to the question [of how gay people can live as faithful Christians], and in the world that we're moving to, we're going to have to face that reality. I spoke at a youth convention of a very significant denomination in the US. The convention of 5,000 youth was meeting simultaneously to the adults going through evaluating the rules and regulations of the church. And [the adults] came out with a very strong statement towards gays and lesbians, saying [the church] would never accept gay marriage. Word drifted over to this youth convention, which was right next door. And [the youth] put their own statement together saying . . . , "We are not going to make a strong statement on this. We are going to be open to a variety of answers, and we don't like that you have come down so strong with one answer. And the last thing we want to say is it's not that long of a time before all of you will be dead." Young people are not thinking the same way as the older people are on this. And they are not necessarily liberal. They are very conservative in many circles. It's just that young people have reached a point where they see something transcending above this issue, and it's the love for Christ that transcends that issue.

Christians need to be reminded to represent Jesus well. Some of the harsh, fearful, critical, demeaning comments that are directed at people with whom there is a disagreement do *not* reflect the character of Christ. This is particularly true in the largely anonymous world of online discussions. If you truly want to learn how to embody hospitality in relating to those who differ from you, then focus your attention on having in-person conversations with people you actually know and with whom you share more than just this topic. All of the tension that we can experience when we disagree is worth it for the sake of our gay brothers and sisters. Honoring them as beloved family members is more important than our own comfort. Regardless of our convictions on Scripture, we need to be willing to consider the ways our attitudes, language, and expectations affect gay people. We realize these things when we actually take the risk, in the context of relationship, to explore this topic with others.

In the church we talk a lot about love and loving each other. But so many things can get in the way of tangibly expressing to someone, particularly someone with whom we disagree, that we really do extend love and care to them. The following list has been adapted from some of Jean Vanier's work[9] and can be helpful for those who genuinely want to stretch and grow in this area.

- See each person's value and beauty. We express love when we demonstrate that we value another person. We can validate someone's value and beauty without necessarily affirming or agreeing with everything they think and do.
- Take the time to understand. Taking the time to carefully listen to why someone believes what they do and to listen to their story is a key way to grow in our understanding. This means we'll avoid coming to quick conclusions, making assumptions, or leaning on stereotypes.
- Invite trust and belonging. Letting another person know that we trust them is a sign that we really do love them. When we embody a mutual sense of belonging it is a sign that we really do love one another, not as a project, not with an agenda, but with a mutual give and take.
- Walk in a spirit of forgiveness. Relationships in which there are philosophical and theological differences can be marked by conflict, hurt feelings, and misunderstanding. So we need to walk in a spirit of forgiveness, eyes alert to how God is at work in the other person's heart but perhaps most importantly in our own heart.

For those who dare to engage new questions around how to relate to gay people, there may be moments when you feel that you just can't stand the tensions or uncertainties of it all for one more minute. The temptation at that moment is to shut down, revert back to uniformity and black-and-white certainty. But in those moments, we have the opportunity to go to the foot of the cross, gaze into the face of Jesus, rest at his feet, listen for his voice, and be filled with his love, patience, strength, courage, and grace to keep moving forward, one step at a time.

The decision to think through different perspectives and engage relationally with diverse people across this spectrum of faith and sexuality should come from a deep desire to embody the love and grace that we see in the person of Jesus Christ. When we believe that God is at work in all sorts of surprising places, we want to have eyes to see what he is already doing. And when we believe that the Holy Spirit truly is more than able to be the energy and motivation behind any transformation or growth in any of us, we have the ability to relate to people where they are, even when they are at a different place than where we are.

Regardless of where anyone is on the continuum of belief and practice in relation to gay relationships, we all need to be challenged to navigate these conversations with a growing maturity. This kind of maturity refrains from lashing out and accusing others as a cover for our own insecurities, hurts, emptiness, or anxiety. This kind of maturity recalls that engaging with the fruit of the Spirit (love, joy, peace, patience, kindness, goodness, faithfulness, gentleness, and self-control) is just as important as a commitment to sexual purity and integrity. And this kind of maturity chooses to move from a self-focused perspective to look for the ways we can serve, bless, and encourage others.

When we long to embody this maturity and to see it develop in others, we quickly experience incompleteness this side of heaven. We all fall short. We all can play the victim from time to time. We all point the finger and blame others, while hiding from our own fear and anxiety. We're all selfish at times and have next to no desire to serve others. There are gaps between who we are and who we want to be.

But in the midst of this mess, we can find grace. And we can find ways to be gracious with one another, giving one another the benefit of the doubt, expecting the best of each other. We are all on a journey.

> Lord, make me an instrument of Thy peace;
> where there is hatred, let me sow love;

where there is injury, pardon;
where there is doubt, faith;
where there is despair, hope;
where there is darkness, light;
and where there is sadness, joy.
O Divine Master,
grant that I may not so much seek to be consoled as to console;
to be understood, as to understand;
to be loved, as to love;
for it is in giving that we receive,
it is in pardoning that we are pardoned,
and it is in dying that we are born to Eternal Life.
Amen.[10]

To be peacemakers in the midst of the diversity and divides within the church is a needed focus in the season ahead.

Jean Vanier says,

> The world is divided into many thousands of more or less hermetically closed groups. *If each group is sure that it is better than others, how can peace ever come?* It is difficult to dialogue with others if we cling arrogantly to the idea that we are right or that our power and technology are a sign of our humanity and goodness. Walls and barriers exist between people because of language, but also because of fear—each group fearful of those who are different, fearful of losing its identity. People resist opening up to others. Aren't we all in one way or another enclosed in a secure group, in our culture, our religion, our family, our network of friends? Family and different types of groups are needed for human growth, but when they become sealed they engender rivalry, conflict, elitism.[11]

How Now Shall We Live Together?

At the congregational level, the call to unity is deeply personal and relational. These are the friends and neighbors with whom you rub shoulders on a regular basis. You pass the peace of Christ to them on Sunday morning. You pray with them, sing with them, serve with them.

You dream with them, hope with them, and long with them for transformation and *shalom* in the community in which you find yourself. You weep with them, you rejoice with them. You celebrate and grieve with them. Unity is not some nice theoretical idea. It is the earthy stuff of everyday life with people you are called to love, honor, and submit to in a spirit of mutuality. Unity is affected by the posture in which you worship, serve, and extend pastoral care to one another.

The ethos of your local congregation affects the tangible expression of unity in the midst of differences of perspective. By *ethos*, I mean the values-shaped environment through which people experience community together. Any given congregation has its own unique ethos, some of which are more conducive to experiencing unity in diversity than others.

Stuart Murray, a catalyzer of church-planting movements in the United Kingdom, describes the specific ethos of church plants as a response to our rapidly changing, post-Christendom, and increasingly post-Christian context. I would submit that such an ethos will also serve us well as we seek to navigate the longing for unity in the midst of our diversity around questions of faith and sexuality. He says, such an ethos will invite an "adventurous spirit of experimentation." This experimentation is not fundamentally about belief or doctrine but rather experimentation in expression, language, style, and paradigm. In such a spirit there is a "freedom to fail," where people are freed from the need to be right, to never make mistakes, or to have it all together. In such communities there is a refusal to adopt the quick, ready-made programmatic solution to the questions and challenges facing the congregation. Rather, the emphasis is on doing the hard work of *listening and waiting* within the community for God to reveal contextualized responses that are birthed and brought to life through the unique group of people—with their particular gifts, talents, experiences, and abilities—God has gathered in that fellowship. Murray goes on to suggest that such an ethos will explore the implications of post-Christendom and thereby recognize the church's "place on the margins," rather than a centralized institution in the community, and willingly inhabit this servant-oriented, powerless position. A church with this type of ethos will be well positioned to engage the unique relationships they will experience with gay Christians and gay neighbors. As a side note, Murray concludes that it is often only church plants that have the flexibility and freedom to embrace such an ethos.[12] But my prayer is that established congregations will prove him wrong. And I can't help but wonder if the conversations around matters of sexuality might not be the catalyst that prompts some congregations to move toward such an ethos. In our current context, such an ethos will enable churches to serve their communities with renewed vitality, responsiveness, and love.

When we focus on nurturing generous spaciousness with those in the Christian community who differ from us, we become part of restoring a unified and loving witness to a watching world. A few years ago New Direction hosted a synchro-blog.[13] We invited bloggers from diverse perspectives and backgrounds to each contribute a post with the following focus: "What positive insights and suggestions can you offer to help us bridge the gap(s) that arise in our conversations at the intersection of faith and sexuality?" We had over sixty bloggers join us. Some writers identified as gay, others did not. Writers came from many different Christian traditions and viewpoints, and some came from atheist, agnostic, or other religious backgrounds. It was a very lively conversation as people visited each others posts and left their comments. A gay Christian pastor wrote,

> We begin by turning our attention and energy to one another; to those on the other side of the gap who are equally committed as we are to meeting in the middle; not in the sense of compromising our convictions but in the sense of approaching the other from a place of compassion and grace that says, "Despite our differences you are my brother, you are my sister. Know me and let me know you." When we who share that same commitment can find a way to come together in Christ then together we can reach out to the edges, to those stuck in their agendas and deafened by their own rhetoric and through our unified spirit and in the Spirit's power and love draw them in.[14]

If churches can wrestle together to find a way to navigate different perspectives in a manner that is loving, respectful, gentle, and caring of one another, then I believe we have hope to influence the many negative perceptions of those outside of the church community. But if we insist on making these differences the line in the sand by which we exclude and judge another's true faith, we will only continue to fracture and fragment our witness. Issues of sin matter. Issues of authority matter. But they are secondary to a shared commitment to welcome and receive the redeeming lordship of Christ in our lives. Our differing hermeneutics, our different emphasis on interpretive priorities, our differing under-standing of justice and equity—while important and significant—are secondary. We are part of the same body, and we are called to humble ourselves, honor brothers and sisters in Christ who differ from us in perhaps many significant ways, and link arms in a shared commitment to be salt and light in a broken world.

13

A Word for Pastors and Leaders

In the world of ideas and concepts it might sound all good and well to extol the virtues of nurturing generous spaciousness in our faith communities, but the rubber hits the road when the ideal meets the reality of people's lives in our congregations, ministries, and schools. In this chapter, I try to be as practical as possible with suggestions for implementing ways to nurture generous spaciousness.

Attributes of a Hospitable Pastor

Nurturing generous spaciousness begins in our own hearts. When we consider the attributes of a hospitable pastor or leader, that is the foundation. Some years ago I was having coffee with a well-respected pastor. He had been part of revitalizing and growing several key churches. He coached other pastors. He taught leadership at a local seminary. I had approached him about serving on New Direction's board of directors.

After praising various aspects of New Direction's work (in particular our support of gay Christians who were seeking to live celibate lives) this older pastor let me know that he was uncertain about board involvement because, he confided in me, the thought of two men engaging in sexual activity was repulsive to him. While I was thankful for his candor, I was rather taken aback by this admission. He had always been supportive and encouraging toward me, regularly asking me how the ministry was going. As we continued to speak, however, it became clear that he was only supportive of the aspects of our work that clearly fit his paradigm—not only of doctrine, beliefs, and ethics, but of how pastoral care ought to be handled. While it is not unusual to encounter straight men who have a rather visceral reaction to the topic of same-sex sexuality, it still doesn't make it right.

In my former days with Exodus, we would explain such a reaction by justifying it as a God-given response to sin. In other words, "we react with repulsion because it is repulsive to God." As I look back, however, I realize that in making that statement, many Exodus leaders that experienced same-sex attraction themselves were essentially voicing their own internalized homophobia and self-loathing. In reality, those who experience such negative, gut-level responses need to be confronted with the truth that gay people are human beings and that through their response they are devaluing and objectifying others. Gay people are not to be reduced to some imagined same-sex sexual act that they may or may not have ever participated in. It is not uncommon for some of the most antigay voices, including many Christian pastors, to draw attention to extremely perverse forms of gay sexual activity that your average, everyday gay person can't imagine ever participating in. Gay couples rightfully protest the comparison of their relatively pedestrian sex lives with such outrageous behaviors.

In a similar vein, it is not uncommon to hear about how disturbed Christians are by the public display of eroticized behavior at many gay pride events. However, there are also plenty of *gay* people who are disturbed by the goings-on at pride parades. I know many gay people who say that pride events do not represent them and their families. Similarly, highly sexualized events that glorify heterosexuality, such as

Mardi Gras festivals, do not represent me or my family. To base one's heart attitude toward an entire group of people based on the extremes of such public events is short-sighted and indifferent to the reality of people's lives.

A leader has to examine his or her own heart. If there is discomfort, it is incumbent upon a pastor to intentionally commit to work through that. You can begin by taking some time for self-reflection. Consider the messages you heard growing up about gay people. Consider any personal experiences you may have had with gay people. If you have obvious negative feelings, you may be able to work through them by intentionally realigning your heart toward gay people in a manner that is consistent with the unconditional love of God. But if the roots of your reaction to gay people seem less obvious, you may want to talk with a counselor about what might be behind some of those feelings. Matters of gender and sexuality are very significant for your own sense of wholeness and your ability to pastor people well. Perhaps this is an opportunity to experience more generous spaciousness yourself as you work through your own internal issues.

For some, there may be a sense of deficiency in one's own masculinity as a male, or femininity as a female, that can be part of the energy driving a negative response toward gay people. Covering up our own insecurities by projecting them onto someone who is different is a normal coping mechanism. But pastors and leaders, particularly, are called to bring such projections into the light. Many heterosexual people, including leaders, have spent little time reflecting on their own sense of sexual identity and/or gender identity. They may be in need of inner work but are able to mask these needs with their competency and confidence. Delving into these matters can be scary. None of us likes to be exposed to insecurities, old wounding, and our own limitations in understanding. Putting resistance and fear aside and stepping into the journey of healing and growth, acceptance, and security can equip a pastor to be used to bring greater freedom and wholeness to others.

A common question that I hear (particularly from male pastors) has to do with the possibility of a gay person who seeks them out for pastoral care becoming attracted to them. When I asked a gay Christian friend about this, he said, "I would tell him not to flatter himself." It seems like stating the obvious, but gay people are not attracted to everyone of their own gender, the same way a straight person isn't attracted to everyone of the opposite gender. If perchance a gay parishioner was attracted to his pastor and expressed that to him, the pastor would need to handle it the same way he would if a woman were attracted to him. When a pastor puts healthy boundaries in place while maintaining a caring pastoral relationship, this can be a model of healthy relating for the church member.

In other situations, the disgust or discomfort that is felt toward gay people has been built on prejudice, bias, and stereotypes. *Prejudice* can be defined as "an adverse judgment or opinion formed beforehand or without knowledge or examination of the facts" or "a preconceived preference or idea." The best way to counteract such prejudice is to become informed about the reality of gay people's lives. New Direction released a DVD series called *Pastors' Conversation: Navigating LGBT Issues and Questions*, which features more than fifteen video interviews with gay Christians. Another helpful DVD, *Through My Eyes*, was produced by the Gay Christian Network; it shares the stories of more than twenty-five young gay Christians. Sometimes I encounter people who are reluctant to hear the stories of gay Christians because they fear being emotionally influenced to change their position to a more progressive stance than they believe the Bible supports. One retired pastor, who felt that he was being called to write a book about homosexuality, interviewed me. He said he wanted his book to be pastorally compassionate toward gay people while exhorting the church to remain firm in holding to a traditional, biblical sexual ethic. He said, "You have to be careful to not love people too much. Loving people changes you." Indeed, loving people does change you. Loving people who are different than you changes you. But it seems to me that such change is consistent with the call of Christ. Allowing your heart to enter the beauty and brokenness of another's life (which really isn't so different from your own), to hear hopes and dreams and disappointments, fears and hurts and joys does change you. One ought not be afraid of that. As you walk in step with the Holy Spirit, you can entrust people to him, you can rely on him for guidance, you can seek his help to guide your words and shape your responses. God can use an open heart. Being enlarged to love people because you better understand your common humanity with them is consistent with growing in the fruit of the Spirit. It is sad, however, that the kinds of messages that have permeated some of our more conservative churches teach people to hold gay people at arm's length.

I was preaching one Sunday morning about befriending and loving the gay neighbors you encounter in your day-to-day life. A woman came up to me after the service and told me about her hairdresser who was gay. She always got her hair done by him and thought he was a nice guy. That week after visiting the salon, she and her two kids went to McDonald's and got the two-for-one sundae deal for the three of them. She had decided to bring the fourth sundae to her hairdresser. As she told me about this, she seemed to want permission and affirmation that she had done the right thing. How is it that the church has so distorted a message of love that churchgoers are unsure of whether bringing an ice-cream sundae to a neighbor is a good thing or not?

One of my colleagues at New Direction encountered a couple whose teenaged son had recently come out. The mother was clearly experiencing a great deal of anguish as she explained that for her, following the Bible's teaching was more important than loving her son. Her son was single and not involved in sexual activity, but since he came out his parents had prevented him from eating meals with the rest of the family; they were applying Paul's teaching (in his letter to the Corinthians) that they should not eat with a sexually immoral brother. Addressing one's prejudices may not mean that your personal convictions about committed same-sex relationships change. What you believe may not change, but *how* you believe what you believe hopefully will.

When examining our own heart, we need to look at how we generally deal with people we disagree with. Are we able to engage in open, honest, and calm dialogue or do these discussions devolve into us trying to convince, persuade, and sway the other to our position? Can we humbly acknowledge that we could be wrong? Are we willing to really listen to the other person with a teachable heart? Do we expect to see God at work in the other person?

Once we have addressed the state of our own heart toward gay people, we need to do our best to educate ourselves. If you've gotten to this point in the book, you've already made a good investment in better understanding the complexities of the intersection of faith and sexuality. But there is much more to consider from scholars in the sciences to better understand gender, sexuality, orientation, and identity. There is much more to dig into in terms of hermeneutics and exegesis. To really serve as a hospitable pastor to gay people means that you commit to be a learner.

As a pastor and a Christian, you may have very traditional and conservative beliefs about same-sex sexuality. But do you know what it is like to have to keep a significant part of yourself hidden? Do you know what it is like to be vigilant every moment you are with your church community for fear that if you let something slip you will experience rejection? Have you ever seen the light return to a person's eyes and a change in their countenance when they are freely able to say, "I'm gay"? Do you understand how to lift the burdens and dismantle the barriers that hinder gay people from more exploring and growing in faith in Christ? It does not mean you must contradict your conscience and change your theological beliefs. But it does mean that you need to hold a posture that is willing to explore hard questions, willing to say you don't have all the answers, willing to allow an individual to make different choices than you want. It means you are willing to focus on equipping that individual to pray, listen to God, engage the Scriptures, and grow in discernment. It means you prioritize, above all else, encouraging the individual to "take God with them" in every part of their journey. It means that you will be willing to explore diverse perspectives with them, not with a sense of coercion, but from a place of deeply entrusting this individual to the leading and guiding of the Holy Spirit. And it means you will have the grace to agree to disagree, without cutting off relationship.

When some leaders engage in this kind of pastoral journey, they do find their conscience affected and their convictions shifting. If this is where you are, I simply encourage you with the words, "Fear not." Don't be afraid of losing your job, your pension, your influence, your friends, or your reputation. "Trust in the LORD with all your heart / and lean not on your own understanding. / In all your ways acknowledge him, / And he will make your paths straight."[1] God will make a way for you. Be strong and of good courage, stay the course of integrity, be prayerful, and wait on the Lord.

Shepherding Your Congregation

As you walk this path, it becomes possible to prayerfully discern how to shepherd your congregation in such a manner that they, too, grow in the grace of being a community of generous spaciousness. One of the most important questions to ask regarding your congregation is, are they ready? You could do pastoral violence within a congregation if they are pushed beyond their readiness to engage such a complex and emotionally charged topic. Exercising wisdom in discerning a congregation's readiness is essential.

Here are some questions to consider when reflecting on a congregation's readiness to have open dialogue about same-sex sexuality:

- Does your congregation have a history of willingness to sacrifice "sacred cows"? Have they demonstrated commitment to move forward for the sake of welcoming others? Do they have a missional heart for their own neighborhood? Do they understand that the church is not for them but for those they are called to reach and engage?

- Is there a sense of "us and them" in your congregation? Do people in the congregation feel like mutual pilgrims in the journey of faith? Are people aware of their own struggles and need for encouragement and support? Are people able to be transparent about the real issues in their lives?

- Is there a healthy level of trust in the leadership and among members?

- How would you describe your congregation's approach to Scripture? Is there a sense of generous spaciousness in conversations around interpretation and application of the text?

233

- What kind of paradigmatic shifts has your congregation engaged in the last five years? How did this process impact the congregation? Was the shift made? Was there resistance? Is there residual fatigue from this process? Some examples of such shifts are: changing worship styles, dealing with women in ministry, navigating divorce and remarriage, and addressing systemic racism by becoming a more ethnically diverse congregation.

- What has been your congregation's response or level of openness to uncomfortable or challenging issues of sexuality? Have you had open conversation about sexual abuse, pornography addiction, premarital sex, or sex education for youth? Are there diverse responses in the congregation, or is there a general sense of openness to address such issues?

- Has the congregation navigated personal experiences together around this matter? Has an individual, known and loved by the community, come out and identified as gay? Has a family had a child come out—and have they openly shared that with the community, or have they kept that fairly private? Has the congregation welcomed people from the community who are gay? In these situations, how did the congregation respond?

- Has there been theological discussion about committed same-sex unions in the past? What was the tenor of this discussion? Were people able to make the jump from theoretical discussion to the reality of people's lives? Were gay people part of the discussion? If not, has there ever been an opportunity for a gay person to tell their story to your congregation?

As you consider these questions, I cannot overemphasize how important prayer is in this process. Not only is the leadership encouraged to pray, but it is important that the entire congregation prayerfully seeks God's guidance in becoming a more open and welcoming place. Times of prayerful listening and waiting will bear good fruit as you submit this journey to God.

As you discern, you may feel that your congregation is ready to have a focused conversation together about how to nurture generous spaciousness and be a more hospitable place to gay people in your community.

234

If so, there are many creative ways to brainstorm, hear people's stories, assess your community, and consider the needs to address and barriers to deal with. You may find that people need the assurance that current theological boundaries are not up for discussion, but that the focus will be on becoming a more welcoming place. In some situations, you may find that there is already a variety of perspectives and that people are looking for the opportunity to explore beyond the current theological position. If this is the case, be encouraged to listen carefully to the variety of stakeholders within your community, including gay Christians in your area.

Perhaps you are feeling that some initial steps need to be taken prior to such an upfront discussion. Certainly, a positive way to begin is to preach and teach on the importance of hospitality in the message of the gospel. Spend some time looking at the stories of Jesus reaching to the margins and engaging with the types of people who were excluded by the religious leaders. It is also helpful to address the matter of how we engage with people we disagree with. This is a great opportunity to spend time looking at the fruit of the Spirit, the virtues, and character development that is needed to be able to respond with maturity and grace. Perhaps another significant area is to look at how the community addresses interpretation of Scripture, including any disputable matters that are relevant to your particular congregation. As you do this kind of preparation, the topic of homosexuality does not need to be the focus but can be touched on as an example.

Engaging this kind of process for your congregation is about more than being better equipped to listen and have open dialogue with gay people you welcome. It is about becoming a more hospitable and mature community, able to be generous and gracious in the midst of differences and diversity, so that you can be a light in your local context.

Moving through this kind of preparation may take longer than you initially expect. Along the way, listen for the stories that emerge. Be ready to offer pastoral care to those who share stories of alienation, hurt, and frustration with the church. Go and seek out the young people and others who have quietly disappeared from your community, have a coffee, and ask for their help in better understanding how the church can be a more hospitable place. Engage the entire community, young and old, in seeking the hospitable heart of God.

When you begin the conversation to specifically open hearts and minds to welcome gay people, not just in theory but in actual real relationships, it will be important to identify the foundation of hospitality that is being built. Hospitality is not about compromise, it is not about tolerance, it is about living the heart of Jesus for everyone in your neighborhood.

It will also be important to create a safe environment for people to share their fears without worrying about being judged or pigeonholed. This may be a season of one-on-one pastoral visits, small groups, or times of prayer. When people are heard, when there is clear information and clear expectations, a lot of fear (based on assumptions) can be addressed. Increasingly, those who hold traditional views are the ones who begin to feel marginalized. They may grieve a loss of influence in the church and culture, they may demand reinstatement of their perspectives as the dominant position of the church, or they may struggle with a sense of hopelessness or resignation. Wherever they are, such folks need wise and sensitive pastoral care as they are invited and encouraged to focus their attention on the person of Jesus, who can be trusted to lead the church.

This may be the time to consider outside resources that can be helpful in engaging congregational members in focused conversation. New Direction's small-group DVD resource was developed with this in mind. It features both gay Christians and pastors, and raises challenging and complex questions at the intersection of faith and sexuality. This may be time to bring in a gay Christian, or a panel of gay Christians who are navigating their journeys in different ways, to share their stories with the congregation and to respond to questions. These experiences aren't meant to promote a particular position but to help the congregation understand and nurture a deeper sense of hospitality that will welcome and include sexual minorities.

Whether the outcome of such a journey is a movement toward greater inclusion of those in committed same-sex relationships or a rearticulation of a welcoming-but-not-affirming position that actually takes the welcoming aspect seriously and intentionally, a question that the congregation should grapple with is, "Would a gay person feel that our church is a place where they can explore and grow in faith in Jesus Christ?" Additionally, a congregation can ask, "Would we as a congregation feel that our welcome and encouragement of gay people is a faithful expression of God's desire for them to experience life and life abundantly in their relationship with him?"

Being an Advocate

The personal reflections of a leader and the commitment to shepherd a congregation or Christian community to be a place of more robust hospitality are important steps for any pastor to take. But there will be other leaders who need to consider whether they are called to be an *advocate* for gay people in this particular season in the life of the church. One might assume that such an advocacy role ought to be filled only by a pastor who holds a clear and fully affirming position. I believe, however, that we need advocates in all parts of the body. For my own purposes, I differentiate between advocacy and activism in this way: advocacy is about people, and activism is about issues. We need pastors across the theological spectrum to prayerfully discern if God is asking them to risk speaking out in their sphere of influence as an advocate for gay people. Regardless of theological position on the appropriateness of committed same-sex unions, gay people need someone who will emphasize the real need for the church to be a welcoming place for them. Gay Christians in a welcoming-but-not-affirming church need an advocate who will speak out about the reality of their faith, their desire to be a fully contributing member of the body, and their posture of willingness to dialogue and honor the position of the congregation.

A pastor or leader willing to be an advocate must possess:

- Conviction: An advocate is convinced that God's unconditional love for all who bear his image calls the church to recognize and create a hospitable environment for those who feel unwelcome.

237

An advocate identifies with those with lower status by being willing to put his or her own status on the line. An advocate believes that the church is impoverished if we do not receive the contributions of our gay brothers and sisters. It requires a sense of calling that God is asking you to raise awareness, challenge hearts, and break down dividing walls.

- Courage: When you speak up for people who are different and who may be perceived to be a threat to the church, there will be a cost. This cost may be your reputation. It may be conflict that arises in your own congregation. It may be push-back from leaders in your denomination. An advocate presses on despite the cost. All of this demands great courage.

- Wisdom: Being an advocate requires that you "be innocent as a dove and wise as a serpent" (see Matt. 10:16). Knowing when to speak and when to remain silent comes from a prayerful commitment to walk in step with the Spirit and to not let your passions be the determining force. Understanding which topics are "essentials" and which are open to challenge will demand wisdom in every unique situation.

- Relationships: Advocates speak out of the context of relationship. They invest in getting to know gay people and gay Christians. Advocates are not driven by a position but motivated by the real lives of people they know, love, and pray for. They speak with an authority that comes from having invested in the pastoral care of gay people.

- Information: Advocates will have a thorough understanding of same-sex sexuality as represented in the current literature and research. They will be well aware of the history and current state of the conversation in the larger church, their own denomination, and their particular congregations. Advocates will be aware of the variety of ministry approaches espoused within the Christian community and be able to articulate a knowledgeable critique of the strengths and weaknesses of each. Advocates will understand and honor the boundaries within their community while presenting a challenge to the status quo in engaging, listening to, and nurturing a spacious place for gay people.

238

The Christian community needs pastors and leaders who will speak out as advocates for a more robust inclusion of gay people. Such inclusion will recognize diverse perspectives and the multiple ways that gay followers of Jesus integrate their faith and their sexuality. This recognition does not demand approval of every choice gay Christians make about relationship and intimacy, but it does acknowledge that pursuit of faith should be encouraged—even when there is disagreement.

I had dinner with a ministry leader the other day. She has been a long-time supporter of my work through New Direction. When New Direction made the transition to embody a posture of generous spaciousness, it was confusing to her. To this leader, either I condoned committed same-sex unions (which she could not in good conscience do) or I disapproved of committed same-sex unions (which she did, but reluctantly). Such a polarized dichotomy does little to equip us for the reality of people's lives. If you actually extend yourself to get to know gay people, you will encounter people with authentic faith or a genuine desire to reengage faith. You will encounter followers of Jesus who have been in long-term, committed relationships. And in their lives you will see good fruit.[2] If you live in an "either/or" world, you must either express your disapproval and hope that people will repent, or you must communicate complete affirmation of gay relationships. If, however, you refuse to capitulate to such a dichotomy, you will find yourself in a more generous space. You will be able to affirm the aspects of faith that you encounter in people's lives, and you will be able to encourage them to continue to move toward Christ. I hope you will also be able to invite them to affirm the faith they see in your life and to receive encouragement from them to know Christ more deeply. Then you will begin to experience life as mutual pilgrims with these friends. And you will know that there are both areas of growth and areas of struggle in each other's lives. Follow the leading of the Holy Spirit as you connect with one another, and you'll live in the freedom of entrusting each other to the Spirit's guiding. It isn't a matter of ignoring the questions of same-sex relationships, it is a matter of submitting them to the Holy Spirit's arena. You can be free to love each person well as you continually entrust them to God and deeply long for them to be close to Christ.

You can be fully confident that God will keep on revealing himself to them—just as he does to you. The focus is people and their relationship with God, not approval or disapproval of positions on committed same-sex relationships. As long as this question continues to play the role of ascertaining another's orthodoxy, gay Christians will feel marginalized by the church. It is not that the question is unimportant. But it is not of *ultimate* importance. Of ultimate importance to God is that every human being has every opportunity to experience God's extravagant, reconciling love through Jesus Christ.

14

A Word to Gay Christians

I encounter a lot of gay Christians who are looking for help in finding a church or making decisions about where they need to be connected. While I am not a fan of those who "church shop" simply to find the fellowship that meets their needs or suits their tastes, I do recognize the importance of a good fit for the gay Christian who is seeking to grow in faith in the context of community. This search also begins with one's own heart.

Finding a Church

When considering what church to connect to as a gay Christian, you need to have a clear sense of where you are in your own journey. Has faith become a vibrant part of your life that you own for yourself? How does faith shape your identity? How does your faith impact how you work through (or have worked through) questions about your sexuality?

241

When you consider faithful discipleship as a gay person, where do you find yourself: Are you committed to refraining from a consummated same-sex relationship? Are you confident about pursuing a same-sex relationship? Are you still wrestling with God and Scripture to know whether the future may include a same-sex relationship? Are you in a committed same-sex relationship?

When I meet with young, single gay Christians, it is common to encounter some degree of uncertainty about being in a same-sex relationship. This is an important part of one's spiritual journey, and many will say that their struggle brought them closer to God and taught them to rely on God and trust him more. So if this is where you are, it may be helpful to see this not as a question to resolve, but as part of the journey in coming to know God and yourself as you experience intimate relationship with him.

As you reflect on where you are in your faith journey and in the process of integrating your faith with your sexuality, you can then begin to consider questions about a potential church. For better or worse, the tone and ethos of a church may be significantly impacted by the leadership. When you meet with a pastor of a potential church, it is not particularly helpful to immediately ask for his or her position on same-sex relationships. It may not even be that helpful to ask about the church's position on same-sex relationships. These kinds of questions are closed ended. You might get an answer you like or don't like, agree with or don't agree with, but you won't really get much of a conversation. Closed-ended questions are the ones most pastors I know dread. They dread them because they don't give much of a chance to show you their hearts or to express the kind of journey that they hope that their congregation might participate in with a gay Christian. Pastors may feel cornered and potentially disregarded by such a question. They may feel you are turning these questions into your own litmus test. I would guess that you don't appreciate it when Christians reduce you to the answer you give to the question of whether you believe God blesses same-sex relationships. So if you are really considering whether this church might be a place for you, you'd be better off asking the pastor more open-ended questions that will invite the two of you to actually have a conversation together.

One such conversation starter is to ask about the ways diversity is embraced in the congregation. Ask about the kinds of people who gather in fellowship. Ask about how they navigate differences between people. Ask about whether the community is open to learning from other people's backgrounds and experiences in their corporate worship. Ask the pastor what some of the challenging conversations have been of late in the congregation and how the group worked to come to consensus or resolution. You could ask if there are specific topics the pastor would recommend you listen to in their sermon archives as examples of how this congregation addresses challenging subjects. The responses to these kinds of questions, and the opportunity to hear archived sermons, will give you a better sense of the pastor's heart and the tone of conversations within the church community.

You will want to hear from the pastor, and experience firsthand by a visit to the congregation, the priority placed on hospitality and the genuineness of the welcome for those who are new. Part of the ethos of hospitality you will want to explore is the comfort level and sense of safety in being honest and transparent. Do people feel free to share what is going on in their lives? If people disagree about choices others are making, is there a safe environment in which to discuss differences and give one another space to wrestle through their discipleship journeys? Would disagreement be threatening to others in the congregation?

It is important to have a sense of your own spiritual gifts and the areas of the church to which you feel most called. You will want to know if your passion and desire to serve are warmly welcomed rather than viewed with some level of hesitation. If children are your passion, would there be any reservation to you being involved in nursery care or Sunday school leadership (following regular safety protocols, such as background checks)? If music is the primary way you express worship, will joining the worship team be encouraged? Are there community outreach programs you can be part of? Is there an opportunity to mentor and encourage youth by serving in the youth ministry? Some of the gay Christians I've talked to have said that once they came out and indicated they were comfortable identifying as gay, they were removed or prevented from serving. These are hurtful decisions that can cause an individual to feel marginalized in the church. It can also negatively affect a person's spiritual journey. There may be hurt and resentment that needs to be processed or that an individual finds difficult to process and release. Additionally, serving others is one of the ways we grow as we learn to trust God, grow in the fruit of the Spirit, and see God's hand at work. Being involved in using your gifts, growing in your sense of calling, and serving others is an essential part of belonging in a faith community.

If the church you are considering is part of a larger denomination that you are unfamiliar with, you may want to have a conversation that brings you up to speed on the history of discussion around the inclusion of gay Christians. You may want to read any denominational position statements. But it may also be important to understand how much autonomy each congregation has in its local context of mission and ministry.

One thing to consider asking the pastor is if there has been any previous political involvement on the part of the congregation or leaders within the church. For example, was the congregation encouraged to sign a petition either against or in support of gay marriage? Is the pastor or congregational members involved in any activism on social issues? Where and how does the congregation address matters of injustice? The responses to these kinds of questions will help you to discern the ethos of the congregation.

Each gay Christian has their own unique journey. This is evident in the choices individuals make about the church they will attend. Finding a church where you feel you can become fully engaged will be a positive step toward sustaining a deep and committed faith. Whether that choice is an affirming church or a church that is intentional in extending hospitality, make sure that you will have a spacious place to continue to grow in Christ. Encountering a pastor who is willing to listen and dialogue may be an important factor in the decision-making process. No church is perfect. In fact, it is the imperfections of our churches that can afford us important opportunities to grow. As we persevere in walking a "long obedience in the same direction" within a fellowship, despite the weaknesses and friction points, we can find ourselves enlarged in our own ability to extend hospitality, grace, and forgiveness.

Should I Stay or Should I Go?

Unfortunately, there are some church environments that tip the balance from being spiritually formational to being spiritually dysfunctional or even abusive. I encounter a lot of gay Christians who have very serious and painful questions about how to discern when it is time to leave a church. Individuals who take their faith seriously often agonize about this decision. Many individuals wrestle with guilt and a nagging sense of selfishness when considering leaving. Others wonder if they are supposed to stay and be agents of change to help their church become more welcoming in extending the good news of the gospel to gay people, even though the current environment is detrimental to feeling like a fully contributing member.

These questions may be helpful in discerning whether to stay or leave your current church:

- Is God still using you in this congregation? Have you had the opportunity to encourage and help stretch leadership and congregational members in their understanding of gay people? Have you remained closeted in the congregation even though you have sensed some nudging to take the risk to speak more honestly about your experience of same-sex attraction? Do you feel that your place in the community is focused on your sexuality in a way that you feel trapped? You may want to ask trusted friends to pray with you as you seek to listen for God's response.

- Are you stalled in your spiritual and personal growth? Is this because of external or internal limitations or barriers? Might there be an opportunity to build your character by working through bitterness and resentment?

- Is it toxic and spiritually damaging for you to stay? Are you encountering systems of fear and shame rather than a foundation of love and trust? Are the power systems inconsistent with your best reading of Jesus's model in Scripture?

- Have you exhausted attempts at dialogue with leadership? Sometimes our perceptions become our reality, even though we haven't actually pursued a better understanding. It may be important for you to meet with your pastor or leader prior to making your decision, to ensure that you have given them the opportunity to hear you, and for you to feel that you have done your best to articulate what you need to feel safe and like a fully contributing member of the church. In these kinds of conversations, sometimes we realize that our expectations have been unrealistic. But we may discover that we can come to a consensus about next best steps toward a shared goal of a more hospitable and spacious environment in which you can continue to grow and thrive spiritually.

- Can you bless and wish this congregation well if you leave?[1] If you feel that you can't, you may need some help to work through past hurts, or there may be internal work to do on issues of unforgiveness. It may be helpful to work with a counselor (not from that particular church) so that you will be able to have clarity about releasing or reengaging with the congregation.

No one can really answer the "shall I stay or shall I go" question for you. If you have come to a place where you are open to a same-sex relationship or are beginning to date, integrity may compel you to transition to an affirming congregation. If you know that your dating will cause disruption and conflict in the congregation, you may choose to leave because of your love for the church. If you know that your relationship will cause you to be removed from positions of service, you may choose to leave to be able to engage in service with another congregation. If you do choose to leave, I encourage you to include your pastor in the transition process. If they are open, involve them in praying with you as you seek a new community to join. If they are willing, try to arrange a time for them to meet your new pastor with you. Wherever possible, try to nurture open and positive relationships for the sake of unity in the body of Christ. Once the transition has been made, guard your lips and do not speak badly of your former church. In as many creative ways as possible, try to honor the congregation you have left. If you can initiate any collaborative partnerships between the two congregations, that may be a way for God to continue to use you and help you to nurture ongoing relationships. This may call for a depth of humility on your part, but the fruit of such extensions of grace will be a living demonstration of the unity Jesus prayed for.

A Word to Would-Be Gay Advocates in the Church

On a regular basis, I receive emails from both gay and straight people who sense a passion and a calling to help the church be a more hospitable and safe place for gay people to explore and grow in faith in Jesus Christ. Perhaps this book has stirred you to communicate a message of generous spaciousness in the churches in your area. I hope that you feel more optimistic and confident that the church can find a way to move forward in the midst of diversity while honoring the fact that people hold different convictions about committed same-sex unions. I pray that the vision of embodying a *posture* rather than a polarizing *position* will help people live in the tension of their own beliefs (or uncertainty), their high regard for the Scriptures, and their desire for the church to extend a hospitable welcome to our gay brothers and sisters.

Do I Love the Church?

But if you're going to try to serve the church with this kind of message, you need to be aware of some key issues. The first question to ask yourself is: Do I love the church? Many people who write to me wanting to be advocates for gay people in conservative, evangelical churches have an unmistakable love for gay people. The challenge is whether or not they love the church as much as they love their gay friends. Sometimes people want to be an advocate for gay people because of the anger and hurt they have experienced in the church. So it is important to check your own heart for resentment, unhealed wounds, defensiveness, or anger.

Additional questions to consider on this topic of loving the church: How do you currently see yourself as part of the church? How are you serving your own church? What can you affirm about the churches you want to engage? In what spirit do you come? As you consider these questions you may need to do a humility check. If you feel that you are coming to the church with the belief that they are stubborn, traditional, homophobic, or self-focused, you will sink before you even try to swim. Engagement with the church needs to come from a servant heart, a loving heart, a respectful heart, and from a deep and abiding commitment to honor Christ by serving his people.

Do You Understand the Church?

The second area of consideration is understanding: Do you understand the church? It isn't enough for you to understand gay people or the diverse theological perspectives on the question of same-sex relationships. You need to understand the particular churches you hope to serve. This requires a willingness to do your homework. This may include researching the particular denomination of which that congregation is a part. It may mean looking at the history of how homosexuality has been addressed in the denomination and in that church. You may need to become familiar with how the leadership structures function and how decisions are made so that you access the appropriate channels when you offer to engage or catalyze conversation on this topic.

You may also need to do some homework regarding the best potential entry point in a given congregation. Ask yourself, "Where is this conversation likely to be best received?" Would it be the youth group? In some churches that is a great place to begin; for example, a church where the youth are asking these questions, and the youth leader is comfortable with being out of the box and pushing the envelope a bit. In other churches, this is the worst place to begin. You can break trust if parents feel that you have begun a conversation without informing them or that they feel is too challenging for their vulnerable youth. One of the best ways to ascertain an effective entry point is to build a relationship with a champion from within the congregation. This will be someone who cares about the subject and will support you and encourage leadership to let you share your passion for hospitality with their church. This person will understand their congregation and may be invaluable as a prayer and discernment partner as you search for the best way to find an open door. This may be the pastor (which is great), or it may be someone who can help connect you with the pastor.

What Is Your Approach?

The third area of consideration is your approach. As urgent as you feel the task to be, it is critical that you commit to wait on the Lord for his timing. You cannot force this work to happen. A rushed and anxious pushing will not bear good fruit. When you think about a church you are hoping to serve, start by considering if you actually know anyone in that church. It is my conviction that serving the church in this area of advocacy must be built on relationships. And relationships take time.

Understanding a church also takes time. How will you be able to hear this church's story? How can you be sensitive to the priorities and commitments of this church? Just because this is a passion of yours, does not mean it will suddenly become priority number one for the entire congregation. Have you considered what risk initializing this conversation may present the church's leadership? I sometimes joke that as a guest speaker, I get to shake things up and then go home while the local pastor has to shepherd the people through the mess. (But I never make that joke in a church if I think that there is real conflict there.) I want to serve the church, and I want to serve the leadership of a church with a shared goal of the congregation moving toward a mature hospitality that nurtures safe and spacious places for anyone on the margins to explore and grow in faith in Christ. That is why it is important for me to ask what kind of follow-up support I can offer to any presentation or meeting that I participate in. When you think about your approach, you will want to quickly reconsider sending mass emails or form letters to every church in your area or making cold calls or drop-in visits. This is work that demands significant investment, ongoing relationship, humble willingness to wait for the right timing, and ongoing commitment to love, serve, and support a congregation in its journey to stretch in its capacity to be more welcoming and inclusive to gay people.

What Credibility Do You Offer?

The fourth issue is that of credibility. Ask yourself, "What credibility do I offer?" I recently had a gay Christian ask me how important I thought credentials were. He was considering going to seminary for a master of divinity because he thought that might help him in his desire to be a bridge-builder in the church. I described for him some of my concerns. On one hand, I know that letters behind a person's name don't necessarily demonstrate credibility or even competence, and I find myself resistant when I consider how higher education can create false divisions between people and perpetuate a sense of elitism. But I am also aware that the nature of this subject raises the issues for pastors and leaders of who they can trust to serve their congregations well. Credentials such as seminary education can indicate at least a minimum of study and critical thought. But certainly credibility to serve as an advocate ought not be solely based on educational accomplishment.

So when you think about the credibility you can offer, ask yourself, "Why should a pastor trust me to speak to the congregation?" Maybe you are gay yourself and have the credibility of your own journey. Maybe you're the parent of a gay child. Andrew Marin, author of the book *Love is an Orientation: Elevating the Conversation with the Gay Community*, begins his story by describing how three of his best friends came out to him within months of one another. But the real credibility comes when Andrew tells of his commitment over the last nine years to live in Boystown, a part of Chicago with a large population of gay people, to learn how to incarnate the love of Christ for his gay neighbors. What do you bring to the table in addition to your passion?

You might also ask yourself what partnerships you can help a church build on its journey to better understand and grow to be a hospitable place. Have you volunteered with any ministries or gay organizations in your area? Can you connect a church with another congregation that is also working intentionally to grow in this capacity? Can you connect them with a variety of resources that will help continue the conversation? If you aren't able to develop your own resources (and you don't want to reinvent the wheel anyway), have you built a relationship with the organizations and ministries whose resources you want to recommend? Are you confident in the scope of the resources you are suggesting? All of this is part of the credibility question—and without credibility, you will make little headway in your goal of serving as an advocate within the church.

What Is My Message?

If you have made it through these four issues, it may be that you find yourself ready to serve a congregation. If so, the next question to ask is, "What is my message?" You may plan to encourage a church to be more hospitable to gay people and keep it that simple. But the reality is that nothing is ever simple when it comes to the church and homosexuality. You may have no intention of making statements about controversial aspects of this conversation, but people will still want to know or make assumptions about your message regarding: civil equality for gay people, the causation of same-sex attraction, the possibility of orientation change, current political and cultural issues in your area, questions of church polity or congregational policy, and gay marriage. I encourage you to think through each of these matters very carefully and have a clear sense of your own heart and mind. That is not to suggest that all of these issues need to be included in any advocacy initiatives you attempt, but to encourage you to be prepared to encounter both questions and potential accusations regarding these things. Do not be surprised if people seem suspicious or expect that you have an agenda regarding these issues. That is par for the course in this polarized arena of conversation. If you are trying to express a willingness to live with tension on some of these matters, many people will be frustrated and demand a clear positional answer. You will need to pray and think through how you will respond to orthodoxy tests in the variety of contexts you may find yourself in.

New Direction has always had a policy of not getting involved in political activism. This means that when gay marriage, for example, was being debated by the Canadian parliament, New Direction did not testify, start petitions, or lobby on any side of the issue. Our concern was to maintain an open door to those across the spectrum of diversity to approach us with pastoral care needs and concerns. But regardless of our clarity on our noninvolvement in the debate, we were nevertheless regularly questioned about our position on the matter.

In one question-and-response session, I was asked for my opinion about the mayor of Toronto not participating in the Gay Pride events that year. Sometimes when you are confronted with these kinds of questions, you might feel like you are in a no-win situation. Whatever your response, you are likely to have supporters and detractors in the audience. The most important thing to remember is to try to model and embody the very postures that you are trying to communicate to the church. Be as hospitable and open to the questioner and the audience as you can be. That means that it will be important to keep your own emotions in check. Do not get defensive, no matter how strong the retort or assumption about you may be. Be generous, be gracious, be gentle. It is okay to say that you do not have an answer to a particular question—but don't hide behind that as an excuse. It is okay to say that your focus is on serving the church in the quest to become more hospitable and welcoming to gay people. But be sure to do your homework and do some critical thinking on these other matters as well. It can be helpful to be able to point to other scholars or practitioners who work in the area that has been raised. But remember that in your response to every question asked, you are trying to open the conversation, to encourage people to listen well—perhaps to ideas and perspectives that may be different than their own—to build up the church and advance the gospel to those who need to hear the good news of reconciliation in Christ Jesus. As often as possible in your responses, you should point back to the centrality of Christ.

Working for Peace

When you are entrusted with the work of advocacy, you have the opportunity to be a prophet of peace. Philosopher and theologian Jean Vanier says,

> We work for peace every time we exercise authority with wisdom and authentic love. This love is not sentimental; it reveals to people who they are, enabling them to make choices and to follow their consciences. It is listening to people and appreciating them just as they are. We need to become humble servant-leaders in order to help others grow in knowledge, wisdom, freedom, and responsibility, so that they may become, in the depths of their beings, more human. When we love people, we liberate them. Prophets of peace are those who in their person and attitudes do not awaken fear, but open people's hearts to understanding and compassion. They are those who are weak and crying out for relationship. In some mysterious way they are breaking down the barriers of fear in our hearts. We become prophets of peace when we discover our weakness. Here we are touching a mystery. Peace doesn't come from superiority and might. It comes from this power of life that flows from the deepest, most vulnerable part of our being, a power of gentle and strong life that is in you and in me.[1]

If you would work to see the church become a safe and spacious place for gay people to explore and grow in faith in Jesus Christ, be prepared to relinquish power and any sense of superiority. Discover your own weakness, the limits of your own love, your own need for a safe and spacious place; discover afresh what it means to be a channel of love, willing to be used by the Master. This is the heart of an advocate.

Concluding Thoughts

Living into Incarnational Postures

In 2007 I read the book *Intuitive Leadership* by Tim Keel. As someone whose Myers-Briggs personality profile takes me off the charts on the intuitive scale, I expected to resonate with it. Keel introduced me to the language of "posture," and it changed the way I viewed the role of the ministry of New Direction in the contentious and complex landscape of faith and sexuality. I was profoundly weary of the polarity and enmity in church and culture on the topic of homosexuality. I wanted to opt out of the "win-lose" setup that pitted conservatives against liberals. I needed a new way to articulate the heart of the ministry without triggering the knee-jerk reactions and shut-down valves that are so common in the discussions around faithful discipleship for our gay brothers and sisters.

After so many years of engaging churches and having coffee with gay people, my priorities had become fairly simple. I wanted to foster a spacious place for those outside the heterosexual mainstream to explore faith. I wanted to encourage disciples in local, contextualized communities. I wanted to dismantle the negative perceptions of those outside of the church. And I wanted to nurture *shalom* for the common good where the issues of faith and sexuality touch the reality of people's lives.

I longed for the goodness and love of God to flow into the lives of gay people and for grace, humility, and generosity to flow into the conversations in the church. But it seemed that wherever I turned, people cared only about what position I held.

Keel says,

> We all have ways that we posture ourselves in life based on how we interpret our environment. It doesn't end with people. Institutions and organizations likewise adopt postures toward the environment around them based on what they have experienced in the past and now believe in and about the present. And these postures we assume are not supplementary to something else. They are a way through which we engage the world—both what we perceive as well as what the world perceives of us. They impact our lives, personally and corporately, in profound ways. These postures reveal something of who we are at the core of our identities and influence what we communicate, verbally and nonverbally, and conversely what we are able to hear.[1]

My experience has shown that the posture of much of the church toward engaging the conversation of faithful discipleship pathways for gay people is a hardened, defensive posture of avoidance. This posture is understandable. Churches have often felt under assault from a secularized or activist push toward a position that they believe is inconsistent with the perhaps difficult but truthful reading of Scripture. This hardened posture, however, preempts the potential of life-giving conversation that could offer space to wrestle, breathe, explore, dialogue, disagree, or live in tension. And this is what I was discovering gay Christians most need. Many of the gay Christians I was in conversation with were not demanding wholesale movement to a fully affirming and inclusive stance. There were those who were uncertain of such a stance even for themselves. What they did desire was space, a safe space without judgment, accusation, condemnation, assumption, and rejection. They desired a generous spaciousness to embrace authentic faith while engaging the quest for an honest, godly, and fulfilling life as a gay person.

Because such space has so often not been the experience of gay Christians, there are those who hold themselves in a guarded, cynical, bitter, or negative posture toward the church. This posture may hide the tender, vulnerable heart that wants a place to belong and be accepted among God's people. It is a posture that makes it hard to trust. This posture is understandable too. But it also makes it difficult to experiment with sharing hospitable space together and exploring new conversations that focus more on Christ and less on who is right and who is wrong.

One year, as New Direction's annual celebration was nearing, the musical artist who was to perform at the event called me to follow up on some details. Then she said, "So I invited one of my lesbian friends to come to this gig—and I was pretty surprised by her reaction. She said that she knew about you and that you were antigay because you expected all gay people to be celibate. I asked her how she knew that, and she said that she'd heard you speak in a church eight years ago." The artist went on to say that she was disappointed by her friend's reaction because, she told her, "I'm a very different person than I was eight years ago, and maybe Wendy is, too." Regardless, the lesbian friend wasn't open to reconsider coming to the event. I explained to the artist that while this kind of reaction was always sad and disappointing for me, it was not surprising. The understandable posture of her friend was to mistrust that I would be a safe and hospitable person. This is the common tenor of interaction between those perceived to be conservative or antigay and those more progressive or affirming. The postures we hold color how we hear one another; they color our ability to extend the benefit of the doubt; and they color the opportunity to enter into meaningful dialogue.

The historical posture of New Direction, despite our more moderate Canadian context, was perceived to be fundamentalist, ex-gay, traditional, and in opposition to the tide of a gay-affirming paradigm. I knew that this needed to change if we had any hope of actually engaging the men, women, and youth I believed God was calling us into relationship with. But on the flip side, if we were perceived to be overtly gay affirming, I knew that we would lose the opportunity to continue to engage with the many churches that needed to have more conversation on this matter. To try to stay in conversation with both gay people and with the church felt like a nearly impossible task.

Learning

The language of *posture* seemed to hold some promise to help us live out our desire to love and serve the church in its response to gay people and to love and serve gay people in their response to the church. In his book, Keel speaks about key shifts in posture he had made in the local context of Jacob's Well, the community he pastors. The postures he seeks to incarnate are in many ways about being open to creativity and a Spirit-ignited imagination. As a leader, Keel wants first to embody a posture of *learning*. This means moving from a focus on giving answers to a focus on asking questions. This means that as a leader, he relinquishes the mantle of expertise and breaks down the barriers between the leader and the community. What Keel discovered is that this seems very much to be the posture that Jesus embodied. Jesus often responded to questions with another question. Keel says, "It takes a lot more *depth*, *presence*, and *creativity* on the part of the leader to ask a well-informed, sensitive, and sincere question that engages the person on the other end of the relationship."[2]

I knew that this is what God had been showing me in the pastoral care and spiritual direction I'd been offering to the variety of gay individuals I was encountering. Not only was I not the expert with all the answers, I didn't want to be. I wanted God to be in control. I wanted God to lead each individual in the way they should go. I wasn't even same-sex-attracted—so who was I to presume to know God's heart for the particular steps in their particular journeys? I learned to ask better questions as I learned to listen much more closely to the working of the Holy Spirit. I knew that this was a posture that needed to be associated with the ministry of New Direction.

Vulnerability

The second posture Keel speaks about is a posture of *vulnerability* that takes us from living inside our heads to living from our hearts. The inheritance many of us are reaping in our churches is an inordinate reliance on our cognition to rightly assess God's direction for our lives through our reading of Scripture. There can be the feeling that our emotional intelligence, those things that arise from our hearts, is suspect. I will often hear from Christians, both gay and straight, who say that they feel they can't argue their position of what they believe about a faithful journey for gay Christians—but they just know it to be right and true. They also know, however, that if they were to express this in the context of their church, they would quickly be silenced with the admonishment that we can't rely on our feelings, we have to rely on the Bible. Perhaps a more open and integrative response, however, acknowledges that we need both our heads and our hearts. Keel says,

> Ignoring the heart for very long is always dangerous because we are emotional and relational people. The heart always finds a way to get what it needs: legitimately or illegitimately. . . . The heart is not engaged or satisfied in the same ways the mind is. It cannot be domesticated, or at least if it can, it is only at great cost and is often the result of violence. To engage the heart, your own and other's, you must be present, and that can be incredibly hard for many of us because it means engaging pain.[3]

Some have described this pain as *cognitive dissonance*, the tension of feeling in your heart something to be right but not being able to square that with what you have been taught about Scripture's position. By adopting a posture of vulnerability, you create space where people don't have to bolt the doors of their hearts. A posture of vulnerability means that people can express the things that arise in their hearts without fear of mockery or accusation. In connection to the first posture of learning, this may raise more questions than it answers—but this posture has room for this kind of searching and wrestling as an intrinsic part of the spiritual journey.

Availability

The third posture is one of *availability*. This posture is particularly calling leaders to a place of formation where they move from spoken words to living words. Here Keel refers to biblical prophets whose entire lives became the actions of God as they laid on their side for a year, walked around naked, or married a prostitute. Though I have not moved into an area of my city known for its large population of gay people, a part of my calling over the last ten years has been to do my best to see with the eyes and hear with the ears of a gay person. Particularly in the context of church or Christian resources, I will consider how a gay person would hear this, what it might trigger for them, and how it might make them feel. While I cannot presume to understand things from a gay person's perspective, especially given the tremendous diversity of experience among gay people themselves, the discipline of this exercise has made me more available to be formed and shaped by God to serve this population. My ministry is focused less on trying to teach the scriptural formula for what faithful discipleship for gay people is, and more about living with my gay friends in the pursuit of faithful discipleship. This means discipleship is much more integrative and holistic than a reductionistic focus on sexuality. As I identify with my gay brothers and sisters in Christ, together we wrestle with how to swim upstream in a privatized, individualistic, and consumeristic world; we work together to seek to alleviate poverty, pursue justice, exercise good stewardship, and lead simple lives of worship and service.

A posture of availability is about being willing to be formed by living in the way of Jesus. Keel says, "While God might work in and shape a person in many different ways, the most consistent way I have engaged God has come through suffering and pain. When I have chosen to embrace rather than evade or anesthetize pain, I die in order that I might live."[4] As leaders, one of the ways we can embrace pain in solidarity with our gay brothers and sisters is to be willing to take the heat for opening up the conversation and challenging status-quo, rigid, theoretical pronouncements. As I have tried to follow God's heart in leading New Direction, I have been accused, rejected, and marginalized by people of influence and power in the Christian community. The ministry has lost credibility with some people of influence. Along the way, we've faced financial stress when donors pulled their support because we weren't stating clear positions that reinforced their beliefs. There were many times I felt scared and unsure and hurt. I did my best to frame these experiences in the greater context of the privilege of serving those who had been marginalized by the church, and while that helped to make meaning of the experiences, it didn't make me feel much better.

But what became clearer over the years is that this posture of availability has blessed me more than I could have imagined. I have grown in a security in the love of God that sustains and grounds me. This, in turn, blesses the lives of those I engage. As challenging as this road at times has been, I am profoundly grateful to have been called to this journey.

Surrender

The fourth posture of *surrender* seems like a well-known Christian principle. I'm sure many Christians share my experience of growing up singing, "I Surrender All." As a kid I used to worry that I'd have to give up my favorite toy or any material thing that gave me pleasure. I'm not sure I ever thought about something as intrinsic as giving up the need to control things. But Keel describes the posture of surrender as moving from control to chaos. Chaos in ministry or in relationships is typically seen as a negative thing. But if we're honest, many of us experience fairly significant levels of chaos. Lives are busy, multifaceted, and undergoing change at a rapid pace. More often than not, in the midst of such chaos we work very hard to re-establish control, to get on top of things, and to bring things back into order. It has been a profound paradigm shift for me to recognize that pausing to be present in the midst of the chaos has allowed me to see the creative spiritual formation that can happen. Clamping down, shutting off the questions, quieting the doubt, or reigning in the desire to challenge the status quo can cause one to gain a false sense of security. But, as I have often seen in the lives of gay Christians, it can be just a temporary suppression of the questions of the heart that refuse to be permanently silenced and that resurface in unhealthy and sometimes downright destructive ways. To live into a posture of surrender means that a leader, an individual, or a community recognizes that the messiness of our lives is the very place God reveals himself and transforms our hearts. If God brought the creation of the world out of the hovering chaos, what creativity might emerge from the tension and mess in our souls and in our communities?

One pastor told me that he had discovered a great metaphor for how his leadership navigated and discerned the Spirit's leading for his newly formed community. He said that a lot of churches have leadership that functions like an orchestra. There are highly competent musicians with different skills who work together as a team under the expert direction of the conductor. The result is beautiful and often flawless music. But his church, he explained, played jazz. That meant that whoever had their *mojo* on (aka moving with the Spirit) would take the lead, with all the other musicians joining in, finding their rhythm, groove, and unique contribution. Sometimes, the music would get kind of funky and sound rather unpleasant and disorganized, but out of this dissonance someone would pick up a new thread, maybe the piano or bass, and carry on with an entirely new riff. The thing about jazz is that expertise is filtered through improvisation. One never knows how long a particular riff is going to last—you can't predict times of transition, you can't plan for who is going to take the lead next, you've got to feel it, you've got to trust your other musicians, and you've got to simply be fully present, with your senses tuned to fully engage the music as it emerges. Jazz is a beautiful example of surrendering to the music and not controlling it.

Cultivation

A fifth posture takes us from being programmers to being environmentalists. It is a posture of *cultivation*. This posture disengages from formulaic expectations to a recognition that nurturing an ethos of authentic community and forming fully devoted disciples takes time and investment in relationship. An environmentalist knows that theoretical linear progression might look good on paper, but it rarely translates into a nice sequential pattern in people's lives. When I first came to New Direction, we offered a variety of program options: individual counseling, support groups, counseling with family members, and informal conversations with those who contacted the ministry. In all these situations—while we would certainly listen to a client's story, goals, and

264

expectations—we always had the clear agenda of helping gay people align with a conservative, traditional understanding, which precluded same-sex relationships. The system was built with an expected outcome: movement toward heterosexuality or (the less desirable but still acceptable alternative) commitment to single celibacy. The system did not welcome any exploration outside of these expectations. When I, rather naïvely, mentioned to another Exodus leader that I helped individuals find gay-affirming churches or organizations when that was clearly in alignment with their convictions and goals, I was chastised with the words, "I would never do anything to help a person live a gay life." Referral to any group that was not in agreement with the stated goals of a program was unthinkable.

If, however, your posture is one of cultivation, there is freedom to consider that it is better for someone to continue to engage with God despite theological differences than to have them walk away from the community of faith altogether. A posture of cultivation trusts that God is more than able to continue to lead and guide an individual into deeper and more intimate relationship with himself.

As New Direction continued to listen and learn, adopting a posture of cultivation meant that we focused less on programs like counseling or support groups and more on organic and flexible investment in relationships. This is not to say that counseling and support groups are wrong or inherently unhelpful. For some people at certain times in their life, these may be the absolute best options for addressing issues and receiving encouragement and accountability. But to assume that every sexual minority person of faith needs counseling or a support group prioritizes a system over the individual. Cultivation means that we meet each person where they are, we expect no quick fixes or simplistic shortcuts, and we discern how to take each step of relational investment with them as they invite us into their journey of faith.

Even today, it is not uncommon for me to receive a panicked phone call from a pastor who has encountered either a gay person or someone with a gay loved one. They want to know what programs we offer. Their fear is palpable. They feel ill-equipped. They don't want this to explode and cause conflict or crisis in their church. And they want the program that will make it all go away so they can regain a sense of normalcy. When you think about the postures we've discussed so far, one begins to see that rather than wanting this to go away, such a disclosure can be viewed as an opportunity to listen for and trust the leading of the Holy Spirit. This is an opportunity to really do the imaginative work of theology together in the particular context of a real person's life. "Communities engaging with the missional context of our age must be aware of the fact that they are *theology-generating* communities. I use the word *aware* because generating theology is not something we choose to do; it is something we do by default. Theology at the most basic level is nothing more than what we believe about God and ulti-mate things and, perhaps more importantly, how we live out of what we believe."[5] If we believe that God is seeking to reconcile all things to himself, and if we believe that he is the source, energy, and power behind any transformation, and if we believe that he will work every-thing together for good for those who love him, then we will cultivate an environment where a gay person can work out the implications of their faith. We'll give God room to complete in that individual the good work that he has started in his time and in his way. And if we believe that God calls us into relationship and into vibrant healthy community, we will cultivate environments where gay Christians can authentically connect with others in the journey of faith without fear of rejection.

Trust

Such cultivation requires a tremendous amount of trust. A sixth posture of *trust* will take us from defensiveness to creativity.[6] This posture is both essential and a great challenge as we seek to respond to the reali-ties of gay followers of Jesus. Keel advises,

> People in our culture are asking very important questions right now about God, about Scripture, about the church, and about many other topics and issues they struggle with. Many of them worship in our churches. Questioning basic assumptions about reality is a by-product of a culture in transition. However, we cannot ask questions and seek God in the

midst of our questions if at the same time we are defending some secured ground that protects the identity of God. The presuppositions and rigidity of such a posture will ultimately render impotent any true seeking.[7]

Gay Christians need the space where they can truly seek the heart of God for their lives without the people around them anxiously putting up barriers in an effort to protect the Scriptures. But such spaciousness is rarely the experience of gay people in our churches. They are allowed to seek only within the narrow parameters of our assumed interpretation of seven passages of Scripture. This can create a circle of shame, frustration, defiance, and then finally either capitulation to external standards or a departure from the church. What such rigid expectations do not do is demonstrate a robust trust that God will lead those individuals where they need to go. When gay Christians feel forced to function from a defensive position, they lack the spaciousness they need to really be accountable for their own spiritual journeys.

One of the women I interviewed for our *Pastors' Conversation* DVD spoke of being a bridge. That is, she felt as if people were actually walking on her, as a gay Christian, to try to navigate the complexities of this conversation. She then said that she often felt that she wanted to defend herself, put her hands up like a boxer ready for a fight, but that she felt God continually tell her to put her hands down. She felt that God was saying to her, "I will protect you." To move out of a gut level desire to defend yourself requires a deep trust that God will do what he has said he will do, that he will protect you. It isn't hard to find untrustworthy people. Some will say they have your back, and perhaps really mean it, until their own back is up against that wall. The litmus test adjudicators demand a certain and clear position. The orthodoxy police don't care about what your posture is, they just want to know what your position is. But we can begin to embody this posture of trust, even in this difficult milieu, when we live into the reality that God will protect us. God is our strong tower, the place we are safe. And when we embody this posture of trust, we are the change we long to see. We model the alternative to the history of polarity, shame, and rejection that marks so much of the conversation at the intersection of faith and sexuality.

267

You may have noticed that Keel describes this posture as the movement from defensiveness to creativity. What might this creativity look like in the journey of a gay Christian? Might it mean that alternatives to single celibacy are explored and tested through prayer and discernment? Might it mean that a community walks with a person, who had previously struggled with depression and unchaste behavior, and who now seems like an entirely different person as they learn the joys and challenges of love and fidelity in a committed same-sex partnership? When our responses to the relationship choices of a gay Christian arise from a posture of defensiveness, we are guaranteed to *not* encounter any creativity in the ways that God might work in people's lives to bring them closer to him. But when we incarnate a posture of trust, we have the space to see with unclouded eyes where God might be at work. We may not understand why or how he works in particular situations, but our spirits will be open to the surprising and unpredictable whispers of the Spirit's presence. We may not be able to dot all the i's and cross all the t's, but rather than controlling the situation, we will be able to entrust our friends and loved ones to God.

I see this posture of trust most poignantly in some of the parents of gay individuals. When they first come to see me, they are often in great turmoil. Their love for their child is unmistakable. They may have always believed that Scripture precluded same-sex relationships. And they just can't make these two things fit together. Often it is the mother who, after some time of processing and coming to accept the reality of their child, will say to me, "I want my child to know the love I have with their father. I want them to know the joy I have had in being their parent. I want them to have love and a family. I don't know how God is going to work this out in their lives, but the most important thing to me is that they have a relationship with Christ. And I want them to know that we love them no matter what." That mother may still have the strong scriptural conviction that same-sex relationships are not God's best, but she is seeking to embody a posture of trust as she submits her child to the love of God and as she stands steadfast in extending her unconditional love. This kind of posture, even where there may be theological differences, is one that nurtures a space where a child knows they are loved. The confidence such love engenders can help to lower defenses so that the child is free to continue to explore and grow in faith in Jesus Christ. Such a posture of trust ought not to be confused with resignation, fatalism, or compromise, as some would suggest. Rather, such a posture loves without fear in deep dependence on God. Love compels us to move toward a more open, spacious place than the systems we may have been taught afford. But such openness is grounded in a robust faith in the trustworthiness and faithfulness of our God.

Joy

A seventh posture that Keel describes is the posture of *joy*, one that moves us from work to play. To be honest, I was tempted to leave this one out. Many of us know how to work and think and be responsible, but many of us have forgotten how to play. I haven't done very well at integrating play into my life, let alone into my ministry with New Direction. So often this work can feel very serious, fraught with tension and the potential for harsh and angry reactions at any given moment. For many years, I felt the great weight of responsibility in promoting a life of discipleship for gay people that seemed to ask so much more of them than was being asked of me. Keel asks,

> But what happens when we start to live in a trust-saturated relationship with God, our church community, and the world around us? One thing I have experienced as a result of trust is relief and joy. Because we can appreciate what is happening around us without needing to manufacture or control it, the possibility of enjoying what we do and who we are enters into the equations of our lives. . . . Joy flows from an acknowledgement that regardless of our circumstances, we are known and loved. And out of that conviction flows not only joy but peace, presence and love. From those manifestations of the Spirit's presence come the ability to relax, celebrate, play and have fun.[8]

Celebration and play are still not real strong points for me. But upon reflection, there has certainly been an infusion of joy and lightness as I have led New Direction into a more generous spaciousness. Posturing ourselves to trust more deeply, let go of our own anxieties and control, and be present to witness the creative ways God is working in the lives of unique individuals has been a very freeing experience. Moving away from a place of dread that I would disappoint God and hurt both the church and the gay people I loved, and moving toward a confidence in entrusting the outcomes to God, empowered me to love and serve without conditions and restrictions. It has been a journey of profound healing and growth.

Dependence

An eighth and final posture that acts as the culmination for all of the others is the posture of *dependence*. Like chaos, many of us might not view the idea of dependence very fondly. Interdependence maybe. But dependence can conjure up images of a whining, overly entitled, immature adult still living with their parents. And those of us with a history of codependence are especially vigilant to avoid even the faint-est whiff of overreliance on someone else. Unfortunately, we can bring such defensive independence into our relationship with God as well. We say that we trust God for everything, but once we peel back the layers of our piety, we see a resistant and resilient core of self-reliance. Moving into a posture of dependence takes us from our clear and firm resolutions into a tension between our not knowing and our trusting that God will eventually lead us to a place of resolution again. Only this posture recognizes that dependence on the leading of God's Spirit will emulate the journey of the Israelites through the wilderness, pick-ing up and following whenever the cloud or fiery pillar moved. This posture will move us from resolution to tension to resolution to tension to resolution, and so on. This posture anticipates moving with God as he reveals himself in the unique facets of gathering his people in a specific time and specific place. A posture of dependence allows us the freedom to focus on our local contexts in the lives of the real and actual people we are walking with on the journey of discipleship. Keel says,

> It is only when we stay in a posture of engaged dependence—of learning, vulnerability, availability, surrender, cultivation, trust and joy—that we

will find real life in all its creative and dynamic glory. This new life will cause us to see God, the Scriptures, our churches, the world and ourselves in new (and old) ways. And the result of these new (and old) ways of seeing will not be maps or visions that let us off the hook by delivering us to freshly secured and resolute terra firma. No, I think the result will be new ways of being that cause us to become more brazenly dependent on God and each other and willing to lean into ambiguity, mystery, and creativity so that we might be faithful to God's work in the midst of a dynamic and ever-changing liquid landscape.[9]

At this point, some may be thinking that I'm throwing out the baby with the bath water. After all, isn't resolution good? Isn't order good? Aren't spoken words through preaching and teaching good? Aren't some programs really good and life changing? Isn't using our intellect good? The simple answer is yes. Part of living into postures that nurture a deep reliance on God's leading is that no good tool is tossed out of the toolbox. But if you've come from such a dominant paradigm that you always find yourself reaching for the same tool regardless of the situation, you may need to leave that tool alone as you learn to listen and follow and make use of the right tool in the right situation. These postures allow us to be responsive to the master carpenter and to use the tools he suggests—even when they seem surprising or uncomfortable or just plain wrong. God wants to cultivate within us such a willingness to depend on him that sometimes it seems he needs to consternate us so that we learn a deeper and more radical obedience and willingness to relinquish our desire for control.

Consider the apostle Peter on the roof as the vision of the sheet unfolding in front of him reveals unclean animals and a voice tells him to "kill and eat." Peter's natural reaction is, "Surely not, Lord! I have never eaten anything impure or unclean." But the voice speaks to him a second time and says, "Do not call anything impure that God has made clean."[10] If Peter relied on his own abilities, he may have disregarded the vision as a likely case of indigestion or extreme hunger. God knew how entrenched the system of law was in Peter's paradigm, so he created a series of events that would open Peter's eyes to see that God was revealing a new thing.

In their book *Colossians Remixed* Brian Walsh and Sylvia Keesmaat portray the story of Scripture as a six-act play: creation, fall, Israel, Jesus, the church, the consummation. They say,

> We are now living in Act V and are on the stage as actors in this divine love story that seeks to restore the covenantal bond between the Creator and his beloved creation. Our task is to keep the drama alive and move it toward Act VI, recognizing that in this final Act God becomes the central actor again and finishes the play. But how do we move the drama forward? We turn to the Author and ask for more script. And the Author says, "Sorry, but that's all that's written—*you* have to finish Act V. But I have given you a very good Director who will comfort you and lead you." So here we are with an unfinished script, at least some indication of the final Act and a promise that we have the Holy Spirit as our Director and we have to improvise. If we are to faithfully live out the biblical drama, then we will need to develop the imaginative skills necessary to improvise on this cosmic stage of creational redemption. Indeed it would be the height of infidelity and interpretive cowardice to simply repeat verbatim, over and over again, the earlier passages of the play.[11]

It is much easier to close the book. It is much easier to play it safe and hide in our own certainty. But not only will this stifle the authentic wrestling of our gay brothers and sisters, it moves us to an idolatrous dependence on ourselves. God moves through history; it is after all his story. The Spirit keeps on revealing Jesus to us, who is the perfect representation of the Father. Will our faith, sharpened by our doubts and questions, be courageous enough to risk seeking him afresh as we journey hand in hand with our gay brothers and sisters? Certainly, my gay Christian friends are struggling to find that same courage as they wrestle and find their own unique places of conviction, belief, and decision. They need the support and affirmation of their straight brothers and sisters to keep seeking Jesus with an adventuresome spirit and uninhibited courage.

This book has never been about trying to convince you of a particular position on the matter of committed same-sex relationships. The intention throughout these pages has been to model a posture that invites generous spaciousness into our own hearts, into our relationships, and into our churches and Christian organizations. These postures may feel very risky, if you are accustomed to the safety and security of certainty. But my prayer is that these risks will seem more than worth it for the opportunity to move out of the house of fear and more fully into the house of love. My hope is that any initial sense that generous spaciousness is just a wishy-washy, weak compromise will have been replaced with a robust vision of living into the discipline of a deep, yet freeing, trust in God. I believe it to be crucial that, as we seek to navigate the conversation around faithful discipleship for our gay brothers and sisters, we focus our hearts on Christ, on his desire that a unified church would be a witness to the world of his reconciling love, and on being the extension of that love to all our neighbors. I believe that hospitality is central to the heart and ministry of Jesus and that to the extent we fail to extend this hospitality to gay people, the church will fail to walk in the way of Jesus. I hope that this book has encouraged, challenged, and strengthened your resolve to break down the dividing walls of hostility and to incarnate a generous and spacious welcome for all.

Notes

Introduction

1. Alan Chambers, then-president of Exodus International, issued a public apology to the gay community and announced the ministry's closure in June 2013. Having known Alan since the early 2000s, I have been aware of his own journey toward a more generous spaciousness. At the time of publication, Alan and others have announced plans to start a new organization. In the year prior to the closing of Exodus, a number of ministries in the network left Exodus to form a new group called Restored Hope Network. These ministries continue to promote an ex-gay paradigm. See http://www.christianitytoday.com/gleanings/2013/june/alan-chambers-apologizes-to-gay-community-exodus.html.

2. Hans Frei cited in Brian McLaren, *A Generous Orthodoxy* (Grand Rapids: Zondervan, 2004), 10.

3. Peter Rollins, *How (Not) to Speak of God* (Brewster, MA: Paraclete Press, 2006), 3.

4. It should be noted that the ex-gay system is hardly monolithic and contains a range of diversity.

5. Justin Lee founded the Gay Christian Network (GCN) as an online support forum in 2001. GCN welcomes gay Christians and their straight allies across a diverse spectrum of belief and practice. They denote those who believe God affirms committed same-sex relationships as "side A" and those who hold to a traditional view of marriage and celibacy for gay Christians as "side B." The vast majority of GCN members are side A or unsure. A small minority are committed to a side B position. GCN is not supportive of an ex-gay paradigm, but they do intentionally invest in building bridges between the church and gay people and hope to see the church, including all denominations, become a more hospitable place for gay people. Since that episode, Justin and I have become good friends, and I respect him immensely.

6. Alan J. Roxburgh, *The Sky Is Falling: Leaders Lost in Transition* (Eagle, ID: ACI Publishing, 2005).

7. Cornelius Plantinga Jr., *Not the Way It's Supposed to Be: A Breviary of Sin* (Grand Rapids: Eerdmans, 1995), 79.

8. Wendy Gritter, "Exodus 2008 Leadership Address," New Direction audio resources, http:///www.newdirection.ca/content.xjp?id=444, accessed July 17, 2013.

9. Warren Throckmorton, "New Direction for Exodus?," *Warren Throckmorton* (blog), February 5, 2008, wthrockmorton.com/2008/02/05/new-direction-for-exodus/.

10. David Roberts, "Wendy Gritter of Exodus Member Ministry New Direction," *Ex-Gay Watch* (blog), February 25, 2008, www.exgaywatch.com/2008/02/wendy-gritter-of-exodus -member-ministry-new-direction/. Minor edits have been made to style and syntax.

11. "Ex-ex-gay" or "ex-gay survivor" are terms describing someone who has invested in the ex-gay process to try to change their sexual orientation and who has left that paradigm and has come out as gay.

12. Since writing that post I no longer use the term "alternative." One of my gay friends helped me to see that this term could give the impression that sexual identity is a choice—an alternative they chose. I do not believe the vast majority of people make a choice about the direction of their attractions. I now try to use the word "diverse" rather than "alternative."

13. This post was written early in 2008. Some of my views and the manner I communicate them have continued to evolve since that time, as you will see in the remainder of this book.

14. Brian McLaren, *A Generous Orthodoxy* (Grand Rapids: Zondervan, 2004), 30.

15. Language is important, and definition of terms can be very important. Use of the term "gay" simply means "experiencing same-sex attraction." I recognize, however, that there are persons who do experience same-sex attraction who are not comfortable describing themselves as "gay." To keep things simple, in much of the book I will simply use the word "gay" as a descriptive term.

16. Walter Brueggemann, *Finally Comes the Poet* (Minneapolis: Fortress Press, 1989), quoted in McLaren, *A Generous Orthodoxy*, 146.

Chapter 1 Reevaluating Evangelical Ex-gay Ministry

1. Alan J. Roxburgh, *The Sky Is Falling: Leaders Lost in Transition* (Eagle, ID: ACI Publishing, 2005), 29.

2. Andy Comiskey is the founder of Desert Stream Ministries and the Living Waters program, which addresses "sexual and relational brokenness." He is now part of the Restored Hope Network.

3. Frank Worthen is considered one of the founders of Exodus International and founder of the Love in Action ministry. He is now part of the Restored Hope Network.

4. Leanne Payne is a pioneer in healing prayer ministry and writes extensively on gender and sexual identity and healing—particularly the book, *Crisis in Masculinity* (Wheaton: Crossway, 1985; Grand Rapids: Baker, 2006).

5. Lewis B. Smedes, "Like the Wideness of the Sea?," Soulforce Archives website, January 1, 1998, www.archives.soulforce.org/1998/01/01/like-the-wideness-of-the-sea/.

6. Exodus Doctrinal and Policy Statements, http://exodusinternational.org/wp-content /uploads/2010/11/EA-Packet.pdf

7. To learn more about the Sexual Identity Therapy Framework, see the website of the same name at http://sitframework.com/.

8. See Mark A. Yarhouse, *Homosexuality and the Christian: A Guide for Parents, Pastors, and Friends* (Bloomington, MN: Bethany House, 2010).

9. See Janelle Hallman, *The Heart of Female Same-Sex Attraction: A Comprehensive Counseling Resource* (Downers Grove, IL: InterVarsity Press, 2008).

10. Patrick M. Chapman, *Thou Shalt Not Love: What Evangelicals Really Say to Gays* (US: Haiduk Press, 2008), 254.

11. To learn more about Evangelicals Concerned, see their website at www.evangelicals concerned.org/.

12. To learn more about Soulforce, see their website www.soulforce.com/.

Chapter 2 Of Doubt, Tension, and Anxiety

1. Peter Rollins, *How (Not) to Speak of God* (Brewster, MA: Paraclete Press, 2006), 36.

2. pursuegod, commenting on "Betrayal," by Wendy Gritter, *Bridging the Gap* (blog), June 11, 2009, www.newdirection.ca/2009/06/betrayal.html.

3. Jeremy Marks, *Exchanging the Truth of God for a Lie* (Weybridge, Surrey, UK: Roper-Penberthy, 2008), back cover.

4. James Alison, "Is it Ethical to Be Catholic?," a talk given February 12, 2006, San Franciso, *James Alison. Theology* (website), www.jamesalison.co.uk /texts/eng27.html.

5. For a critique of this statistic, see Jim Burroway, "Where Did the Ex-Gay One-Third 'Success Rate' Come From?," *Box Turtle Bulletin* v, July 18, 2011, www.boxturtlebulletin .com/2011/07/18/35178.

6. Living Waters is a discipleship/healing program for those experiencing sexual and relational brokenness. It was developed by Andy Comiskey, a man who experienced same-sex attraction. It was a common program used by Exodus ministries.

7. Eugene, "Survivor Narrative," *Beyond Ex-Gay* (website), www.beyondexgay.com /narratives/eugene, accessed July 20, 2013. Eugene's story has been edited for length.

8. Matt. 7:16–20.

Chapter 3 The Power of Stories

1. American Psychological Association. *Definition of Terms: Sex, Gender, Gender Identity, Sexual Orientation.* http://www.apa.org/pi/lgbt/resources/sexuality-definitions.pdf p.1, accessed August 21, 2013.

2. Lisa M. Diamond, *Sexual Fluidity: Understanding Women's Love and Desire* (Cambridge, MA: Harvard University Press, 2009), 137.

Chapter 4 A Complex Spectrum

1. Paul W. Egertson, "One Family's Story," *Veritas et Ratio: Truth and Reason* (website of Scott Bidstrup), July 7, 1990, www.bidstrup.com/stories3.htm.

2. See James Brownson, "Gay Unions: Consistent Witness or Pastoral Accommodation? An Evangelical Pastoral Dilemma and the Unity of the Church," *Reformed Review* 59, no. 1 (August 2005): 3–18.

3. James 2:1, 8, 9.

4. Egertson, "One Family's Story."

5. Lisa M. Diamond, *Sexual Fluidity: Understanding Women's Love and Desire* (Cambridge, MA: Harvard University Press, 2009), 3.

Chapter 5 Coming-Out and the Church

1. "Spiritual Profile of Homosexual Adults Provides Surprising Insights," Barna Group website, June 20, 2009, www.barna.org/barna-update/article/13–culture/282–spiritual-profile -of-homosexual-adults-provides-surprising-insights.

2. Albert Mohler, "Reparative Therapy, Homosexuality, and the Gospel of Jesus Christ," *AlbertMohler.com* (website), July 19, 2011, www.albertmohler.com/2011/07/19 /reparative-therapy-homosexuality-and-the-gospel-of-jesus-christ/.

3. Matt. 23:4.

4. G. Remafedi, M. Resnick, R. Blum, and L. Harris, "Demography of Sexual Orientation in Adolescents," *Pediatrics* 89 (April 1992): 714–21.

5. Cited in "Widening the Circle: Opening to Diversity and Undoing Racism," published by the Christian Reformed Church in North America, Office of Race Relations (Grand Rapids, 2010), 23.

Chapter 6 The Journey of Discipleship

1. Stanley Hauerwas and Charles Pinches, *Christians among the Virtues: Theological Conversations with Ancient and Modern Ethics* (South Bend, IN: University of Notre Dame Press, 1997), 14.

2. Ibid., 31.

3. Jeremy Marks, *Exchanging the Truth of God for a Lie* (Weybridge, Surrey, UK: Roper-Penberthy, 2008), 8.

Chapter 7 Understanding Holistic Sexuality

1. A study commissioned by the Catholic Theological Society of America concluded this from the Vatican's *Declaration on Sexual Ethics*, quoted in Stanley Grenz, *Sexual Ethics: An Evangelical Perspective* (Louisville: Westminster John Knox, 1997), 21.

2. From a statement adopted by the Tenth General Convention of the American Lutheran Church, quoted in Grenz, *Sexual Ethics*, 21.

3. Grenz, *Sexual Ethics*, 21.

4. Grenz, *Sexual Ethics,* 193, cited in Lisa Graham McMinn, *Sexuality and Holy Longing: Embracing Intimacy in a Broken World* (San Francisco: Jossey-Bass, 2004), 70. Based on this phrase: "The drive to bond with others in community is an expression of our fundamental sexuality, a sexuality that goes deeper than body parts, potential roles in reproduction, and genital acts."

5. Grenz, *Sexual Ethics*, 27.

6. James V. Brownson, *Bible, Gender, Sexuality: Reframing the Church's Debate on Same-Sex Relationships* (Grand Rapids: Eerdmans, 2013), 29.

7. Ibid., 31.

8. Ibid., 32.

9. *Bridging the Gap* DVD, available at http://www.newdirection.ca/shop/.

Chapter 8 Our Image of God

1. C. Baxter Kruger, *Jesus and the Undoing of Adam* (Jackson, MS: Perichoresis Press, 2003), 12.

2. John 10:10 NKJV.

3. This quote is an example of Luther's commitment to extol the glorious ways God reveals himself through creation as a means of common grace.

4. "Brennan Manning Live at Woodcrest," *YouTube* (website), uploaded May 30, 2007, www.youtube.com/watch?v=pQi_IDV2bgM.

5. 1 John 4:7–9.

6. 1 John 4:18.

7. Henri J. M. Nouwen, *Lifesigns: Intimacy, Fecundity, and Ecstasy in Christian Perspective* (Garden City, NY: Doubleday, 1986), 6.

8. Ibid., 110.

9. D. S. Reade, *Superheroes, Saviors, and Sinners without Secrets* (Lincoln, NE: iUniverse, 2007), 117.

Chapter 9 The Role of Scripture

1. Tim Keel, *Intuitive Leadership: Embracing a Paradigm of Narrative, Metaphor, and Chaos* (Grand Rapids: Baker Books, 2007), 168.

2. Eugene Peterson, *Eat this Book: A Conversation in the Art of Spiritual Reading* (Grand Rapids: Eerdmans, 2006). This section is adapted from Peterson's work.

3. Dwight Friesen, "Orthoparadoxy: Emerging Hope for Embracing Difference" in *Emergent Manifesto of Hope*, ed. Doug Pagitt and Tony Jones (Grand Rapids: Baker Books, 2007), 202.

4. Peterson, *Eat this Book*, 66.

5. Ibid., 65.

6. Quoted in Stanley Grenz, *Sexual Ethics: An Evangelical Perspective* (Louisville: Westminster John Knox, 1997), 4.

7. Lauren Winner, *Real Sex: The Naked Truth about Chastity* (Grand Rapids: Brazos, 2006), 129.

8. Rob Bell, *Sex God: Exploring the Endless Connections between Sexuality and Spirituality* (Grand Rapids: Zondervan, 2007), 43.

9. 1 Cor. 7:35 NLT.

10. Matt. 5:17–18.

11. Rom. 13:8–10.

12. Justin Lee, "The Great Debate: Justin's View," *The Gay Christian Network* (website), www.gaychristian.net/ justins_view.php, accessed July 23, 2013.

13. Marvin Ellison, *Making Love Just: Sexual Ethics for Perplexing Times* (Minneapolis: Fortress Press, 2012), 67.

14. 1 Cor. 3:16–17 NIV 1984.

15. 1 Cor. 6:18–20 NIV 1984.

16. Peter Ould, "Why James Jones Is Wrong," *An Exercise in the Fundamentals of Orthodoxy* (website), March 6, 2010, http://www.peter-ould.net/2010/03/06/why-james-jones-is-wrong.

17. http://www.fulcrum-anglican.org.uk/445.

18. Lee, "Great Debate: Justin's View."

Chapter 10 The Challenge of Interpretation

1. Gen. 3:1.

2. Saint Peter Damian, *Book of Gomorrah: An Eleventh-Century Treatise against Clerical Homosexual Practices*, trans., introduction, and notes by Pierre J. Payer (Waterloo, ON: Wilfrid Laurier University Press, 1982), 7.

3. Thomas Aquinas: http://www3.nd.edu/Departments/Maritain/ti04/budz.htm, accessed August 21, 2013.

4. Ewald Martin Plass, *What Luther Says: An Anthology*, vol. 1 (St. Louis, MO: Concordia, 2006), 134.

5. http://www.patheos.com/blogs/nakedpastor/2011/02/there-is-no-box/.

6. Martin Luther, cited by Bernard Ramm, *Protestant Biblical Interpretation* (Grand Rapids: Baker, 1970), 56.

7. John 8:11; Mark 2:5; John 4:23.

8. See Patrick M. Chapman, *Thou Shalt Not Love: What Evangelicals Really Say to Gays* (US: Haiduk Press, 2008), 132–36; Jack Rogers, *Jesus, the Bible, and Homosexuality: Explode the Myths, Heal the Church* (Louisville: Westminster John Knox, 2006), see

chapter 5: 69-90; Pim Pronk, *Against Nature? Types of Moral Argumentation Regarding Homosexuality* (Grand Rapids: Eerdmans, 1993), 267–80.

9. J. Richard Middleton and Brian Walsh, *Truth Is Stranger Than It Used to Be: Biblical Faith in a Postmodern Age* (Downers Grove, IL: InterVarsity Press, 1995), 71.

10. Jenell Williams Paris, *The End of Sexual Identity* (Downers Grove, IL: InterVarsity Press, 2011), 40.

Chapter 11 A Disputable Matter?

1. John L. Allen Jr., "Interview with Anglican Bishop N. T. Wright of Durham, England," *National Catholic Reporter* (website), May 21, 2004, www.nationalcatholicreporter.org /word/wright.htm.

2. The origin of this quote is contested, but it is often attributed to St. Augustine.

3. Matt. 5:43–45, 48.

4. David Kinnaman and Gabe Lyons, *unChristian: What a New Generation Really Thinks about Christianity . . . and Why It Matters* (Grand Rapids: Baker Books, 2007), 92.

5. Rom. 10:9.

6. Albert Mohler, "The Osteen Moment—Your Own Moment Will Come Soon Enough," *AlbertMohler.com* (blog), January 27, 2011, www.albertmohler.com/2011/01/27/the-osteen -moment-your-own-moment-will-come-soon-enough/. See also http://www.newdirection .ca/blog/disputable-matter-part-5//.

Chapter 12 Engaging the Church

1. "Our Beliefs," *Highlands Church* (website), highlandschurchdenver.org/about/our -beliefs/, accessed July 26, 2013.

2. I have changed or deleted identifying details.

3. Anonymous, "A Third Way? Beyond the "'Affirming/Not Affirming' Dichotomy," *Red Letter Christians* (website), December 6, 2011, www.redletterchristians.org/a-third -way-beyond-the-affirming-not-affirming-dichotomy/.

4. Jean Vanier, *Becoming Human* (Mahway, NJ: Paulist Press, 1998), 63, 65.

5. Jenell Williams Paris, *The End of Sexual Identity* (Downers Grove, IL: InterVarsity Press, 2011), 43.

6. Miroslav Volf, *Exclusion and Embrace: A Theological Exploration of Identity, Otherness, and Reconciliation* (Nashville: Abingdon Press, 1996), 214.

7. Transgender—a person feels an incongruence between their biological sex and their sense of gender identity.

8. Cisgender—A person feels a congruence between their biological sex and their sense of gender identity. The majority of people are cisgender, that is, a biological male feels like a man.

9. Vanier, *Becoming Human.*

10. The words of this famous prayer (popularly attributed to Saint Francis, someone who emptied himself by living a life of poverty) can remind us to extend grace to others. The prayer in its present form cannot be traced back further than 1912, when it was printed in Paris in a small spiritua magazine called *La Clochette* (*The Little Bell*), published by *La Ligue de la Sainte-Messe* (*The Holy Mass League*). The author's name was not given, although it may have been the founder of *La Ligue,* Fr. Esther Bouquerel.

11. Jean Vanier, *Finding Peace* (Toronto, ON: House of Anansi, 2003), 16, emphasis added.

12. http://lci.typepad.com/leaders_resourcing_leader/files/ChurchAfterChristendom .pdf.

13. The archives of this initiative can be found at Wendy Gritter, "This Is It . . . Synchroblog Mania," *Bridging the Gap* (blog), June 24, 2009, www.newdirection.ca/2009/06/this-is-it-synchroblog-mania.html.

14. www.sisterfriends-together.org/bridging-the-gap/.

Chapter 13 A Word for Pastors and Leaders

1. Prov. 3:5–6 NASB.

2. It should be noted that you may also encounter gay Christians who have had a string of broken relationships or infidelity in relationship—the same way you may encounter this in straight Christians. You may encounter gay Christians who have a deep conviction that they should not be in a consummated relationship. So this statement is not intended to be a blanket generalization but an acknowledgment that there are indeed vibrant Christians who are also in long-term, committed same-sex relationships.

Chapter 14 A Word to Gay Christians

1. If an individual is leaving a spiritually abusive religious system, this may be unhelpful phrasing. What might be a better alternative in such a toxic situation is to ask whether or not you will be able to "let go" and entrust the group to God.

Chapter 15 A Word to Would-be Gay Advocates in the Church

1. Jean Vanier, *Finding Peace* (Toronto, ON: House of Anansi, 2003), 69.

Concluding Thoughts

1. Tim Keel, *Intuitive Leadership: Embracing a Paradigm of Narrative, Metaphor, and Chaos* (Grand Rapids: Baker Books, 2007), 226.

2. Ibid., 229.

3. Ibid., 231.

4. Ibid., 234.

5. Ibid., 163.

6. Ibid., 243.

7. Ibid., 244.

8. Ibid., 248.

9. Ibid., 251.

10. Acts 10:13–15.

11. Brian Walsh and Sylvia Keesmaat, *Colossians Remixed: Subverting the Empire* (Downers Grove, IL: InterVarsity Press, 2004), 133–34.